AMERICAN W

1941–1

AMERICAN WAR PLANS 1941–1945

The Test of Battle

Steven T. Ross
Naval War College, Newport, Rhode Island

FRANK CASS
LONDON • PORTLAND, OR.

First published in 1997 in Great Britain by
FRANK CASS & CO. LTD.
Newbury House, 900 Eastern Avenue, London IG2 7HH, England

and in the United States of America by
FRANK CASS
c/o ISBS, Inc.
5804 N.E. Hassalo Street
Portland, Oregon 97213-3644

British Library Cataloguing in Publication Data:

Ross, Steven T.
    American war plans, 1941–1945: the test of battle
    1. World War, 1939–1945 – Campaigns 2. United States –
    Military policy – History
    I. Title
    355.4'8'0973

ISBN 0 7146 4634 2 (cloth)
ISBN 0 7146 4194 4 (paper)

Library of Congress Cataloging-in-Publication Data:

A catalog record for this book is available from the
Library of Congress

Printed in Great Britain by
Bookcraft (Bath) Ltd., Midsomer Norton, Avon.

To Bea and Jay

Contents

List of Maps

Acknowledgements

No scholarly monograph is written alone. Many individuals contributed to the writing of this study. At the National Archives Mr John Taylor and Mr Wilbert Mahoney helped me find many important documents. Mr Dean Allard performed a similar service at the Naval Historical Center. Professor George Baer, Chairman of the Strategy and Policy Department at the Naval War College gave me encouragement, time and financial support. Professor C.J.M. Goulter, an expert on the Second World War, read and commented on the manuscript. Finally Mrs Barbara Atkins and Mr Thomas Buiak typed the book.

No bibliography dealing with the Second World War can pretend to be complete. The selected bibliography for this volume does include the documents upon which the book is based. The secondary works are but a partial list of books and articles consulted or previously used. To those whose works doubtless provided indirect help but who are not listed my apologies. To those whose works are listed my thanks.

Introduction

One of the most important functions of a military staff is creating war plans. Staffs produce war plans for many reasons. Creating a war plan is often ritualistic – it is simply something that staffs do. The ritualistic aspect of war planning does, however, serve a useful purpose – training. Staff officers learn in the process of planning the military and bureaucratic mechanisms involved in a large military organization as well as the requirements of a variety of operations. Writing plans as a training exercise also prepares officers for the real thing. The planning process also seeks to encourage strategic thinking about the generation, deployment and use of armed forces to achieve political objectives. During the inter-war years, for example, American staff officers dealt with problems ranging from relatively minor operations in the Caribbean to a global war against a hostile coalition. The most critical aspect of war planning and war plans, of course, takes place in a real conflict when strategic and operational plans are put to the test of battle. Planning in war ceases to be a paper exercise and takes on a critical political and strategic role.

An effective war plan contributes directly to the accomplishment of a state's political and strategic objectives. It also enables a nation's armed forces to fight under favorable circumstances. A viable war plan must encompass a wide variety of factors including national objectives, the size and strength of the country's armed forces and those of the enemy, logistics, individual service requirements and perspectives, and frequently the interests and strategy of allies. Intelligence and deception play significant parts in the planning process. In putting a plan into action the abilities of commanders and random factors, defined by Clausewitz as friction, influence the execution and outcome of a plan. The independent will of the enemy has, of course, a major impact on the results of a war plan.

The size and composition of a country's armed forces is the result of a process involving judgments concerning political objectives, human and material resources and the power of allies and enemies. Prior to America's entry into the Second World War, for example, planners recognized that the United States might well become involved in a two-ocean war. Service planners therefore devised a war plan and a mobilization plan to wage a war against both Germany and Japan. In the Korean conflict Washington chose to fight a limited war. The government therefore restricted assets sent to Asia.

Logistical considerations have always played an important role in war plans. Napoleon's defeats in Spain and Russia were at least partially caused by logistical problems. The growing complexity of warfare in the nineteenth and twentieth centuries enhanced the importance of logistics. Grant in Mississippi and Sherman in Georgia could improvise and live off the country, whereas armies in the First World War were engaged in a conflict of material and required constant and massive logistical support.

During the Second World War logistics were a major factor in operational planning. The Americans, for example, in discussing the invasion of north-western Europe with the British, frequently noted that their logistical preparations stretched from England all the way back to the Mississippi River. In fact, every major Allied operation in Europe and the Pacific involved extensive logistical preparations. The slowing of the Allied offensive in Europe in the late summer and fall of 1944 was in large measure due to growing supply and distribution problems.

War plans must accommodate individual service requirements and perspectives. During the American Civil War, Union army and naval forces operating on the Mississippi established effective *ad hoc* co-operation. By contrast, the German army and navy during the First World War rarely collaborated and with few exceptions fought separate conflicts. The German air force and navy experienced a similar failure of co-ordination during the Second World War. Allied amphibious operations during the Second World War required extensive inter-service co-operation on the operational and tactical levels of conflict although differing army and navy views on the conduct of the Pacific war resulted in many time-consuming arguments. The debate in the months preceding D-Day over the role of heavy bomber squadrons is still another case illustrative of the difficulties involved in mounting multi-service operations.

The personality of a commander often influences the formulation and execution of a war plan. Napoleon's belief in his operational invincibility led him to make several crucial strategic blunders. General MacArthur's Pacific strategy was, for example, influenced by his desire to avenge his earlier defeat in the Philippines. Admiral King's views of Pacific strategy were in turn influenced by many years of pre-war naval planning.

Coalitions must devise plans that are acceptable to all the major members. In 1799, for example, a coalition failed to defeat France because, in part, one of the partners decided to pursue its own particular objective at the expense of the coalition's overall strategy. In 1813 by contrast, the Allies devised and followed a common strategy in the German campaign against Napoleon. Policy differences led to strategic disagreements in the 1814 invasion of France. The coalition came close to dissolution but did finally manage to pursue the campaign to a successful conclusion.

During the First World War both the Central Powers and the Allies experienced serious problems in devising coalition strategy. The Germans, for example, did not co-ordinate their 1914 offensive with the Austrians and in 1918 even came to blows with the Turks over control of vital areas in the Caucasus. In the Allied coalition a divisive issue arose after the United States entered the conflict. The British and French wanted to employ American troops as reinforcements for their own depleted divisions. The Americans insisted upon the creation of complete American divisions, corps and field armies. Long and difficult negotiations finally produced a compromise: in an emergency American divisions would serve in British and French armies, but eventually the Americans would establish their own armies with their own sector of the Western Front.

In the Second World War strategic planning for the European and Mediterranean areas was, after 1942, a combined Anglo-American effort. Even before the United States entered the war, Washington and London had agreed that in a war against Germany and Japan the Allies would focus their efforts on defeating Germany first. Differing strategic views of how to accomplish the defeat of the Third Reich did, however, lead to constant, often heated, arguments between the British and the Americans. The invasion of North Africa, campaigns in Italy and the timing of the cross-Channel invasion were the subject of serious Anglo-American controversy. The course of post D-Day operations in Western Europe also roiled Anglo-American relations. The Allies, however, did manage to arrive at the compromises necessary to maintain the coalition's unity.

War plans must also be based on accurate assessments of enemy strengths and vulnerabilities. Countries have typically devoted substantial resources to intelligence gathering and analysis. In the 1920s and 1930s, for example, the French Republic made substantial efforts to obtain and analyze information from Germany. French intelligence created a remarkably clear picture of German intentions and capabilities. The Republic's failure to respond effectively to German expansionism was not a result of faulty intelligence. The failure to understand Japanese capabilities caused major problems for the Allies during the early part of the Pacific War. Throughout the Cold War, the United States devoted vast resources to gathering information on all aspects of the USSR and its satellites with mixed results.

Deception is a vital factor in war planning. In 1805 Napoleon convinced the Austrians that French armies would operate primarily in Italy and southern Germany. The Emperor then concentrated the bulk of the Grand Army in the Rhineland, crossed the river and moved to the southwest to outflank and encircle the Austrians. In the First World War the British, prior to the second Battle of Gaza, convinced the Turks to deploy against a false threat, and in 1918 the Germans deployed in great secrecy for the March offensive in order to achieve tactical surprise.

Deception played a significant role in the Second World War. The German attack in the west in May 1940 relied heavily on convincing the Allies that the offensive would essentially replicate the strategy of 1914. Thus, while the British and French moved to counter an invasion of Belgium, the Germans would deliver their main blow south of Namur at Sedan. The Overlord Plan included a major deception operation designed to convince the German high command that the Normandy landings were a feint and that the main blow would subsequently be delivered at the Pas de Calais.

In the execution of a war plan, friction plays a significant role. Staffs and commanders cannot hope to forecast chance events and luck, good or bad, and all they can do is prepare themselves as far as possible to respond to the unexpected. Prior to the Battle of Antietam, for example, General George B. McClellan obtained a copy of General Robert E. Lee's orders. He failed to profit from this lucky accident. By contrast at Utah Beach on D-Day American troops landed at the wrong location. Finding it lightly defended, the commander on the scene ordered the landings to continue.

The independent will of the enemy is often a crucial variable in determining the success or failure of a war plan. During the Second World War, for example, Allied plans for operations in Italy often achieved initial surprise but rapid and violent German responses usually created severe problems for the Allied forces.

The problems of friction and the independent will of the enemy have led to two basic responses by commanders. Some have emphasized the use of initiative by subordinates coupled with a willingness to improvise. Others have tried to eliminate friction and dictate enemy responses by precise and detailed planning.

Many leaders have viewed plans as the basis for improvisation believing that no plan could possibly account for or eliminate friction or entirely dominate the will of an opponent. Failure or unexpected success could occur at any time and leaders had to be ready to respond to the unexpected.

In the spring of 1864 General Ulysses S. Grant decided to concentrate the bulk of his military assets against the eastern part of the Confederacy in order to strike at the main southern field armies and the resources that sustained them. Accordingly, he ordered a near simultaneous advance of the Federal armies. Sherman was to advance from Chattanooga against Johnston's army and Atlanta. Banks was to move from New Orleans against Mobile. Sigel was to move up the Shenandoah Valley to deny the area's resources to the Army of Northern Virginia. Butler was to advance from the James River against Richmond, and Meade was to engage directly Lee's army. All forces were to begin their operations early in May.

Beyond ordering simultaneous attacks against the main centers of Confederate power Grant did not specify particular operations in detail. On 4 April 1864, for example, he telegraphed instructions to Sherman explaining, 'I do not propose to lay down for you a plan of campaign but simply lay down the work it is desirable to have done and leave you free to execute it in your own way.'[1] Five days later he informed Meade that, 'Lee's army will be your objective point. Wherever Lee goes, there will you go also.'[2]

Grant's design did not initially succeed. Banks, involved in the Red River Campaign, did not advance on Mobile. The Confederates defeated Butler and Sigel. Sherman and Meade did, however, move forward. Grant quickly found another commander – Sheridan – who defeated Confederate forces in the valley, and the Union navy finally neutralized Mobile. After the capture of Atlanta, Grant approved Sherman's proposal to march through Georgia to the sea. Later he approved another of Sherman's suggestions – an overland march from Georgia into the Carolinas.

Count Helmuth von Moltke (the Elder) believed that no war plan could with certainty look beyond the first meeting with the major forces of the enemy. The initial clash of arms combined with an opponent's decisions and actions created an inherently unpredictable situation. Consequently, campaigns and even battles could not simply be executions of premeditated plans. Rather they were spontaneous actions influenced by specific circumstances and directed according to the will and intelligence of the commander.

If operations and tactics reflected a clash of wills, Moltke also believed that mobilization and initial concentration of forces, the establishing of strategic objectives and the establishment of general lines of advance were within the realm of rational calculation and planning. The rational elements of strategy, if executed properly, would enable a commander to seek battle under favorable conditions.

On 6 May 1870, for example, Moltke issued orders in anticipation of war with France:

> The operation against France will consist simply in our advancing closed up as much as possible, a few marches in French territory until we meet the French army and give battle. The general direction of this advance is Paris because in that direction we are most certain to find our objective – the hostile army. On the direct road from the Palatinate to Paris is Metz. This place will be circumvented on the left and will be observed only. The next strategic advance insofar a battle does not ensue sooner is the line of the Moselle ...[3]

On 5 August 1871 Moltke informed the commander of the 1st Army that any forthcoming clash with the French was dependent upon the interaction of French and Prussian movements. The King and the General Staff would control the combined advance of all the field armies but 'in those orders the freedom of executing them will be left entirely in the hands of the different army headquarters, and they can act according to the situation'.[4]

Other commanders have operated on the premise that proper detailed planning could virtually eliminate the frictions of war. A well designed plan could dominate the will of the enemy and dictate the entire course of operations. A plan could in fact attain precise strategic and operational objectives.

The Schlieffen Plan employed by the Germans in 1914 was intended to dictate the course of the war against France from the beginning of mobilization until the moment of victory in the West. Mobilization flowed directly into operations in which each field army had a precise timetable and set of objectives. The swift concentration of forces coupled with strategic surprise would, the General Staff assumed, dominate enemy actions throughout the entire campaign. The German armies would, therefore, be able to execute their strategic design against a steadily weakening and progressively demoralized foe.

Extrapolating from their experiences during the First World War, the French army, after 1919, devised the concept of the methodical battle designed to eliminate friction at the operational level of war. Officers presumed that carefully planned combined arms assaults with precisely delineated objectives could substantially reduce, if not eliminate, the impact of chance and friction on major operations. Advanced weapons – modern tanks, artillery and aircraft – were fully integrated into this strategic concept. In the spring of 1940 the French High Command intended to halt the expected German thrust into the Low Countries and then mount a series of carefully orchestrated counterblows.

The ultimate test of any war plan is whether or not it succeeds. Intelligence assessments, inter-service interests, alliance politics and a host of other factors do indeed influence a plan's creation, but only victorious execution really matters. The planning process may be turbulent or smooth, but victory or defeat is what really matters. German planning for the western offensive in 1940 involved heated debates among the OKH, OKW, a number of senior officers and the head of state. The final product was, however, crowned with success. French planning for the 1940 campaign was by contrast a model of bureaucratic efficiency, but the French and British suffered a stunning defeat.

Depending upon the nature of a particular war, there are many substitutes for victory. The Second World War was, however, a total unlimited conflict and the Allies could achieve their political objective of the unconditional surrender of the major Axis powers only in the wake of military victory. Thus, strategy and policy became almost identical and war plans either helped or hindered the overall effort.

The United States during the Second World War waged campaigns on a global scale from the islands of the South Pacific to the plains of Germany. Every major operation was based on a war plan that was either a combined Anglo-American effort or a purely American concept. Some of the plans – Torch and Overlord – are well known, while others – Shingle and Cartwheel – are remembered primarily by participants and scholars. There were, of course, literally hundreds of war plans each with its own code name. The plans ranged from broad strategic concepts to small unit operations. The major plans dealing with theater level operations form the subject of this volume which will attempt to do a number of things. It will describe initial American strategic designs and their modification as a result of inter-Allied disagreements, internal debates and enemy actions. It will then set forth the means and objectives of the major war plans and discuss their execution. Finally, it will attempt to explain the gap, where it existed, between the war plans and the reality of battle.

NOTES

1. E.B. Long, ed., *Personal Memoirs of U.S. Grant.* New York, DaCapo Press, 1952, p. 366.
2. Ibid., p. 367.
3. Helmuth Graf von Moltke, *Strategy; Its Theory and Application: The Wars for German Unification, 1866–1871.* Westport, Greenwood Press, 1971, p. 172.
4. Ibid., p. 187.

1

The Grand Design

The United States and Great Britain reached a fundamental agreement on global strategy early in 1941 even before America became a participant in the Second World War. Washington and London agreed upon the paramount strategic importance of the Atlantic and European area, and in case of a two-ocean conflict the powers agreed upon the necessity of defeating a European enemy before seeking victory in the Pacific. The Anglo-American ABC 1 agreement and the American Rainbow 5 Plan set forth the basic assumptions that were to guide at least in broad outline the conduct of American strategy from 1941 to 1945. American military planners also produced a general plan for national mobilization in a global war.

The primacy of the Atlantic and European areas had been a cardinal element in American strategic thinking for many decades. During the interwar years American strategic planners had dealt with two broad categories of problem. The Joint Army and Navy Board produced a series of war plans to deal with possible contingencies including internal subversion, revolution in the Philippines, intervention in China and war against Mexico. United States forces could execute most of the plans with existing forces. The second set of plans dealt with war against a major power – Britain or Japan. The United States lacked the forces to cope with either country unless there was a major mobilization of human and economic resources. The planners, however, did not believe that war with either power was likely. Plan Orange for war against the Japanese Empire and Plan Red for war against the British Empire were essentially paper exercises designed to train staff officers in the complexities of waging a major conflict.

Almost all the Joint Board's plans dealt with a conflict with a single power. The plan for intervention in China did have the United States acting in concert with other countries, but projected forces were small, and China was the single focus of Plan Yellow. The sole exception was the Red–Orange Plan, an exercise for a global war. Although a training effort, the Red–Orange Plan did establish a strategic concept that had a major impact on American thinking about a real global war.

Plan Red–Orange assumed that a hostile coalition consisting of the British Empire and Japan would be based on expediency. The European war would start first, and Japan would strike at the United States only after American forces were engaged against the British.[1] The initial phases of hostilities in the Pacific would involve naval operations to contain the American Navy, air attacks against Hawaii and invasions of Guam and the Philippines.[2]

An invasion of continental United States was unlikely, but at the commencement of hostilities the country would be unprepared for a global war. The nation would have to mobilize its resources for a long war, and the development of adequate forces would tax its resources. As the nation mobilized for a maximum effort, forces in being would have to cope as best they could.[3]

Initially, the United States would have to accept territorial losses which might be regained later or at a peace conference. Available forces would focus their initial efforts on securing the north-eastern portion of the United States thereby defending the heart of American industrial might and the hub of the country's commercial activity. US forces would also hold the Panama Canal. Outlying possessions including Guam, the Philippines and even Alaska would be defended by unreinforced local garrisons, and Orange forces would probably capture them.[4]

Once America had generated adequate forces she would take the offensive as soon as possible. The Joint Board rejected the strategy of standing on the defensive against both Red and Orange until the country was fully mobilized since such a course of action would leave the initiative to the enemy. Planners also rejected the concept of attacking Orange first. Orange was the weaker member of the hostile coalition and thus easier to defeat, but geography alone precluded a rapid defeat of Orange while doing little to weaken Red which was geographically much closer to vital areas in the continental United

States. Consequently, the Joint Board decided to assume a defensive posture against Orange and concentrate on obtaining a favorable decision over Red.[5] By defeating Red first American power would have developed to a point where the defeat of Orange was a foregone conclusion.

The Red–Orange Plan was not, of course, a precise forecast of the strategy of the Second World War. Since Britain was a presumed enemy, much of the plan dwelt on operations against Canada and British colonies in the Caribbean. Moreover, the plan never defined the conditions of victory. It presumed that the exhaustion of enemy resources would ultimately produce favorable, if undefined, peace terms. The plan also assumed that major fleet actions would be sought in the Atlantic and that the United States would fight without major allies of its own.[6]

Nevertheless, the Red–Orange Plan did establish the concept that in a global war an enemy in Europe posed a greater danger to the United States than an Asian opponent. Furthermore, the nation would seek to defeat the European foe first while standing on the defense and even accepting significant territorial losses in the Pacific. Thus, geography and resources led American war planners to adopt a 'Europe first' strategy. Finally, the plan enabled staff officers to identify and attempt to resolve a range of problems associated with waging a global war.

Written in the benign international environment of the 1920s and early 1930s, the Red–Orange Plan was little more than a staff problem. By the late 1930s, however, many American political and military figures came to view German, Italian and Japanese expansionism as potentially dangerous to the national interests of the United States. Although there was no national consensus on how to respond to the new disquieting security environment, military planners had to respond to changes in the international situation.

Shortly after Munich – 12 November 1938 – the Joint Board ordered its planning staff to undertake exploratory studies and estimates as to possible responses by the armed services to violations of the Monroe Doctrine by one or more of the Fascist powers and a simultaneous Japanese effort to expand further in the Pacific. Planners were to assume that the European democracies would remain neutral and that the United States would have to act unilaterally.[7]

3

Completed early in 1939, the exploratory studies dealt with three scenarios: Japanese aggression in the Pacific, German and Italian aggression in the Atlantic and combined action by all three powers. Unilateral Japanese aggression would make substantial initial gains including the seizure of the Philippines and Guam and sea and air attacks on Hawaii. The American response involved a counter-attack across the Central Pacific, reconquest of the Philippines and the ultimate blockade of the Japanese home islands[8] – a replay of the Orange Plan which the Joint Board had been working on and revising for many years. German and Italian aggression would be limited by geographic constraints to submarine warfare and subversion in South and Central America. Germany and Italy might also attempt to seize bases in West Africa and the Atlantic islands in order to mount air raids on the Panama Canal. The American response involved naval action to deny the enemy access to the Americas and the creation of expeditionary forces to recapture German and Italian airheads and establish in their place American bases.[9]

In the case of a three-power attack the planners again emphasized the overriding importance of the Atlantic and European areas. The estimates explicitly stated that in the event of concerted aggression there was no doubt that American vital interests required offensive measures in the Atlantic against Germany and Italy to preserve the Caribbean and the Panama Canal. Consequently, at the start of hostilities, the United States would have to assume a defensive posture in the Pacific. Thus, despite the incongruity of the studies the Joint Board dealt for the first time with the prospect of a global war against likely enemies. Moreover, the Board again emphasized the strategic concept of the primacy of the Atlantic and the consequent requirement of defeating European opponents before dealing decisively with threats in the Pacific.

In July 1939, as war drew closer in Europe, the Joint Board ordered its planning staff to draw up a series of plans – the Rainbow Plans – based on a variety of strategic assumptions. Originally the Board established scenarios that required four different plans, but in April 1940 it agreed with the planners that the advent of war in Europe required a fifth scenario to enable the military to respond to an increasingly complex and dangerous situation.[10]

Rainbow 1, the only plan completed before the start of the Second World War, based its terms of reference on the need to protect the

United States and the Western Hemisphere down to latitude 10 °S, just below the bulge of Brazil, from German and Italian aggression. At the same time, American forces would have to protect the Aleutians, Midway and Hawaii from Japanese attacks. The Philippines and Guam were not included within the American defense perimeter and would have to rely on local resources for their defense. In Rainbow 1 the United States would act alone.[11] The army and navy would secure American bases in the Caribbean, occupy Natal in Brazil to deny potential air bases to the enemy and establish American bases in the area, and deny the enemy sea or air access to the Western Hemisphere north of latitude 10 °S. Action in the Pacific would be defensive. American forces would seek to hold Batan and deny Japan access to Manila Bay as long as possible.[12]

Rainbow 2 presumed that a European war was in progress and that the United States would enter the conflict on the side of England and France once Japan attacked the Far Eastern interests of the democratic powers. America's major effort would be to operate almost exclusively in the Pacific in co-operation with the British, French and Dutch.[13] Rainbow 3 dealt with a similar situation, but in this case American forces would at the start of hostilities conduct primarily defensive operations.[14] Due to the rapidly changing global strategic situation, the government never approved Rainbow 2, and Rainbow 3 was never written.

In the wake of the German victories in Western Europe Rainbow 4 sought to protect the Western Hemisphere and the eastern Pacific up to and including Midway Island. The planners presumed that Germany and Italy had defeated England and France and would join Japan in a war against the United States which would have to fight alone. The US Navy with fifteen battleships, six aircraft carriers, eighteen heavy and nineteen light cruisers, 156 destroyers and 1,741 aircraft of all types would have been hard pressed to fulfill its missions under the Rainbow 4 scenario. The Army with eight infantry and one cavalry division supported by 2,200 aircraft would also have found it difficult to respond to the demands of the plan.[15] America's basic strategy closely resembled the concepts in Rainbow 1 with the significant difference that forces required for Rainbow 4 were much larger.[16]

Rainbow 5 originally focused on the Atlantic and Europe. The purpose of the plan was to provide for the projection of American forces to the eastern Atlantic as rapidly as possible. The United States forces in conjunction with Great Britain and France would operate either in Africa or Europe or both continents to accomplish the decisive defeat of Germany.[17] The plan did not initially envisage a two-ocean war. Rather, American forces were to defend the Western Hemisphere and project power against European enemies in conjunction with Allies much as had been done during the First World War.

The Rainbow Plans were quite limited in scope. Rainbows 1 and 4 were essentially defensive in orientation. The United States, acting alone, would counter attacks coming from Europe and the Pacific. Both plans in some respects resembled the old Red–Orange Plan. Rainbows 2 and 3 did have the United States operating as a member of a coalition, but action in both plans was confined to the Pacific. Initially, Rainbow 5 projected a scenario of war against European powers. The United States would operate within the framework of a coalition. Action would be confined to Europe and North Africa but there would be no simultaneous war in the Pacific. It was not until late 1940 that the Joint Board began to focus on the problems of acting as an alliance member within the context of a global war.

German victories and Japanese expansion convinced the government to undertake measures of military expansion including the introduction of peacetime conscription and the construction of a greatly enlarged fleet. The administration also began to supply ever increasing amounts of aid to Great Britain. After the elections of 1940, Admiral H.R. Stark, Chief of Naval Operations (CNO), submitted to the Secretary of the Navy, a paper later known as Plan Dog, in which he discussed the strategic options open to the United States.

Admiral Stark's basic premise was that Britain's survival and success in the current conflict was of vital importance to the United States. If Britain won the war, he argued, the United States could win everywhere. If Britain lost, the United States would confront grave strategic dilemmas, and while the country might not lose everywhere, it might possibly not be able to win anywhere.[18]

Admiral Stark asserted that the physical security of the United States and the Western Hemisphere was a fundamental requirement. The balance of power in Europe was in turn essential to American security. The collapse of Britain and the surrender or destruction of the Royal Navy would destroy the balance and free hostile military power for operations against the Western Hemisphere.[19] Thus, the future of American security was linked to the fate of Britain.

In late 1940 it was by no means a foregone conclusion that Britain would be able to continue to resist German power or avoid defeat in other parts of the world. A British victory would require offensive operations on the European continent, but Britain lacked the resources to defeat the Germans alone and therefore required the help of powerful allies. Should the United States enter the war, aid to Britain would of necessity involve the deployment of land armies to Europe or Africa or even both continents.[20]

The CNO recognized that the American government and people wished to remain at peace, but he insisted that national leaders had to face the possibility that the country might at any moment become involved in the war. The government and the military, therefore, had to devise a policy and a strategy for this eventuality. If war came, where and for what objectives should America fight?[21] The Admiral then presented four alternative strategies for war against both Germany and Japan.

Plan A called for hemispheric defense which would allow the nation to stay out of war unless directly attacked. No major military effort would be required, and aid to Allies would consist of material support. Under Plan A, however, the United States could exert little influence on the outcome of the war.[22]

Plan B called for a full-scale offensive against Japan in conjunction with British and Dutch forces in the Far East and a strict defensive posture in the Atlantic. Geography alone dictated that a Pacific war would be a conflict of long duration. It would also restrict the flow of aid to Britain, and if Britain were defeated, America would in any case have to reorient its efforts to the Atlantic.[23]

Plan C called for the United States to undertake major campaigns in both the Atlantic and Pacific. Given the current state of the armed forces, a dual offensive ran the risk of being too weak in both oceans. America in 1940 lacked the military resources to fight offensively in both the Atlantic and Pacific, and one or both offensives risked the grim possibility of defeat.[24]

Plan D called for a strong offensive in the Atlantic in conjunction with the British and a defensive campaign in the Pacific. Any strength diverted to the Pacific, Admiral Stark argued, would reduce forces available for operations against Germany. Operations in the

7

Atlantic would require the United States to send naval and air forces to the British Isles and the Mediterranean. The Americans and British might also have to seize the Portuguese and Spanish islands in the Atlantic. The Allies would also have to mount large-scale land operations on the European continent. The plan provided for the concentration of American might in a single decisive theater. It sacrificed the American position in the Pacific at least until the European war was successfully concluded.[25]

Admiral Stark concluded that Plan D best suited American national interests and recommended that the United States Army and Navy undertake immediate talks with the British, Canadians and Dutch in order to devise common plans and promote Allied unity of effort if and when the United States entered the war.[26] Using the CNO's memorandum as a foundation, the Joint Board approved on 21 December 1940 a paper dealing with the National Defense Policy of the Unites States. The paper reached the same conclusions as Plan Dog.[27] Though not formally approving the paper, President Roosevelt agreed to hold informal secret staff conversations with the British.

On 21 January 1941, the Joint Board approved a paper providing instructions for the American representatives to the forthcoming talks. The Board described the nation's strategy in terms that closely resembled the approach taken in Plan Dog. The fundamental principle of American policy was the security of the Western Hemisphere, and to this end the American government would continue to offer material and diplomatic support to the British Commonwealth. By diplomatic means the United States would continue to oppose any further extension of Japanese rule in Asia. If the United States entered the war, American strategy would emphasize the primary importance of the Atlantic and Europe and would seek the defeat of Germany and its allies as the first call upon the nation's resources. If Japan joined the conflict, the United States would conduct Pacific operations in such a manner as to facilitate the execution of the major military effort in the Atlantic. President Roosevelt approved the instructions on 26 January 1941.[28]

Thus, for the first time an American government agreed to devise a common strategy with a prospective ally prior to entering a war. The basic American view – the Atlantic and Germany first – was a function of previous experience and the prevailing strategic situation in early 1941. During the First World War American military efforts had been primarily focused on the Western Front. Inter-war staff studies of a global war had emphasized that threats from Europe were more dangerous than threats from Asia. German victories in 1939 and 1940 and the possibility of British defeat further strengthened the view of military planners that in a global conflict America first had to deal with a European menace even at the expense of initial sacrifices in the Pacific.

The British and American military delegations met in Washington from 29 January to 29 March 1941. The talks, known as the ABC 1 Conference sought to provide a strategic framework for a future Anglo-American war effort if and when the United States became involved in hostilities.

The Report of the Staff Conversations stated clearly that the goals of the conference were: to determine the best methods by which the forces of the United States and the British Commonwealth could defeat Germany and its allies, to co-ordinate plans for the employment of British, American and other allied forces and to reach agreements concerning areas of responsibility, military strategy and the strength of British and American forces. The American and British delegates also agreed to work together continuously in the formulation and execution of operational plans and that even operations conducted by a single allied power would be subject to Anglo-American co-ordination.[29]

The British and Americans readily agreed to the 'Germany first' concept, and the report bluntly stated that the broad strategic objective of any Anglo-American coalition would be the defeat of Germany and its allies.[30] As a prerequisite to offensive operations the two powers agreed that they first had to accomplish a number of essential defensive tasks.

The United States had to protect the Western Hemisphere from European or Asiatic enemies, a task that appeared feasible as long as Britain remained in the war. The British had to provide for the safety of the United Kingdom, the dominions and the colonies in order to sustain the war effort. In 1941 the security of Britain and the Commonwealth was not a foregone conclusion. Finally, the Allies had to maintain the security of their sea lines of communication against a growing U-boat menace.[31] The Allies realized that although difficult to achieve, the security of the sea lanes was essential. Winning the Battle of the Atlantic might not guarantee victory, but losing the struggle would lead to almost certain defeat.

The British and Americans agreed to a number of offensive strategic concepts to achieve their basic objective – the defeat of Germany. The concepts generally matched current Anglo-American capabilities but several of them were not particularly effective.

The Allies agreed to wage economic warfare against Germany using blockade and control of vital resources at their source. Blockade was a traditional strategy. The British had often used it in previous wars. Economic warfare was, however, a long-term undertaking, and in 1941 German control of Western Europe and Berlin's *de facto* alliance with Moscow would make efforts to undermine the German economy exceedingly difficult.[32]

The British and Americans also called for a sustained air offensive against German military power including attacks on targets in occupied countries. Until 1941 RAF attacks on German targets had been generally ineffective, and neither the British nor the Americans fully understood the massive requirements involved in a sustained and effective aerial offensive.[33]

Because of their concern for their strategic position in the Mediterranean, the British were particularly concerned to eliminate Italy from the war as soon as possible. The Americans accepted this strategic concept since it was important to the overall security of the British Empire which Americans regarded as vital to the security of the United States.[34] Although London and Washington reached agreement easily on the issue of driving Italy from the war, the formulation of Mediterranean strategy would later become very contentious.

The Conference also agreed to mount raids and minor offensives against the Axis powers and to support resistance movements on the European continent.[35] Raids were withering the British and American military capabilities in 1941 but they could not produce decisive results. Nor could resistance movements defeat the Germans without the direct intervention of Allied armies in Europe. The British, however, placed great hope in the efficacy of guerrilla operations perhaps because there were no other alternatives in 1941.

Finally, the British and Americans agreed to capture positions from which to launch eventual offensives against Germany.[36] In early 1941 both Washington and London were concerned that Germany might seize bases in West Africa and in the Spanish and Portuguese Atlantic islands. If the Germans obtained bases in these areas, they could greatly expand the scope of their U-boat operations. Additionally, the Americans were concerned that the Axis might use advanced bases as stepping stones to intervene in Latin America. Thus, Anglo-American concern for the capture of advance bases was in 1941 governed as much by defensive as offensive considerations.

The ABC 1 Conference also reached agreement on overall guidance for future military operations. Participants agreed that since Germany was the predominant Axis power, the Atlantic and European area would be the decisive theater, and the principal United States effort would be exerted in that theater. If Japan entered the war, military strategy in the Far East would be defensive although forces in the region could act aggressively to contain Japanese thrusts. Finally, the Conference agreed to maintain the current British position in the Mediterranean and to counter and prevent the expansion of Axis power in North Africa.[37] The British and Americans also divided the globe into major operating regions wherein one commander would direct all allied forces. To avoid the problems that arose concerning the deployment of American troops during the First World War the Conference agreed that when forces of one power served under the strategic direction of the other, the forces involved would serve under their own national commanders and would not be distributed in small formations to units of the other ally.[38]

The Conference also produced the United States–British Commonwealth Joint Basic War Plan[39] which did not attempt to go beyond the opening stages of the projected conflict and dealt primarily with initial defensive tasks and force deployments. The United States Navy would operate in the Western Atlantic securing sea lines of communications, protecting the Western Hemisphere and preparing to occupy the Azores and Cape Verde Islands. A force including three battleships and eighteen destroyers would operate out of Halifax, and a strike force of two aircraft carriers and escorts would, according to circumstances, operate from Newport, Trinidad or Bermuda. A small force of four cruisers, nine destroyers and thirty-six seaplanes was assigned to protect the coastal frontiers. The Army, which was in the process of creating a thirty-three division force, would have only six ready by September. Initial army missions included defense of Caribbean bases and the Canal Zone and continued expansion for offensive operations against Germany. The Army Air Corps while in the process of creating twenty-three bombardment and seventeen fighter groups would contribute to the defense of the Western Hemisphere and send forces to Britain as soon as possible.[40]

In the Pacific the fleet would, in case of war with Japan, secure Hawaii and prepare to attack the Marshall Islands. The Army and Army Air Force in the Pacific would contribute to the defense of Hawaii and the West Coast. Hawaii and Alaska would receive additional ground forces, but Guam and the Philippines would have to rely on forces already present.[41]

The United Kingdom and British home waters were, naturally, British responsibilities. The bulk of the Royal Navy including three battleships, two battlecruisers, two aircraft carriers, twenty cruisers and over 200 destroyer types served in the Home Fleet or in other commands around the British Isles. If America entered the war, the US Navy would commit 27 destroyers and 48 patrol planes to the North-Western Approaches. The United States would also relieve British forces in Iceland and send an infantry regiment to England as soon as possible. The Air Corps would send thirty-two squadrons of bombers and pursuit aircraft to England after the start of hostilities.[42] The United States would also relieve the Royal Navy's Force H which guarded the Straits of Gibraltar with a force built around three battleships and an aircraft carrier.[43]

The British would control allied operations in the Mediterranean and Far East. There were no plans for the United States to send ground and air units to the Mediterranean or Middle East. If American naval units entered the Mediterranean, they would operate under British command. In the Far East, British, Dutch and American forces remained under individual national control. Commanders were to co-ordinate their activities when possible.[44] Thus, overall British strategic control in the Far East was at best nominal.

The Allies, of course, underestimated the extent of the U-boat threat and American forces guarding the Atlantic coast were inadequate. Moreover, Anglo-American planners substantially underestimated Japanese capabilities. No serious planning for offensive operations against the Germans in Europe had been undertaken, and the emphasis on Mediterranean strategy was later to cause serious problems between Washington and London. On the other hand, nobody was clairvoyant, and detailed planning for a European campaign was simply not feasible in early 1941.

12

Despite its shortcomings, the ABC-1 Conference with its Basic War Plan re-emphasized the American commitment to the 'Germany first' strategy and provided guidance for initial steps if and when the United States entered the conflict. The ABC 1 Conference thus provided a basic reference point from which the Allies could evolve future strategy.

In April 1941 American, British and Dutch planners met in Singapore to devise a strategic plan to cope with possible Japanese aggression. The planners noted the strategic guidance set by ABC 1 but, nevertheless, called for local offensive operations to stem any Japanese advance. These ADB Conversations called for the rein-forcement of Luzon, an expansion of the bomber force in the Philippines and the creation of a substantial bomber force in China. The small US Asiatic Fleet would operate from Manila, and if necessary, retreat to Singapore and operate with British naval forces sent from European waters. The American Pacific Fleet would also act offensively to halt Japanese moves into Southeast Asia.[45]

In August the Joint Board approved a Canadian–American Defense Plan, ABC 22, to provide for the defense of North America and for combined action against Germany. ABC 22 presumed that Canadian–American co-operation would conform to the strategic guidelines set forth in ABC 1. ABC 22 dealt mainly with measures of military co-ordination and the establishment of unity of command following the methods of ABC 1. The plan also provided for mutual reinforcement of vital areas. The Americans agreed to send some 54,000 troops to Newfoundland and the Canadians promised 9,100 men to reinforce Alaska.[46]

While conducting talks with the British and Canadians, the Joint Board also undertook an estimate of the forces the United States required to defeat Germany and Japan. President Roosevelt had directed the Board to study production requirements on 9 July.[47] The Joint Board approved the staff study entitled *Joint Board Estimate of the United States Over-all Production Requirements* on 11 September 1941, and the Secretaries of War and Navy forwarded it to the President on 25 September.[48]

The Joint Board Estimate, known as the Victory Program, dealt with the size of the armed forces as a necessary basis for deriving production requirements. The Joint Board assumed that future strategy and force levels would also be based upon the political objective of defeating Germany. The Board next defined the defeat of Germany in terms tantamount to a call for unconditional surrender. The Board stated that the United States should strive for the complete military defeat of Germany. Doubtless, recalling the results of 1918, the Board noted that an inconclusive peace would lead to another war and would not provide for long-term American security. Moreover the German government was unlikely to collapse short of defeat. Therefore, the complete military destruction of Germany was the only alternative. Furthermore, it was an alternative that the United States should pursue even if Britain and the Soviet Union were defeated and America had to fight alone.[49] Thus, American military leaders called for a policy of unconditional surrender, or something close to it, and the Service Secretaries agreed. The President accepted the victory program without comment indicating that the Estimate did clearly define forthcoming policy and strategy in the war – total mobilization directed toward the complete destruction of German power.

American strategy also included maintaining control of the sea lanes in the Atlantic. A new element – the Eastern Front – received serious attention for the first time in American planning. The Joint Board noted that the Soviets were engaging the bulk of the German armed forces. The outcome of the war in the east was unclear, but if Soviet forces, even if driven beyond the Urals, could continue organized resistance, there would remain the hope of a final and complete defeat of Germany by land operations. Sustaining the Soviet war effort was, therefore, an important, even vital, consideration in American strategy.[50]

To achieve the country's overall objectives the Navy calculated its manpower requirements to be 1.1 million sailors and 150,000 Marines. By 1946 the Navy required a fleet of thirty-two battleships, twenty-four aircraft carriers, 111 cruisers, 444 destroyers, 238 submarines, 1,093 utility craft and 1,329 patrol vessels. The Navy currently possessed or had under construction most of the required forces but needed an additional six carriers, eighty destroyers and fifty-four submarines to fulfill requirements. The naval air arm required 8,714 combat aircraft and 8,136 replacement planes. The Navy also needed 4,218 trainers and miscellaneous airplanes and an annual replacement rate of 18,000 planes. Finally, the Navy called for a merchant marine of 27 million gross tons. By 1943 existing programs would provide 10.7 million tons and 6.7 million tons were currently available. Thus an additional 9.6 million tons of shipping had to be constructed by 1944.[51]

The Army also set requirements for very large forces based on a very pessimistic strategic assessment. The Joint Board staff believed that the Soviets might not be defeated or, if defeated in European Russia, might continue to offer resistance east of the Urals, whereas the Army Staff was convinced that the Germans would, by July 1942, destroy all vestiges of Soviet power. By 1 July 1943 the Germans would have begun the economic exploitation of European Russia and, leaving minimal occupation forces in the east, would begin the process of moving forces back to Europe. Army planners, therefore, set 1 July 1943 as the date when the United States had to be prepared to conduct major operations.[52]

Faced with an estimated 300 to 400 Axis divisions, the Army called for the creation of a force of approximately 215 divisions, over sixty of which would be armored. Support and service units included over 300 anti-tank and more than 125 separate artillery battalions. Ground force manpower requirements totalled 6,745,000 officers and men. About 2,199,000 men would serve in task forces for operations abroad; 1.2 million would man fixed defenses in the Western Hemisphere, and 3 million would constitute a strategic reserve for use where required.[53]

The Air Force, though part of the Army, submitted its own strategy and estimates. Known as A-WPD1, the plan identified a number of bottlenecks in the German economy which, if heavily damaged, could do irreparable harm to the German war economy. A-WPD1 therefore called for sustained precision bombing of a series of target sets including oil and electricity production.[54]

To execute A-WPD1 the Air Force needed 2,050,000 personnel, eighty-one heavy and twenty-six light bomber, and fifty-four fighter groups. The Air Force also requested two observation and thirty-two transport groups and 37,051 training aircraft. By 1943 the Air Force estimated that aircraft in service would have to include 7,097 heavy and medium bombers, 2,201 light bombers, 8,775 fighters, 2,043 observation planes and 2,560 transports plus aircraft used for training. Moreover, each category required replacement at a rate of twenty-five percent a month.[55]

The numbers predicted by the armed services were not

particularly accurate. The Navy, for example, ended the war with over 3,383,000 men and the Marine Corps with 476,000. The Navy also underestimated the need for aircraft carriers and ended the war with twenty fleet, eight light and seventy escort carriers in service.[56] The 1941 estimates never dealt with the need for more than 60,000 landing craft of various types. The naval air arm by 1945 contained 29,583 combat aircraft and 8,195 trainers.[57]

The Army wound up smaller and the Air Force larger than the original projections. By mid-1945 the Army contained eighty-nine divisions and 5,946,000 men. The Army Air Force by mid-1945 had 243 groups with 13,390 heavy bombers, 5,384 medium bombers and 3,079 light bombers as well as 16,799 fighters, 1,971 observation, 9,561 transport and 9,558 training planes. Manpower included 2,354,000 officers and men.[58]

That specific figures differed from 1941 estimates is not surprising. The vast number of imponderables in a global war made precise prewar estimates impossible. The Victory Program, however, came remarkably close to predicting the total number of men and women needed to wage a global war. Moreover, the Estimate helped make the government and the military vividly aware of the magnitude of the tasks they were contemplating. The effort required to wage a global war would necessitate the mobilization not only of combatant power but also the nation's economy on a scale never before undertaken.

Meanwhile, the strategic consensus reached with Britain at the ABC 1 Conference was reasserted at the Argentia Conference in August. The growing probability that the United States would enter the war in the not too distant future led the Joint Board to order a revision of the Rainbow 5 Plan so that it might conform to the strategy of ABC 1.

Approved by the Joint Board on 19 November 1941, Rainbow 5 was specifically based upon the conclusions of the ABC 1 Conference. Thus Rainbow 5 had as its basic strategic premise the probability of a two-ocean war in contrast to the original 1940 scenario which contemplated only American participation in a European conflict.[59] In its final form the basic strategic approach of Rainbow 5 was that the Atlantic and European area would be the decisive theater and the United States would exert its principal efforts in that region. If Japan entered the war, strategy in the Far East would be essentially defensive although the Pacific Fleet would conduct tactical offensive operations to divert Japanese strength away from the Malay barrier.[60]

Rainbow 5 also followed ABC 1 concepts concerning the necessity of controlling the Atlantic sea lines of communication with the US Navy concentrating its major efforts on the north-western approaches. Rainbow 5 accepted the need to help the British to retain their position in the Mediterranean and to prevent the expansion of Axis control in North Africa. Finally, it called for the creation of large land and air forces for major offensives against the Axis powers.[61]

Rainbow 5 set forth boundaries of American land and sea defense commands and provided a troop list of forces destined to serve overseas during the first three months of deployment which might or might not be coincidental with the beginning of hostilities. The Army planned to send during the first forty-five days of deployment 51,700 men and 349 aircraft to England, 17,300 men and 108 aircraft to Northern Ireland, 10,100 to Alaska, 17,300 to Hawaii and 59,300 men to destinations stretching from Iceland to the West Coast of South America. After the first set of deployments, Rainbow 5 called for the dispatch of 86,000 troops to the east coast of South America and the formation of a ten-division contingency force.[62] The planners finally noted that if the deployments began before 1 July 1942 the orderly movement of forces would not be possible.[63]

By late November 1941 American strategic planners had created a strategic framework for the conduct of the Second World War. Pre-war plans had established the paramount importance of the European theater and the necessity of working in close collaboration with the British. The threat of Japanese aggression though serious, was secondary. Planners also noted the importance of the Russian front although they remained divided on the Soviet Union's ability to survive the German invasion. Finally, military strategists were agreed that if America became involved in a two-ocean war, its primary efforts had to be devoted to defeating Germany first.

Pre-war plans, however, left many issues unresolved. A specific approach for defeating Germany was not proposed in either ABC 1 or Rainbow 5. A detailed plan to defeat Germany was not possible in 1941, for there were simply too many variables, but the absence of a basic operational approach left much room for disagreement between British and American military leaders.

The British tended to favor a peripheral approach while the Americans tended to emphasize concentration of force. The Americans accepted the need to maintain the British position in the Mediterranean and Middle East. The Americans also agreed upon the need to acquire advanced bases and to drive Italy out of the war. The Americans, however, regarded these tasks as necessary preconditions, defensive moves to stem Axis expansion, prior to striking at the core of German power. The British tended to view direct thrusts at Germany as the culmination rather than the start of a process to be undertaken only after Germany had been seriously weakened by losses sustained in peripheral operations and on the Eastern Front. This divergence of approach was not resolved in 1940 and 1941 and was to be an element of discord throughout the war.

American and British planners alike drastically underestimated Japan, believing that if Japan attacked, the Allies could hold the Malay barrier and attack the Japanese mandates without having to deploy major forces to the Far East and Pacific. This failure of perception was to have far-reaching consequences for American and Anglo-American strategy. The United States would have to send significant forces to the Pacific simply to check the Japanese offensives and thus delay the generation of forces for service in the Atlantic and Europe. The pull of the Pacific would also affect American ability to influence Allied decisions concerning operations in the European area.

Pre-war planning did, however, provide the United States with a sense of the magnitude of the forthcoming conflict. Strategists understood that the war would be long, global and difficult. It would be a war of production, of material and of coalitions. Furthermore, pre-war planning did stress the importance of coalition unity and 'Germany first' – principles that were to guide American strategic thinking throughout the conflict.

NOTES

1. Joint Army and Navy Basic War Plan Red and Orange in Steven Ross, ed., *American War Plans 1919–1941*, Vol. 2. New York, Garland Publishing, 1992.
2. Ibid.
3. Ibid.
4. Ibid.
5. Ibid.

6. Ibid.
7. Joint Board 325 (Serial 634) in Steven Ross, ed., *American War Plans 1919–1941*, Vol. 3. New York, Garland Publishing, 1992.
8. Ibid.
9. Ibid.
10. Joint Board 325 (Serial 642) and Serial 632-1 in Ross, op. cit.
11. JB No. 325 (Serial 642–1) Joint Army and Navy Basic War Plan Rainbow, No. 1 in Ross op. cit.
12. Ibid.
13. JB No. 325 (Serial 642–2) Joint Army and Navy Basic War Plan – Rainbow No. 2 in Ross, op. cit.
14. JB No. 325 (Serial 642) op. cit.
15. JB No. 325 (Serial 642–4) Joint Army and Navy Basic War Plan Rainbow No. 4 in Ross op. cit.
16. Ibid.
17. JB No. 325 (Serial 642) in Ross, op. cit.
18. Navy Department Op-12-CTB in Ross, op. cit.
19. Ibid.
20. Ibid.
21. Ibid.
22. Ibid.
23. Ibid.
24. Ibid.
25. Ibid.
26. Ibid.
27. JB No. 325 (Serial 670) in Ross op. cit.
28. JB No. 325 (Serial 674) in Ross op. cit.
29. U.S. Serial 011512-12(R) B. U.S. (J) (41) 30 Short Title ABC-1 in Steven Ross, ed., *American War Plans 1919–1941*, Vol. 4. New York, Garland Publishing, 1992.
30. Ibid.
31. Ibid.
32. Ibid.
33. Ibid.
34. Ibid.
35. Ibid.
36. Ibid.
37. Ibid.
38. Ibid.
39. The Joint Basic War Plan appeared in Annex III of the ABC-1 Report.
40. Ibid.
41. Ibid.
42. Ibid.
43. Ibid.
44. Ibid.
45. American–Dutch–British Conversations, Singapore, April, 1941 (Short Title – 'A–D–B') in Ross, op. cit.
46. Joint Canadian–United States Basic Defense Plan, No. 2 (Short Title ABC-22) JB No. 325 (Serial 717) in Ross, op. cit.
47. JB No. 355 (Serial 707) contains President Roosevelt's letter to the Secretary of the Navy requesting him to join with the Secretary of War in estimating production requirements. This document is to be found in Steven Ross, ed., *American War Plans 1919–1941*, Vol. 5. New York, Garland Publishing, 1992.

48. JB No. 355 (Serial 707) in Ross, op. cit. contains both the estimate and various letters of transmittal.
49. Ibid., Appendix I.
50. Ibid.
51. Ibid.
54. Ibid.
55. Ibid.
56. *Annual Report Fiscal Year 1945. The Secretary of the Navy to the President of the United States.* Washington, D.C., 1946, pp. 15–31.
57. Ibid., p. 54.
58. Russell Weigley, *History of the United States Army*, New York, Macmillan Publishing, 1967, pp. 439–40 and M. Mauer, *Air Force Combat Units of World War II*, Washington, D.C., Office of Air Force History, 1961, p. 7.
59. JB No. 325 (Serial 642–5) Joint Army–Navy Basic War Plan – Rainbow No. 5 in Ross, op. cit.
60. Ibid.
61. Ibid.
62. Ibid.
63. Ibid.

2

Response to Catastrophe

The United States entered the Second World War committed to the strategy of devoting the nation's primary efforts to the Atlantic and European areas. If Japan entered the war, strategy in the Pacific would be defensive until the fate of Germany was sealed. It was then ironic that the first significant American offensives took place in the Pacific against Japan and in North Africa against the Vichy French.

For the United States and the Allies the months following 7 December 1941 were disastrous. On the Eastern Front the Germans were again on the move. In the Middle East the British were on the defensive, and at sea the U-boats were enjoying great success in North American coastal waters. In Asia and the Pacific the situation was, if anything, even more bleak as Japanese forces swept aside all opposition in the Pacific and Southeast Asia. Consequently, the British and Americans had to re-examine and substantially modify their pre-war plans and agreements.

Between 24 December 1941 and 14 January 1942, Anglo-American political and military leaders met in Washington. The Arcadia Conference attempted to reformulate Allied strategy in the light of recent events. On 31 December 1941, the United States and British Chiefs of Staff agreed that America and Britain, despite recent events, would continue to adhere to the 'Germany first' doctrine and that only the minimum force necessary would be diverted to the Pacific to halt the Japanese.[1]

The British and American participants, however, realized that they could do little more than execute essential defensive tasks: securing the United Kingdom, guarding essential sea lanes and supplying material aid to the USSR. Offensive moves included aerial bombardment, support of resistance movements, and possibly a move into North Africa, Operation Gymnast, to secure the Mediterranean. No major land offensive on the European continent was feasible in 1942.[2]

Anglo-American planners also had serious reservations about the feasibility of Gymnast. They noted that if the Allies undertook landings in French North Africa, shipping and escort shortages would preclude major movements in the Atlantic for at least three months. British reinforcements to the Middle East and India would also have to be severely curtailed. Reinforcements being sent to the Pacific and Australia further limited shipping available for use in the Atlantic.[3] Anglo-American planners agreed that for the immediate future Gymnast was simply not feasible, and on 13 January 1942, British and American planners bluntly stated that the Allies did not possess the resources to force an entry into French North Africa.[4]

In dealing with problems in the Pacific, military planners noted the need to protect a series of island air bases stretching from Hawaii to Australia. The Japanese had the capability to attack several places including New Caledonia and Fiji at an early date. Reinforcement of the island bases was, therefore, a pressing immediate requirement. Since Australia and New Zealand lacked sufficient resources, the United States would have to assume the task of providing garrisons to protect the air route.[5]

On 10 January 1942, the British and Americans established a new strategic area officially entitled the ABDA (American British Dutch Australian) area. The ABDA Command included Burma, Malaya, the Dutch East Indies and the Philippines. The Commander of the area was to maintain as many key positions as possible and to take the offensive as soon as feasible. Specifically, he was to hold the Malay Barrier, Burma and Australia and to attack north from the Dutch East Indies in order to re-establish communications with Luzon and support the Philippines garrison.[6] Given the existing military situation the military directive was at best overly optimistic.

The Arcadia Conference also established the structure for the future conduct of Anglo-American strategy. This Conference established the Combined Chiefs of Staff which was defined as the British Chiefs of Staff, or in their absence from Washington their duly accredited representatives, and their United States opposite numbers. Henceforth, the term 'Joint' applied to a single nation's inter-service co-operation and the word 'Combined' to collaboration between allied nations.[7]

The Combined Chiefs of Staff had a planning committee, a secretariat, and an intelligence committee. Tasks included recommending a program of requirements based on strategic considerations, settling issues of priority of overseas movements and establishing policy for the distribution of available weapons.[8] It soon became clear that control of material could not be separated from control of strategy, and by March the Combined Chiefs of Staff received authorization to deal with the entire strategic conduct of the war. The Combined Chiefs were to meet weekly or more often if necessary. The United States Chiefs of Staff were designated on an *ad hoc* basis the Joint Chiefs of Staff and developed their own national committee structure which resembled but was not precisely identical to the Joint Board system.

The Arcadia Conference participants recognized that the actual course of events rendered many elements of pre-war plans unfeasible. The orderly expansion of the American armed forces and their deployment overseas according to a precise timetable had of necessity to give way to a series of emergency expedients. Rainbow 5 deployments were to have begun in July 1942 whilst the rearmament program was initially to reach full development in mid-1943. The timing and course of the war imposed significant changes on American force generation, deployments and strategy. The creation of a permanent structure for Anglo-American strategic collaboration was an important achievement, but at the start of 1942 strategic initiative was in the hands of the Axis, and in both the Pacific and Atlantic the Allies had to wage a desperate struggle to restore a strategic equilibrium.

In the Pacific and Southeast Asia, Japanese advances made a mockery of Allied strategy. Singapore fell on 15 February 1942. The Japanese took over 100,000 prisoners. Less than a month later Japan had destroyed Allied naval power in the East Indies and was well on its way to overrunning the islands. By early April the Japanese were ashore on Luzon and quickly forced American and Filipino troops to surrender. Corregidor fell in early May while in Burma the Japanese rapidly overran the country and moved towards the Indian frontier. The ABDA Command ceased to exist, and if Europe remained the most important focus of Allied strategy, the Pacific was the most urgent area of concern.

On 30 March 1942, Australia, New Zealand, Great Britain and the

United States established a new command area – the southwest Pacific. Initial objectives for the new command were essentially defensive. The Commander was to secure Australia, check the Japanese conquest of the area, hold essential lines of communication and strike at enemy forces and bases in eastern Malaysia and the New Guinea–Bismarck–Solomon Islands region. The Commander was also to maintain the American position in the Philippines, wage economic warfare against Japan and support Allied operations in the Pacific Ocean area and the Indian theater. Finally, the Allies were to prepare to take the offensive.[9]

Despite the reduction in scope the tasks assigned to the Southwest Pacific Command were beyond the capabilities of Allied forces. The Allies had no realistic hope of holding the Malay Barrier or the Philippines and lacked the warships necessary to wage an effective campaign against Japanese shipping. In the spring of 1942 the Allied ability to mount counter-offensives was virtually non-existent.

An American Intelligence Committee report of 1 April 1942 described the Allied dilemma. The Committee noted that the initial reversals sustained by the United States and the British Empire required a sharp revision of earlier estimates of Japanese capabilities.[10] The Committee concluded that based on recent gains the Japanese had the ability to mount further campaigns to the south, east and west and that exploitation of recent conquests would render Japan virtually invulnerable in the raw materials required to sustain a long-term massive war effort. Moreover, Japan's conquests ranging from Burma to the Solomons provided her with a strategic defense in depth that would be very difficult to break.[11] Japan would soon become economically and militarily invulnerable and only by blocking or preferably reversing current Japanese expansion could the Allies forestall the serious consequences that would stem from Japan's ability to organize and exploit the recent gains.[12]

The need to check further Japanese advances began to draw growing numbers of men, ships and aircraft to the Pacific. In January 1942, the United States sent 3,927 Army and 507 Navy officers and men to Bora Bora to develop a fueling base.[13] In February the Joint Chiefs decided to send 54,250 men to Hawaii, increasing the garrison to 100,000 Army personnel, and in March the armed forces sent 6,400 Army, 650 Air Force and 800 Navy personnel to Tonga to set up an airfield and an anchorage.[14] Later in the month, the Americans undertook to reinforce Samoa with over 10,000 Marines and 4,000 Air Corps officers and men.[15] On 20 March the JCS ordered 4,700 troops and 1,200 sailors to reinforce the New Hebrides garrison.[16]

The British supported the American decision to rush forces to the Pacific. In the face of the Japanese advance, Australia threatened and New Zealand declared the intention to bring home forces serving in the Western Desert and Middle East. In early March, Prime Minister Churchill "asked President Roosevelt to send additional American forces to the Pacific to protect Australia and New Zealand thereby allowing the Dominion troops to remain in the Mediterranean. The President agreed, thus adding to the flow of troops to the Pacific.

The American public, angered and frightened by the Pearl Harbor attack and subsequent defeats, demanded action against the Japanese. Washington had to respond to public opinion, which, coupled with strategic considerations, made it politically impossible and strategically unwise to adhere to the pre-war plans that called for a purely defensive posture in the Pacific.

The Battle of the Coral Sea, an American strategic victory, halted Japanese attempts to capture New Guinea by sea, but the battle did not wrest the strategic initiative from Japan. Japanese forces soon began an overland march designed to capture Port Moresby and continued to move forces into the Solomon Islands. The US Navy's victory at Midway in June 1942 stopped the Japanese advance in the Central Pacific and evened the balance of naval forces. The Japanese, however, were still capable of offensive operations especially in New Guinea and the Solomons where ground operations could be supported by land-based aircraft. Thus Japan still retained the ability to threaten the sea lines of communication to Australia, and if unchallenged, Tokyo would organize and fortify recent gains making subsequent Allied offensives far more difficult and costly.

Pressures in the Pacific and the force of public opinion led Washington to commit more assets to the Pacific than to Europe throughout 1942 and well into the following year. Furthermore, strategic planners, in addition to organizing essential defensive tasks began to contemplate launching counter-offensives to prevent the Japanese from fortifying and exploiting economically their conquests.

As early as 27 April 1942, the Joint Planning Staff noted that American Pacific strategy involved four separate but interrelated tasks: maintaining the line of communications and supply to

Australia, maintaining a chain of fortified island bastions from Hawaii to New Caledonia, in order to assist in the first task and to achieve the third task of halting further Japanese advances to the south. Finally, the services had to assemble an amphibious force in the South Pacific to achieve the fourth task of offensive operations to the north-west.[17] On 29 April the Navy noted a requirement for an amphibious corps of two Marine divisions for use in minor landing operations and counter-attacks.[18] Thus, even before the victories of the Coral Sea and Midway, planners were considering operations to regain the strategic initiative in the Pacific.

On 2 July 1942, the Joint Chiefs of Staff issued a directive for offensive operations in the Pacific. The ultimate objective of the offensive was the seizure and occupation of the New Britain–New Ireland–New Guinea area. Due to the lack of sufficient forces, the Joint Chiefs divided the offensive into three separate tasks. Task One involved the seizure and occupation of the Santa Cruz Islands, Tulagi, and adjacent positions. Task Two called for the seizure and occupation of the remainder of the Solomon Islands and the northeast coast of New Guinea, and Task Three involved the capture of Rabaul and adjacent positions in the New Guinea–New Ireland area.[19] The Commander of the South Pacific Area which was a subordinate element of the Pacific Ocean Area would execute Task One. Tasks Two and Three were to be executed under the command of General Douglas MacArthur, who commanded the Southwest Pacific Area. The Joint Chiefs set 1 August 1942 as the date for the start of Task One.[20]

Intelligence reports indicating that the Japanese were building an airfield on Guadalcanal convinced operational commanders in the Pacific to add the island to the list of objectives of Task One. On 8 July 1942, the Commander of the Pacific Ocean Area noted that Task One objectives included the occupation of Santa Cruz, Tulagi and Guadalcanal and the establishment of advanced airbases to assist in halting Japanese offensives and the support of subsequent counterblows.[21] On 16 July the South Pacific Command directed that the landings on Tulagi and Guadalcanal, Operation Watchtower, would commence on 7 August.[22]

On 7 August 1942, the 1st Marine Division landed successfully on Guadalcanal, establishing a beachhead which included the half-completed Japanese airstrip. Elements of the division also seized

Tulagi and two small nearby islets. The Americans evidently expected that operations into the Solomons would soon follow the successful seizure of Guadalcanal, but the Japanese were determined to repel decisively the American offensive.

Guadalcanal, not even mentioned in the 2 July JCS directive and added as an objective almost as an afterthought, became a bitter battle of attrition that lasted until February 1943. The Japanese responded violently to the initial landings. They did not, however, carefully co-ordinate ground, naval and air attacks. Assaults on the Marine perimeter were often mounted with forces on hand without adequate gunfire support or reinforcements. Nevertheless, fighting was bitter; both sides fought tenaciously, and both sides suffered heavy casualties.

At sea the Americans lost two aircraft carriers, five heavy cruisers, an Australian cruiser, two light cruisers and fifteen destroyers. Japan lost a light carrier, two battleships, one light and three heavy cruisers, and eleven destroyers. The Americans also lost a transport and three auxiliary vessels, and the Japanese lost thirteen transports and an auxiliary. About 4,900 American and 3,500 Japanese died in the sea battles around Guadalcanal.[23] On land the Americans lost 1,769 men killed. The Japanese had 25,600 killed. The Americans lost 615 aircraft and 420 pilots and crewmen. The Japanese lost 683 planes and a large number of pilots including 125 of their most skilled carrier aviators.[24]

The United States had mounted Operation Watchtower hastily, in order to contain Japanese expansion and regain the strategic initiative in the South Pacific. Troops were not fully trained especially in the techniques of amphibious warfare and inter-service co-operation was far from being a finely honed skill. Moreover, in August 1942, the Americans did not initially have superiority at sea or in the air since new ships and aircraft that were coming off the production lines had yet to reach the fighting forces. Thus the risks involved in Watchtower were substantial but acceptable in the light of potential strategic benefits.

For the United States, victory was expensive, but America was better able to absorb and replace losses than Japan. New production and military expansion would soon replace American losses, and in the long run the Japanese simply could not match America's ability to wage a war of attrition and material. Japanese losses in the

27

Southern Solomons, especially in trained personnel, were largely irreplaceable. Thus the ability of the United States to cope with unexpectedly strong Japanese resistance paid substantial strategic dividends.

The decision to abandon the defensive Pacific strategy called for in ABC 1 and Rainbow 5 had a major impact on American strategy in the Atlantic. Although the US continued to adhere to the 'Germany first' concept, the flow of substantial forces to the Pacific and serious differences with the British concerning specific campaigns to defeat the Third Reich compelled American military leaders to accept major modifications of their European strategy.

To defeat Germany, American military leaders wanted to concentrate forces in Britain, invade France and drive into the heart of Germany. On 27 March 1942 the Army Staff completed an outline plan, the Marshall Memorandum, for operations in Western Europe. The plan called for an immediate concentration of forces in Britain, Operation Bolero, and a 1943 cross-Channel attack, Operation Round-Up, by thirty American and eighteen British divisions supported by 5,800 aircraft. The plan also made provision for an emergency invasion, Operation Sledgehammer, if the Soviets were on the verge of collapse and needed a diversion to pull German troops away from the Eastern Front.[25] General Marshall presented the outline plan to the President on 1 April and obtained approval.[26]

The British, however, had already produced a very different version of Operation Round-Up. On 24 December 1941, the British planning staff presented to the War Cabinet a plan for an invasion of northern France between Deauville and Dieppe. Forces required were much smaller than in the American version. Five infantry brigades, five tank battalions and two airborne battalions would execute the assault landings followed by twelve divisions, six of which would be armored; thirty-four fighter and ground support squadrons would support the operation.[27]

The British plan involved fewer forces than the American version because it was based on a very different strategic premise. Whereas the Americans viewed the cross-Channel assault as a first step, the British assumed that the invasion would be the culmination of a series of campaigns that sapped the ability and the will of the Germans to resist. The object of the plan was to land a force quickly on the Continent and advance rapidly to the Ruhr after German military power had deteriorated substantially.[28] In the British strategic view, the Allies would invade France in 1943 after the German will to resist had collapsed, and if German power remained intact, the operation would have to be postponed.[29] Thus, memories of World War 1, the defeats on the European continent in 1940 and 1941 and current problems in the Middle and Far East convinced the British that only severe attrition of German military power and morale would allow a cross-Channel assault to be launched with a reasonable prospect of victory.

The British were also wary of the Sledgehammer Plan, but on 13 April the Chiefs of Staff Committee in commenting on the Marshall Memorandum agreed that if Russia was being defeated Anglo-American forces would be compelled to make a supreme effort to draw off German forces from the Eastern Front.[30] Although they had little faith in Sledgehammer, the British agreed to it in order to solidify the American commitment to 'Germany first'.[31]

Putting aside for the moment their differences of opinion, the British and Americans agreed on 28 April 1942 to the preparation of the Bolero Plan for the movement of an American expeditionary force to the United Kingdom under the overall guidance of a Combined Bolero Committee.[32] The Committee held its first meeting on 6 May and agreed that seventeen American divisions would arrive in England by the spring of 1943.[33] On 9 May the Committee revised its estimates to fourteen divisions and 3,464 aircraft plus service troops, a total of 585,515 men, in the United Kingdom by April 1943.[34] In examining troop deployments for the current year the Committee reported on 13 May 1942 that there would be only 51,000 American personnel in England by 31 July 1942. By September 105,000 American troops were scheduled to be in the British Isles, but most of the men would be service and support troops and air corps personnel.[35] A report of 7 June noted that by the late summer of 1942 the United States expected to have three divisions in England.[36] The relatively slow build-up of American forces in the United Kingdom meant that the British would have to supply most of the troops for the assault phase of either Round-up or Sledgehammer thus reducing American leverage in Anglo-American strategic discussions.

On 3 April 1942 the Combined Planning Staff reported that by September forces in the United Kingdom would not be adequate to mount Sledgehammer. Supplies of troops, aircraft, and landing craft were such that any landings in northwest Europe could not seize and hold a bridgehead with reasonable assurance.[37] On 9 April the British Chiefs of Staff met General Marshall who emphasized the need for arriving at a decision on cross-Channel assaults as soon as possible in order that American production, allocation of material, training and troop movements might proceed as part of a co-ordinated plan.[38] The British replied that any landing in 1942 would be at risk of major defeat because of insufficient forces.[39] On 9 June Lord Mountbatten personally informed President Roosevelt that troop and landing craft shortages precluded a landing in France in 1942 large enough to divert any appreciable German strength from the Eastern Front.[40]

President Roosevelt, however, was insistent upon putting American forces into action against Germany in 1942. He had already suggested an operation against Dakar in French West Africa and in June he called for a re-examination of Operation Gymnast.[41]

On 20 June 1942 the Combined Chiefs of Staff met in Washington and failed to reach agreement on the future course of Anglo-American operations. General Alan Brooke stated that the Allies would not be strong enough to execute Sledgehammer in September 1942 and that German success in Russia might even prevent Round-Up in 1943. The Allies should therefore examine Gymnast as an alternative.[42] Admiral King and General Marshall continued to argue against diverting forces into numerous non-supporting areas and argued for focusing Allied efforts on concentrating forces in England. Additional diversions would not only prevent Sledgehammer but also Round-Up.[43]

The following day, news of the fall of Tobruk reached Prime Minister Churchill and President Roosevelt in Washington. Churchill insisted on something being done for the 8th Army. At a White House meeting the British and Americans agreed to continue the Bolero build-up until September at which point plans would be re-examined. If Sledgehammer proved to be impossible, the Allies would turn to Gymnast as an alternative.[44] Ironically, the Combined Chiefs of Staff rejected Gymnast on 21 June, but on 8 July the British War Cabinet rejected Sledgehammer and called for the execution of Gymnast and the examination of the possibility of invading Norway.[45]

The Joint Chiefs reacted strongly to the British proposals. In a meeting of the JCS held on 10 July, General Marshall stated that

Gymnast would be expensive and ineffectual and that it would be impossible to carry out either Sledgehammer or Round-Up without full British support. If the British position were accepted, Marshall proposed that the US should turn to the Pacific for decisive action against Japan. Focusing on the Pacific would concentrate rather than scatter US forces and would be highly popular with the American public. Moreover, concentrating on the Pacific war would be the operation, second only to Bolero, which would have the greatest effect on relieving pressure on Russia.[46] Admiral King fully agreed adding that a North African campaign would divert large naval forces from the Pacific where Japan was planning further expansion and that any departure from the Bolero Plan would in any case result in failure in Europe. The Joint Chiefs sent a memorandum of their views to the President.[47]

President Roosevelt completely rejected the strategy of virtually abandoning Europe for the Pacific. He ordered Marshall and King to go to London to examine Sledgehammer and if the operation was not feasible to agree to an alternative either in North Africa or the Middle East that would being American forces into action against the Germans in 1942.[48] War Department instructions of 15 July to Marshall and King emphasized the importance of bringing US ground forces into action against the Germans in 1942. Marshall and King were also directed to arrive at some agreement with the British at the forthcoming conference.[49]

At a Combined Chiefs of Staff meeting held in London on 24 July the British and Americans agreed that Sledgehammer could not be undertaken. If by mid-September the Russian front appeared to be collapsing, the Allies would make a decision to launch Gymnast by the end of the year. The American Chiefs of Staff pointed out that a North African operation as a substitute for Sledgehammer would also render Round-Up impractical in 1943 and commit the Allies to a defensive encircling strategy for the European theater.[50] The decision to wait until September to decide whether or not to launch Gymnast was a compromise to avoid a complete breach between the British and American service chiefs, but President Roosevelt would tolerate no further delays and insisted that the Allies launch Gymnast, now known as Torch, no later than 30 October 1942.[51]

American strategic planners had to accept significant modifications to their strategy of defeating Germany first by mounting a major cross-Channel invasion by 1943. Defensive operations and counter-offensives in the Pacific drew forces away from the Atlantic, and the overarching necessity of retaining Anglo-American unity compelled the Americans to accept at least for the moment the British peripheral approach to operations against the Reich. Public pressure for some action against Germany and the need to reassure the USSR that the Allies were serious about the European war added further compelling reasons for the President to overrule his military chiefs and commit American forces to the Torch operation.

Operation Torch was both complex and dangerous. The distances involved in voyages to North Africa were immense. It was about 1,500 miles from the British Isles to Algeria and over 4,000 miles from the continental United States to Morocco. The theater of operations was also huge. It was over 1,000 miles from the Atlantic coast of Morocco to the Libyan frontier. Invasion convoys would be at risk from submarine attack as well as possible air attacks as they neared the coasts of French territory. British shipping losses in efforts to sustain Malta had been very heavy, and invasion convoys risked similar problems. Moreover, the Allies were unsure of the French reaction to an Anglo-American invasion of North Africa. Vichy officials might view the invasion as an opportunity to rejoin the Allies or they might, as they had on several previous occasions, resist Allied invasions of their territory. Finally, the nature and extent of the German response to Torch and the possibility of hostile Spanish intervention posed additional threats.

Nevertheless, the Combined Chiefs agreed to place General Dwight D. Eisenhower in command of Torch and on 13 August issued a directive describing his mission. General Eisenhower was to conduct operations in Africa with a view to gaining in conjunction with Allied forces in the Middle East complete control of North Africa from the Atlantic to the Red Sea.[52] The Allies would first establish firm lodgements in the Oran–Algiers–Tunis area on the north coast and in the Casablanca area on the northwest coast of North Africa. From their initial lodgements the Allies would move to acquire complete control of French Morocco, Algeria and Tunisia while also preparing to occupy Spanish Morocco in the event of hostile action by Spain. Finally, the Allies would launch offensive operations through Libya against the rear of Axis forces in the Western Desert.[53]

With German and Italian forces deep in Egypt, the British in the summer of 1942 were willing to take substantial risks to capture Tunisia. On 27 August the British Chiefs of Staff proposed cancelling landings in Morocco and concentrating all operations in Algeria by seizing Algiers, Oran, Bonne and Philippeville in order to reach Tunisia before the Germans could react.[54] The Americans, however, were obsessed by the consequences of failure and insisted on pursuing a more cautious approach. At a Combined Chiefs meeting of 28 August General Marshall pointed out that the American public would understand defeat of an invasion attempt in France but defeat in Africa would lead to a loss of confidence in the American military. Moreover, the prospect of severe naval losses – 1942 was the most successful period for U-boats during the entire war – would create major problems for operations elsewhere.[55] Admiral Leahy added that the failure of America's first major expedition would have an appalling impact not only in the United States but also in China and Russia.[56] The Joint Chiefs, therefore, suggested that in light of the dangers involved and limited resources available, the scope of Torch should be reduced to two landings – Casablanca and Oran.[57]

General Eisenhower and his staff in London had produced on 21 August a preliminary plan with a target date of 15 October for landings at Oran, Algiers and Bonne. After the initial landings, the Allied forces would move west to Tunisia and east to take Casablanca.[58] In a separate letter written to the Combined Chiefs on 23 August, General Eisenhower noted that forces available for Torch were probably insufficient to accomplish the operation's goals. Determined French resistance coupled with Spanish intervention would place the expedition in jeopardy. The addition of a landing at Casablanca would increase the chances of success by reducing the prospect of French or Spanish intervention and improving Allied communications by land and sea. Simultaneous attacks in the Atlantic and Mediterranean, however, would require a delay in launching Torch and push the landing date back to the first week in November.[59]

The British insisted that landings at Algiers, Oran, Bonne and Philippeville were essential if the Allies were to reach Tunisia before the Germans. They agreed to a Casablanca assault only if the Americans supplied the necessary additional shipping, but Admiral King asserted that naval battles in the Solomons precluded additional commitments in the Atlantic.[60]

The British and Americans thus reached an impasse. The British wanted to confine the Torch landings to the Algerian coast and would agree to an assault on Casablanca only if the Americans provided the additional shipping. The Americans insisted on a secure port on the Atlantic and refused to agree to an assault on Algiers in the absence of the seizure of Casablanca. Roosevelt and Churchill, however, were determined to mount Torch as soon as possible and overruling their military advisors acted quickly to produce a compromise on 1 September. Churchill proposed that plans to attack Bonne and Philippeville be abandoned and that the Allies land at Oran, Algiers and Casablanca. Roosevelt agreed, and on 5 September the British Chiefs accepted the Roosevelt–Churchill compromise.[61]

After the agreement of 5 September, the planning process moved quickly. On 20 September Allied Force Headquarters, which was in charge of Torch, submitted an outline plan to the Combined Chiefs of Staff. The plan called for the seizure and occupation of French Morocco and Algeria and a rapid advance into Tunisia. The Allies would also establish a striking force in Morocco to insure continued control of the Straits of Gibraltar by moving, if necessary, into Spanish Morocco. The plan called for simultaneous landings near Casablanca, Oran and Algiers followed by an advance to Tunisia based on Algiers. In hopes of reducing or perhaps avoiding French resistance, the initial landings would be conducted primarily by American troops. The British would provide naval and air support and follow-up ground forces for the advance on Tunisia.[62]

On 8 October 1942 General Eisenhower's headquarters completed a detailed outline plan for the North African invasion. The plan was quite complex, involving three naval task forces sailing from different ports to different destinations to conduct simultaneous landings on beaches near Casablanca, Oran and Algiers followed by an overland campaign to Tunisia.[63]

The Western Naval Task Force was to sail directly from the continental United States to the Moroccan Atlantic coast. The Task Force included one fleet and four escort carriers, three battleships, seven cruisers, thirty-four destroyers, four submarines and thirty transports. The Task Force's mission was to support attacks by elements of three US divisions, 34,000 men, on beaches north and south of Casablanca. Once firmly ashore, the troops would advance on the city while the warships supplied air and gunfire support.[64]

The Center Naval Task Force was to assist in the attack on Oran. The Task Force consisted of British ships including a fleet and a light carrier, a battleship, two cruisers, two anti-aircraft ships, thirteen destroyers, six corvettes, twenty-eight light combatants and forty-four transports carrying 37,800 soldiers from two US divisions and a ranger battalion. The task force would sail in two echelons, link up on D-1 and land troops on three beaches while a small force entered the harbor to seize critical port facilities by a *coup de main*. The main forces, after occupying outlying aerodromes, would then move on the city.[65]

The Eastern Naval Task Force, assigned to seize Algiers, was also to sail in two echelons and join together just before the landings. British warships included one fleet and one light carrier, a battleship, a monitor, four cruisers, three anti-aircraft cruisers, thirteen destroyers and thirty-five smaller warships. Thirty-three transports carried 10,000 American and 45,000 British soldiers. The ground forces were to land at several points around the city and secure airfields and other important sites while a special force launched a direct assault on the harbor. The following day the main body would move on the city.[66]

Two follow-up convoys were to set forth prior to the landings, timing their arrival in North African waters for D+3 and D+4.[67] The Royal Navy also supplied a number of covering forces for Torch. Force H with three battleships, two aircraft carriers, four cruisers, and fifteen destroyers would guard the Central and Eastern Task Forces against possible sorties by the Italian fleet and French naval forces at Toulon. Two cruisers and three destroyers would cover the Azores and help protect follow-up convoys, and a Gibraltar escort force of sixteen destroyers, eight minesweepers and nineteen patrol craft would provide local patrols prior to the Algiers and Oran landings. British submarines would operate off Sicily to watch for the Italian Navy.[68]

On 13 October the JCS issued a joint plan, Operation Rooftree, conforming to General Eisenhower's Torch plan.[69] General Eisenhower's headquarters issued instructions on 24 October for the post-landing organization of the North African theater. After securing initial objectives, the Allies would bring in reinforcements and begin the advance on Tunisia. The British 1st Army with attached American divisions would execute the eastward drive while the US

5th Army would organize itself and guard the Moroccan border. Air support would at first come exclusively from carriers, but as airfields fell to the Allies the US 12th Air Force and the RAF Eastern Air Command would deploy squadrons to North Africa and conduct both tactical and strategic missions.[70] Finally, General Eisenhower asked the British to establish a special force in the United Kingdom to invade Spanish Morocco if Madrid opposed the Allied landings. The Combined Chiefs approved the request on 30 October[71] by which time the assault forces were already at sea with a D-Day date of 8 November.

Operation Torch was a massive undertaking. It was to date America's largest amphibious operation and the first major venture with the British. The Americans had insisted upon a rather cautious approach of conducting one of the landings on the Atlantic coast rather than attempting all assaults within the Mediterranean as the British had proposed. American caution was based on the desire to have a direct line of communications back to the United States and the intent of avoiding the risk of defeat in the first major operation in the war against the European Axis. Despite American caution Torch still faced serious risks, and Vichy's response to the Allied landings and German reactions to the invasion were unknown quantities that could in large measure influence the results.

The Vichy regime had substantial forces at its disposal in North Africa. There were 40,000 troops in Morocco, 52,000 in Algeria, 15,000 in Tunisia and 12,000 reserves and desert units. Most equipment, including more than 200 tanks, was obsolete. Morale was by no means uniform, but Vichy troops had fought vigorously against the British and Free French at Dakar, in Syria and on Madagascar. They might again offer substantial opposition. Air strength included more than 300 aircraft, about half of which were modern fighters and the rest twin-engine bombers. The pilots were well trained.[72]

Vichy's naval assets also posed a serious potential threat for Torch. Despite the losses sustained at Mers-el-Kebir and the neutralization of other ships at Alexandria, Vichy could still call upon large modern naval forces. At Casablanca the French had a modern battleship, immobile but with a functioning main battery, a cruiser, nine destroyers and eleven submarines. Four destroyers and three submarines plus five more in drydock were stationed in Oran, while in Algiers there were two submarines and two light vessels. At Dakar the French had a modern battleship, three cruisers, three destroyers and seven submarines. Toulon contained the largest concentration of warships including two battlecruisers, a battleship, seven cruisers, thirty-two destroyers, sixteen submarines, and numerous light vessels.[73]

The Americans hoped that the Vichy authorities would regard Torch as an act of liberation rather than a hostile attack. American officials undertook secret talks with French commanders in North Africa and sought to use General Giraud, who had escaped from mainland France, as a rallying point for French forces in North Africa. Allied commanders were directed not to engage Vichy forces unless the French fired first.[74]

Full-scale resistance by Vichy forces would not in the long run have defeated the Torch operation. It would, however, have inflicted substantial casualties on Anglo-American forces, delayed the occupation of Morocco and Algeria, slowed the advance to Tunisia and provided the Germans and Italians additional time to deploy ground and air forces to North Africa. A lengthy campaign against the French would also have provided the German navy time to redeploy U-boats operating in the North Atlantic to African waters. The French navy might also have inflicted losses on Allied shipping.

The British victory at El Alamein in October and the failure of the Axis high command to discover where and when the Allies would strike were significant advantages for the Allies. Success, however, required not only surprise but also rapid exploitation of the initial landings. The response of Vichy and Berlin to Torch would also play a major role in the ability of the Allies rapidly to conquer North Africa.

Allied convoys reached the Atlantic and Mediterranean coasts without detection, and when American troops began their assault on 8 November 1942, they achieved near complete surprise. Recovering quickly, the French began to resist. Allied efforts to enter and seize Oran and Algiers were crushed with heavy American losses. French army units also began to fight at other landing sites, and the French Navy attempted to attack the Allied naval task forces. There were fairly heavy casualties on both sides.

The dilemma of having to wage a major campaign against the French forces in North Africa was resolved by a stroke of good fortune. Admiral Darlan, Chief of the Vichy armed forces, was in

Algeria at the time of the invasion to visit his seriously ill son. On 10 November he ordered an end to hostilities against the Allies. Seeing the way the tide of battle was shifting, Darlan in effect switched sides and emerged as the French High Commissioner of North Africa committed to fighting alongside the Americans and British.

Darlan's shift of allegiance resolved one Allied dilemma, but the German reaction to Torch was both rapid and effective. Fearing the collapse of Italy and an attack on Europe from the South, Berlin, despite the grim battle being fought at Stalingrad, directed forces to overrun the unoccupied zone of metropolitan France and also moved to seize Tunisia before the Allies arrived. There was no resistance in France itself. Darlan's shift of sides did not include Tunisia, and despite the German invasion of the unoccupied zone of France, Vichy officials in Tunis offered no resistance to the arrival of Axis forces. Thus on 9 November, one day after the Allied landings, the Germans had troops in Tunisia. In the following weeks the Germans expanded their bridgehead and rushed in additional reinforcements. By the end of November about 21,000 German and 11,000 Italian troops held fairly strong positions in Tunisia including the excellent ports of Tunis and Bizerte and a complex of excellent all-weather airfields. Ultimately the Axis sent over 142,000 German and 30,000 Italian troops to Tunisia where they linked up with German and Italian troops who were retreating from Libya.

The Allies sought to prevent the creation of a strong Axis position in Tunisia, but their advance was hampered by bad roads, steadily worsening weather, a serious shortage of trucks and a lack of hardened airfields. British troops occupied Bone on 12 November and leading elements of a brigade crossed the Tunisian frontier. US airborne troops crossed the border three days later, but the Germans had won the race for Tunisia. Allied advance forces were essentially spearheads operating at the end of a long tenuous line of supply. The German build-up was faster and forces were operating much closer to their bases. Consequently, the Germans were able to halt Allied incursions and push British and American forces back towards the Algerian frontier. By mid-December the Allies abandoned efforts to take Tunisia in a single bold operation. They began to consolidate their positions and build up forces for a major deliberate attack.

It was the Axis, however, who held the tactical initiative during the first months of 1943. German forces in Tunisia launched several successful local attacks against the British 1st Army while German forces from Libya escaped the pursuing British 8th Army, entered Tunisia and linked up Axis forces in the area. In mid-February the Germans attacked and defeated an American corps at Kasserine Pass and in March attacked but failed to defeat the 8th Army at Médenine.

The Allies, while halting enemy attacks, built up their forces, improved road and rail systems and expanded the capabilities of their air bases. On 20 March the 8th Army began an offensive in southern Tunisia which by mid-April had driven the Axis back into a shallow bridgehead around Tunis and Bizerte. The final Allied blow fell in the last days of April, and by 7 May both Tunis and Bizerte had fallen. After a few more days of mopping up, the Allies counted over 275,000 German and Italian prisoners – the largest number of Axis troops captured on any front up to that time.[75]

The North African campaign was a major Allied victory. It cleared Axis power from the south shore of the Mediterranean and in the process eliminated thousands of German troops who might otherwise have fought on the Eastern Front. The Allies learned valuable lessons about amphibious operations and inter-Allied co-operation, and several American divisions received their baptism of fire.

Nevertheless, Operation Torch did not go as planned. Instead of a rapid seizure of Tunisia and the quick destruction of Axis forces in Libya, the Allies, because of the unexpected rapidity of the German reaction, were compelled to fight a difficult and lengthy campaign. Moreover, the duration of operations put an end to all hopes of launching a 1943 Round-Up. The JCS had earlier stated that Torch would delay a cross-Channel attack until 1944, yet some continued to believe that something might be accomplished in North-western Europe in 1943. The failure to reach Tunisia before the Germans put an end to any such thoughts.

Even as the North African campaign was being fought Allied political and military leaders met to discuss their next moves. They had to accept the fact that the German reaction to Torch imposed a new reality on their future plans, and American strategists faced strategic choices very different from those described in pre-war plans.

Prior to 7 December 1941, American global strategy called for a concentration of assets in the Atlantic and European area which was to be the major theater of war. Operations in the Pacific permitted tactical offensives but were strategically defensive. Theater strategy in Europe called for a build-up of forces in the United Kingdom and an invasion of France as soon as possible but probably in 1943. Pacific strategy required the Allies to restrain Japanese advances until Germany was defeated whereupon forces would be redeployed to the Far East and the Pacific.

Enemy actions and inter-Allied politics changed these plans dramatically. Early Japanese victories forced the United States to deploy large forces to the Pacific and convinced the JCS that a purely defensive strategy would allow Japan too much time to strengthen its position. Thus by the spring of 1942, American planners were committed to major offensive operations in the Pacific. In Europe the Americans encountered British reluctance to undertake an early invasion of France coupled with an insistence on operations in the southern Mediterranean where large British, Imperial and Dominion forces were already engaged. The JCS opposed peripheral strategies, but the President, concerned with getting American forces into action against the Germans in 1942 and determined to maintain Anglo-American unity, overruled the Joint Chiefs and agreed to Torch. Consequently, by the early months of 1943 the Allies had restored the global strategic equilibrium, but the Americans found themselves committed to major offensives in the Pacific and a peripheral strategy in Europe.

NOTES

1. U.S. Serial ABC-4/CS1 British Serial WWI (Final) Washington War Conference, December 31, 1941.
2. Ibid.
3. Ibid. and U.S. Serial ABC-4/1 British Serial WWI (JPC) Report by the U.S.–British Joint Planning Committee, December 29, 1941.
4. U.S. ABC-4/6 British WW-14 Joint Planning Committee Report, January 13, 1942.
5. U.S. Serial ABC-4/8 British Serial WW (JPC) 8 Joint Planning Committee Report for the Chiefs of Staff, January 10, 1942.
6. U.S. Serial ABC-4/5 British Serial WW-6 Directive to the Supreme Commander in the ABDA Area, January 10, 1942.
7. U.S. ABC-4/CS4 British WW-16 Washington War Conference Post-Arcadia Collaboration, January 14, 1942.
8. Ibid.
9. Directive to the Supreme Commander in the Southwest Pacific Area CCS57/1, 30 March 1942.

10. JIC8 Joint U.S. Intelligence Committee Japanese Logistic Capabilities, April 1, 1942.
11. Ibid.
12. Ibid.
13. Cominch File A16-3 (0010) 8 January 1942 Operation Bobcat.
14. Cominch Serial 00178 A16-3CD Bleacher, March 12, 1942.
15. JCS11 February 12, 1942, and Cominch A16-3 Serial 00191 Straw, March 17, 1942.
16. Cominch A16-3CD Serial 00209 Roses, March 20, 1942.
17. JPS21/8 April 27, 1942.
18. Cominch A16-3 (5) Serial 00322 Lone Wolf, April 29, 1942.
19. Joint Directive for Offensive Operations in the Southwest Pacific area, July 2, 1942, and July 2, 1942 Naval Message King to CINCPAC.
20. Joint Directive of July 2.
21. CINCPAC File 01994 July 8, 1942.
22. COMSOPAC Serial 0017 OpPlan No. 1–42, July 16, 1942.
23. Richard B. Frank, *Guadalcanal*. New York, Penguin Books, 1990, pp. 601 and 614.
24. Ibid., pp. 611 and 614.
25. Mark A. Stoler, *The Politics of the Second Front*, Westport, Greenwood Press, 1977, p. 35.
26. Ibid.
27. JP(41) 1028 24th December, 1941. War Cabinet Joint Planning Staff Operation "Round Up."
28. Ibid.
29. Ibid.
30. C.O.S. (42) 97 (0) 13th April 1942, Chiefs of Staff Committee Comments on General Marshall's Memorandum.
31. Stoler, op. cit., pp. 40–41.
32. CPS 26/2/D April 28, 1942.
33. Bolero Committee Meeting, May 6, 1942.
34. Tentative Movement Schedule Army Ground Forces Bolero Plan, May 9, 1942.
35. CPS 26/3 May 13, 1942, First Report of the Bolero Combined Committee.
36. CPS 26/4 Bolero Embarkation Schedule, June 7, 1942.
37. CPS 26/1 April 3, 1942, Offensive Operations in Europe.
38. CCS (42) 23rd Meeting.
39. Ibid.
40. Stoler, op. cit., p. 49.
41. Ibid., and Cominch A16-3(4) Serial 00362, May 9, 1942.
42. CCS 28th Meeting, June 20, 1942 Minutes.
43. Ibid.
44. Stoler, op. cit., p. 53.
45. C.C.S. 83, June 21, 1942 Offensive Operations in 1942 and 1943 and J.C.S. 24th Meeting, July 10, 1942.
46. J.C.S. 24th Meeting.
47. Ibid.
48. Stoler, op. cit., p. 56.
49. War Department Draft of Instructions for London Conference, July 15, 1942.
50. C.C.S. 94 Operations in 1942/43, July 24, 1942 and C.C.S. 32nd Meeting. Minutes July 24, 1942.
51. Stoler, op. cit., p. 58.
52. C.C.S. 36th Meeting, August 13, 1942 Directive for Commander-in-Chief Allied Expeditionary Force.
53. Ibid.
54. Telegram from the British Chiefs of Staff, 27th August 1942.

55. C.C.S. August 28, 1942, Combined Chiefs of Staff 38th Meeting.
56. Ibid.
57. Ibid.
58. Headquarters European Theater of Operations United States Army Outline Plan Operation 'Torch', 21 August 1942.
59. Eisenhower to CCS August 23, 1942.
60. British Chiefs of Staff, 27 August 1942.
61. Stephen E. Ambrose, *The Supreme Commander. The War Years of General Dwight D. Eisenhower,* Garden City, Doubleday and Co., 1970, pp. 94–6.
62. AFHQ Outline Plan Operation Torch, 20 Sept. 1942.
63. AFHQ Outline Plan Operation Torch, 8 October 1942.
64. Ibid.
65. Ibid.
66. Ibid.
67. Ibid.
68. Ibid.
69. JCS127/1 Joint Army and Navy Plan for U.S. Participation in Operation 'Torch', Short Title – 'Rooftree', October 13, 1942.
70. AFHQ Operational Memorandum Number 30, 24 October 1942.
71. C.C.S. 103/13 Proposed Action if Spain becomes Hostile at an Early Stage in 'Torch', October 27, 1942 and C.C.S. 103/15 November 4, 1942.
72. National Archives Military Archives Division Record Group 165 Box 1819.
73. Ibid.
74. JCS 127, 5 October 1942 'Rooftree' Draft.
75. For an excellent general account of the operations in North Africa see: Gerhard L. Weinberg, *A World at Arms*, Cambridge, Cambridge University Press, 1994, Chapter 8 *passim*. A more detailed account is to be found in the U.S. Army's official history: George F. Howe, *Northwest Africa: Seizing the Initiative in the West*, Washington, D.C., Center of Military History, 1985.

3

Seeking a Strategy – 1943

In January 1943, as fighting raged in Tunisia and the South Pacific, British and American political and military leaders met at Casablanca to discuss global strategy and decide upon the next moves in the war. Washington and London had already agreed upon grand strategy, but the Allies had yet to develop theater strategies that would enable military planners to create specific operational plans designed to achieve clear strategic objectives.

On 15 January 1943 President Roosevelt met the Joint Chiefs of Staff who told him that after the capture of Tunisia the British favored continued operations in the Mediterranean. Since the Germans could reinforce France faster than Italy and Sicily, a cross-Channel attack was still, according to the British, too risky. Continued operations in the Mediterranean offered a more feasible means of striking at the Axis and would also compel the Germans to disperse their air power.[1]

The following day the President again met the JCS whose members agreed that the next logical step after Tunisia should be the invasion of Sicily. Round-up was essentially out of the question, and if the Allies were to act in 1943 they would have to continue operations in the Mediterranean.

General Marshall noted that American forces in England lacked training and were too few to attempt a cross-Channel attack. Nevertheless, the Allies had to do something in 1943 to assist the Russians who were bearing the brunt of the fighting. A Sicilian operation, though far from ideal, was feasible and was probably the best alternative for effective use of Allied troops in North Africa after the fall of Tunisia.[2]

Admiral King also agreed with the British position. He pointed out that there were sufficient troops in North Africa to invade either

Sicily or Sardinia and that Allied forces should not remain idle after the conclusion of the African campaign. Of the two options Sicily was preferable because its capture would reduce the threat posed by Axis air power to convoys in the Mediterranean. The arrival of new landing craft would allow the Allies to lift 90,000 troops in an initial assault over an open beachhead and attacking Sicily with troops available in North Africa would permit the Bolero build-up to continue.[3] The Admiral also suggested a tacit bargain with the British. Since the Americans were willing to agree to an attack on Sicily, the British in return should approve American plans for operations in the Pacific.[4] Admiral King understood that the British wanted a minimum of American deployments to the Pacific at the expense of the European and Mediterranean areas, and he, therefore, proposed a trade-off offering additional Mediterranean operations for increased activity in the Pacific.

On 19 January 1943, the Combined Chiefs of Staff agreed upon a series of measures for the conduct of the war in 1943. As the JCS had previously predicted, a commitment to Torch rendered unfeasible both Sledgehammer and Round-Up, thus postponing an invasion of northwest Europe until 1944 and committing the United States to additional operations in the Mediterranean.

The first issue for the Allies was, however, the U-boat menace. In January sinkings were running at disastrous rates. Failure to secure the Atlantic sea lines of communication would impose severe delays on all Allied efforts in all parts of the globe.[5] Closely tied to the U-boat war was the issue of Lend-Lease convoys to the Soviet Union. The western Allies recognized the critical importance of the Eastern Front. Failure to cope with the U-boat offensive would make casualties on the convoy routes prohibitive thus limiting the number of convoys to the USSR, with dangerous consequences for the war in the east.[6]

The Combined Chiefs also agreed to invade Sicily in order to secure the Mediterranean lines of communications, divert pressure from the Russian front, and increase pressure on Italy.[7] Operations from Great Britain would include a continuation and intensification of the bomber offensive against Germany, commando raids, and the assembly of forces to re-enter the European continent as soon as German resistance was weakened to the extent that an invasion was feasible.[8] In the Pacific the Combined Chiefs agreed to extended

American offensive operations to include the capture of Rabaul and attacks into the Marshalls and Carolines.[9]

The Combined Chiefs of Staff issued a final report to President Roosevelt and Prime Minister Churchill on 23 January 1943 in which they provided a more detailed explanation of their strategic approach for 1943. The basic strategic framework rested upon the anti-submarine war at sea, further offensives in the Mediterranean and attacks in the Pacific.

In the Battle of the Atlantic, the CCS concluded that adequate escort vessels for convoys would not be available until August or September 1943, and until then the Allies would not be able to destroy U-boats at a rate in excess of the rate of construction until the end of the year. Consequently, if the Allies provided adequate escorts for offensive operations, they would have to accept the risk of increased losses for other convoys.[10] Providing that a shipping loss rate of not more than 2.4 percent a month could be maintained, convoys to the Soviet Union could continue.[11]

In the Mediterranean the Allies would invade Sicily with the favorable July moon as the target date. General Eisenhower would be in Supreme Command with General Alexander acting as his deputy responsible for the detailed planning and execution of Operation Husky. A special planning staff was to be established forthwith.[12]

The CCS agreed that the air offensive from the United Kingdom would be conducted under the general direction of the British Chief of Air Staff with the American air commander free to decide on the techniques and methods employed by his forces.[13] A previous directive had already established a set of target priorities. Attacks on German submarine bases and construction yards were the first priority, followed by the aircraft industry, transportation, synthetic oil plants and other targets in the German war industry. Essentially, the Combined Chiefs approved what amounted to be two separate air bombardment campaigns based on separate doctrinal approaches. The US Army Air Corps was committed to the doctrine of daylight precision bombing of crucial targets. The RAF was wedded to the concept of area bombardment of cities and had little room for other approaches, including large-scale efforts to impede the flow of high-grade Swedish iron ore – vital to the German war industrial effort – by an extensive campaign against German shipping. The lack of co-ordination between the British and American bomber forces probably reduced the effectiveness of the bombing campaign as a whole during 1943.[14]

Other operations from the British Isles during 1943 involved continuing the Bolero build-up to fifteen American divisions and 938,000 troops in Britain by the end of the year.[15] Plans for offensive operations included raids, attacks to seize and hold a bridgehead and, if low morale and resources of the German forces permitted, exploiting successes and returning to the European continent to take advantage of a sudden German disintegration. The Combined Chiefs additionally agreed to set up a Combined Staff to prepare plans for such a return. The staff was also to plan an invasion in force of the Continent for 1944.[16] In the Pacific the CCS approved American plans for the reconquest of the Aleutians and for a dual advance on Rabaul from the South Pacific and towards Truk and Guam via the Central Pacific.[17]

In May 1943 the Combined Chiefs of Staff met in Washington for the Trident Conference to decide upon post-Husky operations. The American and British Chiefs of Staff presented their views of global strategy which continued to diverge substantially. Both the British and Americans remained committed to the general approach of defeating Germany first, but the British wished to conduct additional operations in the Mediterranean while the Americans wanted to pursue a cross-Channel invasion or in the absence of an invasion, conduct intensified operations in the Pacific.

On 13 May the Joint Chiefs set forth their position calling for a determined attack against Germany at the earliest practicable date. All other operations in Europe should therefore be judged primarily on the basis of their contribution to the cross-Channel attack.[18]

The British Chiefs of Staff responded that the Combined Chiefs had already approved the planning of a full-scale assault against the Continent in the spring of 1944. It was, however, unsound to do nothing between the occupation of Sicily and the invasion of France, a period that might last for nine or ten months. The Allies, therefore, should use the time to seek to eliminate Italy from the war.[19] Forcing Italy out of the war would compel the Germans to dissipate their forces if they intended to retain their positions in Italy and the Balkans where the Italians currently had thirty-five divisions. The elimination of the Italian navy as a threat would allow the Allies to move naval assets elsewhere, and the collapse of Italy might even convince Turkey to enter the war.[20] A campaign on the Italian mainland after Husky would, the British admitted, impose delays on Bolero, but the advantages outweighed this drawback. Finally, operations against Italy in 1943 were the most effective means of assisting the Russians.[21] Thus, in the British view, the logic of Husky called either for an unacceptable delay in the war against Germany while forces were concentrated in England or continued operations in the Mediterranean.

The JCS planning staff accepted the British logic, arguing that there was little benefit to be derived from amassing forces and landing craft in England if they were not going to be employed in 1943. The planners, therefore, suggested that the United States continue the tacit bargain struck at Casablanca by supporting the proposed Mediterranean operations against Italy and using excess landing craft for further offensive operations in the Pacific.[22]

A draft of agreed decisions of 21 May and a final report to the President and Prime Minister of 25 May 1943 reflected the Anglo-American compromise. As usual there was an almost ritualistic agreement on the 'Germany first' strategy, and the Americans and British also agreed on pursuing the Combined Bomber Offensive which by 1 April 1944, the CCS hoped, would have caused such destruction and demoralization as to undermine fatally the German capacity for further resistance.[23] Continuation of the U-boat war and Lend-Lease shipments to the USSR and China were readily accepted.[24]

In dealing with future operations in Europe the Combined Chiefs agreed to establish in the United Kingdom a force of twenty-nine divisions with the object of mounting an operation to secure a lodgement on the Continent from which further offensive operations would be conducted. The target date for the landings was 1 May 1944. The Combined Staff was further directed to keep up to date plans for an emergency crossing of the Channel in the event of a sudden German collapse.[25]

In the Mediterranean, the Combined Chiefs of Staff decided that after the conclusion of Husky, the Allies would mount additional operations in order to eliminate Italy from the war. By the summer of 1943 the Allies would have twenty-seven divisions, excluding four American and three British which were to be transferred to the British Isles, available for garrisons and operations in the Mediterranean with air support supplied by 1,060 bombers and 2,012 fighters.[26]

47

At the Trident Conference the Combined Chiefs accepted American demands for extended operations including the recapture of the Aleutians, seizure of the Marshall and Caroline Islands and the capture of the Solomons, Bismarck Archipelago and Japanese-held portions of New Guinea, where American and Australian forces were currently engaged in operations in the eastern part of the island.[27] The British would undertake operations from Burma in an eventual effort to reopen the Burma road.[28]

The Trident Conference again revealed the serious differences between the American and British views of European strategy. Although the British agreed to a specific date for the invasion of North-western Europe, it was clear that London hoped that strategic bombing coupled with losses sustained in the Mediterranean and above all on the Eastern Front would produce an internal German collapse. Any invasion would then be an emergency operation to destroy shattered remnants of the Reich's military machine. The Americans viewed a cross-Channel attack as the first step in a much longer campaign. The Trident decisions incorporated both views thus avoiding the possibility of a serious rift between Washington and London.

The bargain struck at Casablanca was maintained at the Trident Conference. The Americans accepted the fact that once committed to the invasion of Sicily it made sound strategic sense to move on to Italy especially since forces could not be redeployed from the Mediterranean after Husky in time to participate in a cross-Channel attack. The JCS had, after all, already predicted that commitment to Torch would delay an invasion of France until 1944. In return for agreeing to continued Mediterranean operations the Americans successfully insisted on an even more vigorous series of campaigns in the Pacific, and the British agreed to the JCS approach.

The Trident Conference avoided any split in the Western Alliance and established a set of operational priorities for the remainder of 1943. The Combined Chiefs did not, however, establish a coherent theater strategy for either Europe or the Pacific. Additional conferences and inter-Allied negotiations would have to attempt to hammer out specific approaches to achieve the broad political and military objectives of the Grand Coalition.

By the time the Trident Conference ended the Allies were on their way to turning the tide in the Battle of the Atlantic. This was the longest campaign of the war, beginning in September 1939 and lasting until 5 May 1945 with the sinking of U-881.[29] At the time of the Casablanca and Trident Conferences the Germans were having great success. Between July 1942 and May 1943 U-boats sank 780 merchantmen of some 4.5 million gross tons. Moreover, German submarine construction was progressing rapidly, and by May of 1943 the German Navy could put 120 U-boats into the Atlantic.[30]

American production, however, gradually turned the tide. The first Liberty Ship, a prefabricated 7,176 gross ton vessel was launched in September 1941. By July 1942 the United States was able to build more ships than the Germans could sink, and by October 1942 American shipyards were launching three ships a day.[31] All told, by 1945 the United States had launched 2,708 Liberty Ships and 2,893 other types of cargo and transport vessels.[32]

Growing numbers of destroyer and carrier escorts and the commitment of additional squadrons of long-range aircraft to anti-submarine patrols helped even the odds against the U-boats. Signals intelligence also played a crucial role in the war at sea. The ability to read German naval codes, though sporadic, enabled the Allies to reroute convoys away from U-boat concentrations and enhanced the ability of anti-submarine forces to prosecute attacks against submarines.

Consequently, the Allies gradually turned the tide in the Battle of the Atlantic. The bleak picture at the time of the Casablanca Conference changed so that by 25 May, the day before the end of the Trident Conference, the German Navy withdrew its U-boats from the North Atlantic and ordered them to concentrate on the route between the USA and Gibraltar.[33] The U-boat war continued of course, and substantial numbers of ships were lost or damaged, but the Allied sea lines of communication became progressively more secure.

The Combined Bomber Offensive called for at the Casablanca and Trident conferences was in 1943 not nearly as successful as the anti-submarine campaign. The need for more heavy bombers and the lack of long-range escort fighters hampered the US 8th Air Force which suffered appalling losses on some of its missions. Moreover, the German economy was not fully mobilized for total war, thus providing the Reich with residual capabilities to recover rapidly from bomb damage.

Strategic bombing in the first half of 1943 did do some damage to the German war economy. Bombing also forced the Luftwaffe to assign assets to home defense that might otherwise have been used on the battlefronts. The ground-based air defense system absorbed guns and personnel that might also have been so engaged. Still the strategic bombing effort fell far short of the hopes and expectations of the Allied planners.

While the long-term campaigns on the seas and in the air over Europe were progressing, American and British planners were devising theater level operations. In both the South Pacific and Mediterranean allied forces were preparing major operations.

By February 1943, American forces had captured Guadalcanal in the Solomons and, after a very difficult fight, Australian and American troops had driven the Japanese out of eastern New Guinea. Commanders and their staffs then began to contemplate further operations aimed at fulfilling the JCS directive of 2 July 1942 which called for the capture of Rabaul, the major Japanese stronghold in the South Pacific. Before the armed services could do anything, however, they had to resolve several interrelated problems ranging from issues of command and control to specific operational plans.

Both the Army and the Navy advocated a unified command structure for the Pacific but could not agree on a designated commander. The Army wanted to place General MacArthur in overall command, and the Navy wanted Admiral Nimitz to direct Pacific strategy. The services failed to resolve the issue which in turn forced them to adopt a piecemeal strategic approach. The Commanders of the Southwest Pacific and the Pacific Ocean areas wrote their own separate plans which were then submitted to the JCS. The JCS in turn rendered a final decision which was often a compromise, thereby committing the United States to an *ad hoc* approach to Pacific strategy.

Planning for forthcoming operations in New Guinea and the Solomons reflected the fragmented command structure. In early 1943 the reduction of Rabaul was the next objective, but specific plans and command relationships still eluded American strategists. On 15 February 1943 JCS planners presented a proposal calling for further advances toward Rabaul. The Southwest Pacific forces were to move towards western New Guinea while South Pacific forces were to take New Georgia and Bougainville to provide air bases for subsequent operations. The planners did not, however, prescribe operations beyond the middle of 1943, nor did they delineate a command structure for the projected campaign.[34] To resolve a number of problems dealing with force allocations, command structure, and specific operations, a Pacific Military Conference met in Washington in mid-March 1943. Representatives from the South and Southwest Pacific commands met the JCS and the joint planners to iron out the pattern of the next months of the Pacific War.

At the Conference, General MacArthur's Chief of Staff presented the Elkton Plan for the seizure of the New Britain, New Ireland and New Guinea areas. Southwest Pacific forces would seize the Huon Peninsula in New Guinea in order to establish air bases to support further advances. South Pacific forces would take New Georgia to provide land-based air support for advances on Bougainville and New Britain.[35] The two theater forces would then join in an attack on Rabaul. General MacArthur would be in overall command of both theaters.[36]

The Elkton Plan required massive forces including ten divisions for the South Pacific and twelve and two-thirds divisions, ten of which were trained for amphibious operations, for the Southwest Pacific. Additional naval forces including two carriers and several battleships were also required. Finally, the Elkton Plan called for the use of forty-five air groups and fourteen independent squadrons.[37] Its requirements went well beyond American force availability. By the end of 1943 only eight divisions were scheduled to be in the South Pacific. The Southwest Pacific Area would have seventeen divisions but eleven of them would be Australian. Moreover, only three of the Australian divisions would be available for offensive operations. Air strength also fell far short of Elkton's requirements. By the year end there would be six groups in the South and twenty-four in the Southwest Pacific – twenty-four short of estimated needs.[38] The Air Force objected to sending more units to the Pacific because of the necessity of building up forces in Europe, and the navy was reluctant to commit major combatants to the constricted waters of the Solomons. The Conference could not resolve the issues and passed the whole question of Pacific strategy to the JCS with the recommendation that the Joint Chiefs either increase force allocations or modify American strategy.

The JCS decided upon a compromise. They agreed to send two additional divisions to MacArthur and more aircraft to both theaters.

The reinforcements were, however, not sufficient to capture Rabaul thus rendering unfeasible step three of the July 1942 directive. The JCS therefore revised strategic objectives, and on 28 March 1943 issued a new directive for operations in the South and Southwestern Pacific areas.

The JCS abandoned Rabaul as an immediate objective. Instead, both theaters would seize positions that would allow American air power to move to within striking range of Rabaul. Specific objectives were the Woodlark and Kiriwina Islands to the east of New Guinea, the Lae–Salamaua–Finschhafen–Madang area on the northeast coast of New Guinea and the rest of the Solomon Islands including the southern portion of Bougainville.[39] Consequently, any offensive against Rabaul was delayed until 1944.

The JCS placed operations outlined in the directive under the overall control of General MacArthur. Admiral Halsey, Commander of the South Pacific area was to control directly operations in the Solomons under General MacArthur's general supervision. The JCS would assign specific naval assets to operations in one or both areas while the Commander of the Pacific Ocean area retained control of all other naval vessels and air squadrons.[40]

Thus the JCS created an opportunistic strategy to deal with an immediate situation. Rabaul, the key Japanese bastion in the South Pacific remained the ultimate target, but regional commanders in the Pacific and the JCS still lacked a long-range plan for Rabaul's capture. Nor did the United States have an overall strategy for the Pacific war as a whole. By March 1943 all that American strategists could devise was a step by step advance determined primarily by the radii of land-based aircraft. Fortunately for the Americans, the rather chaotic planning and command system was offset by the ability of the commanders and staffs of the South and Southwest Pacific to collaborate effectively.

Planners from the two areas began devising operational plans, completing their work on 26 April. The new plan, Elkton III was essentially a revision of General MacArthur's original plan designed to accommodate the forces and objectives allocated by the JCS. Elkton III known by the code name Cartwheel called for a complex series of operations covering the next eight months. MacArthur's forces were to advance along the northern New Guinea coast while Halsey's men moved into the Solomons. Each area would advance in successive stages in support of each other and always under the cover of land-based air power.[41] The final phase of Cartwheel called for landings on Western New Britain, the capture of a second foothold on Bougainville and the neutralization of Buka Island just to the north of Bougainville.[42]

Cartwheel involved thirteen separate operations which were to be completed by 1 December 1943. The planners recognized that the timing of particular operations could only be tentative and would vary from the plan if necessary. Moreover, if special circumstances presented themselves, commanders would deviate from the plan to profit from fleeting opportunities. The two areas deployed a combined strength of eight Army and two Marine divisions; a New Zealand and three Australian divisions were also available. Between them MacArthur and Halsey had 686 fighters, 879 bombers and 275 transport aircraft. New landing craft, including seventy-eight LSTs, 156 LCIs and 138 LCTs had reached the Pacific. Fleet elements varied in size and composition according to the nature of a particular mission.[43] Warships in the South Pacific consisted primarily of cruisers, destroyers and patrol boats. The ships were well suited to operating in the constricted waters of the Solomons.

The Japanese had used the time spent by the Americans in devising their Pacific strategy and organizing their forces to strengthen and expand their positions. A web of air bases – five at Rabaul, six on Bougainville and one each on New Georgia, Kolombangara, Santa Isabel, and the Shortlands – spanned the northern Solomons. Additional fields existed on New Guinea. In addition to the 390 combat aircraft stationed in the region, the Japanese Combined Fleet at Truk could fly in reinforcements to meet American attacks. To defend the airbases the Japanese deployed large ground forces from other areas into the Solomons and New Guinea. Three divisions and supporting troops served in New Guinea in a number of fortified base areas along the north-western coast. Some 5,000 troops held New Georgia, and 4,000 garrisoned nearby Kolombangara. Japanese Army and Navy ground personnel at Bougainville numbered 50,000, and 55,000 Army and 35,000 naval troops held positions in and around Rabaul.[44]

The Japanese had thus bolstered their positions, but their garrisons were relatively static. Cruiser and destroyer forces operated in the area but, unless the Japanese could retain air superiority in the region, their naval units could not operate safely or effectively, and the web of garrisons would be isolated and not capable of mutual support. Consequently, the Japanese fully intended to contest the airspace over New Guinea and the Solomons as well as wage major engagements on land and sea.

While the services were debating strategy, theater commanders were executing preliminary moves for the forthcoming campaign. On 21 February 1943 Army troops from the South Pacific command landed unopposed in the Russell Islands. The mission of Operation Cleanslate was to enhance the defense of Guadalcanal and to use the islands as a point of departure for future advances.[45] By mid-April the Americans had constructed two airfields and a radar installation in the Russells plus a number of naval facilities.[46]

Operation Cartwheel proper began on 21 June when forces from the South Pacific area landed a few troops at the southern end of New Georgia. On 23 and 25 June MacArthur's forces began to occupy the Woodlark and Kiriwina Islands without opposition.[47] On 30 June Southwest and South Pacific forces struck simultaneously. In New Guinea American troops landed in Nassau Bay. They were to join Australian forces which were moving overland in an attack on Japanese positions at Salamaua. In the Solomons American forces landed on Rendova Island just off the coast of New Georgia. Rendova was to be a staging area for the main assault on New Georgia and its air base at Munda. Other forces landed on Vanguna Island just south of New Georgia in order to secure the line of communication to Rendova.[48]

On 2–3 July Admiral Halsey's forces established a beachhead on New Georgia near Munda.[49] Planners expected that Operation Toenails would involve the swift conquest of the island and presumed that by D+4 American forces would be preparing for further advances to the north.[50] Operations in both New Guinea and New Georgia were, however, far more difficult than originally predicted. A combination of difficult terrain, filthy weather and tenacious Japanese resistance turned operations in both New Guinea and New Georgia into slow and costly battles of attrition.

In New Guinea American and Australian forces had to struggle for more than two months before securing Salamaua and its airfield. On New Georgia Japanese resistance was so effective that the Americans had to commit elements of three divisions in order to take

Munda which did not fall until 4 August. Most of the remaining Japanese garrison escaped to the nearby island of Kolombangara, but rearguards forced the Americans to fight until 25 August in order to secure all of the island.

Reluctant to become involved in another campaign of attrition, Admiral Halsey decided not to assault Kolombangara which had a large garrison, and instead invaded the lightly held Vella Lavella Island. Reconnaissance of Vella Lavella at the end of July indicated the absence of strong defenses, and US troops executed their assault on 15 August.[51] The island was quickly secured, and while engineers began building an airfield, New Zealand troops finished the task of destroying remaining pockets of resistance. Halsey's forces took Baga Island off the southern coast of Vella Lavella on 16 August and on 27 August landed on Arundel Island which was located between New Georgia and Kolombangara; it was secured by 21 September.

Meanwhile, MacArthur's forces were also on the move. Even as Allied forces battled forward against Salamaua, MacArthur struck at Lae, a major Japanese base at the bottom of the Huon Peninsula. Between 4 and 6 September Australian troops landed east of the town, and on 5 September American airborne forces executed the first parachute assault of the Pacific war, seizing Nadzab, northwest of Lae, and its airfield. Taken by surprise, the Japanese offered only sporadic resistance. Australian troops were quickly flown into Nadzab. They advanced on Lae joined by other Australian units advancing along the coast and took the town on 16 September. The Japanese garrison, joined by troops who had escaped from Salamaua, retreated north across the Huon Peninsula towards Sio on the island's north coast.

As the Allies built new airstrips in the Lae–Nadzab area to support attacks on Rabaul, MacArthur ordered Australian divisions to take Finschhafen. The Australians landed near the town on 22 September and occupied Finschhafen on 2 October. After beating back a Japanese counterattack, the Australians began to move on Sio.

In the South Pacific Halsey sent New Zealand soldiers on 27 October to occupy a position in the Treasury Islands in preparation for his forthcoming attack on Bougainville. Bougainville was an essential stepping-stone for the attack on Rabaul. He also sent a raiding force to attack Choiseul Island to divert Japanese attention from the major assault on Bougainville.[52]

Since the Japanese had concentrated their defense forces on Bougainville, primarily in the southern part of the island and on Buka Island just to the north, Admiral Halsey decided to avoid the obvious and strike at Empress Augusta Bay in the west central portion of Bougainville.[53] The invasion force was to carve out a beachhead and immediately begin to construct airfields to extend the range of Allied airpower to the northern Solomons and Rabaul.[54]

On 1 November 1943 American troops landed at Empress Augusta Bay.[55] Caught by surprise, the Japanese were unable to offer significant resistance. The Americans quickly established a beachhead and began to build airfields, the first of which became operational in early December. The South Pacific Command did not attempt to conquer the entire island; instead the Americans fortified their foothold on Bougainville and prepared to hold it and defend the air bases until the end of the war.

The last major Cartwheel operation in 1943 was the 26 December landing on Cape Gloucester at the western end of New Britain in order to tighten further the ring around Rabaul. The Southwest Pacific Command was still thinking in terms of a final assault on Rabaul, but the strategic situation in the region had changed substantially. Central Pacific forces had begun their long awaited advance, and Japanese air power in the South and Southwest Pacific had suffered grievous losses. Consequently, planners began to re-examine American strategy in the light of new developments.

The product of extensive debate not only among the services but also among operational commands and planners in Washington, Cartwheel was subject to much delay which gave the Japanese time to enhance their defensive positions. Aided by excellent defensive terrain, the Japanese were able to force the Americans and Australians to fight costly battles of attrition. The Allies did by-pass a number of strong Japanese positions, but by the end of 1943 had not advanced very far in either New Guinea or the Solomons. Moreover, Rabaul remained in Japanese hands.

Japan had, however, committed the flower of the naval air arm to the defense of what had become the outer perimeter of its empire. Starting in April, the Japanese mounted numerous massive air attacks against the American advance. The attacks increased in intensity after the Bougainville landing: the Americans, of course, struck back. MacArthur's 5th Air Force, Halsey's AIRSOLS – a joint service organization controlling aircraft in the Solomons – and carrier air wings, some sent from the Central Pacific, not only fought defensively but also struck telling blows at targets in and around Rabaul. The air war reached a peak of intensity in early November when American aircraft struck a series of major blows at Rabaul, but throughout the entire Cartwheel operation, the war in the air was a constant battle of attrition.

Better training coupled with the arrival of advanced fighter types gave the Americans an ever increasing edge over their enemy. The Japanese naval air arm, which did most of the fighting, consequently suffered disproportionate losses until by the year's end the Japanese Imperial Navy withdrew its ships and aircraft from Rabaul. During the 1943 campaign Japan lost over 2,500 aircraft and nearly as many pilots. Since Japan's aircraft production was increasing in 1943, airframe losses were relatively easy to replace. The loss of naval aviators, however, was little short of catastrophic.

The Japanese Combined Fleet had committed its best pilots to the South Pacific and New Guinea, and by the end of the year there were few survivors. It would take at least six months before the Japanese naval air arm could again challenge the American advance, and even then the pilots would lack the skill and combat experience of their predecessors, or as Saburo Sakai, a leading Japanese ace put it: 'Many appeared gifted in the air as the great aces in 1939 and 1940 had been. But their numbers were distressingly few, and there would be no painless interval for them to gain many hours in the air or any combat experience before they were thrown in against the Americans.'[56] Thus, as the Americans prepared for new offensives, Japanese air power could initially offer no effective resistance. As with Watchtower, Cartwheel had the unexpected consequence of weakening the most significant component of Japanese power in the Pacific.

As fighting raged in the Pacific, Anglo-American forces on the other side of the globe prepared to execute the Casablanca and Trident decisions to strike across the Mediterranean at Italy. On 23 January 1943, as fighting continued in Tunisia, the Combined Chiefs of Staff appointed General Eisenhower as the Supreme Commander for the invasion of Sicily known as Operation Husky. His immediate subordinates were British – General Alexander was placed in charge of the detailed planning and execution of Husky; Fleet Admiral

Cunningham led Allied naval forces, and Air Chief Marshal Tedder controlled and directed Allied air components.[57] The Allies were to attack in early July.[58]

The initial Husky Plan was derived from a British study of 10 January and called for two major landings on Sicily. The British 8th Army would land on the south-eastern corner of Sicily, seize airfields around Gela and then move on Catania; the American 7th Army would land in the south-eastern part of Sicily, take a number of airfields and seize Palermo. Finally, both Armies would drive on Messina.[59] The planners were quite concerned that the Germans would reinforce the Italian garrison and stated clearly that if large German formations were sent to Sicily, chances of a successful campaign would become very doubtful.[60]

After examining the plan, General Montgomery and General Alexander called for major changes. The Allies, they believed, had to capture airfields and ports in south-eastern Sicily, and the four divisions assigned to the landing in the south-eastern part of the island were not sufficient to take and hold a position stretching from Catania to Gela. Moreover, there was not enough assault shipping to execute and sustain two widely separated landings. The best solution, therefore, was to cancel the American assault in the Palermo area and concentrate the landings in the southeast with the American army coming ashore on the British army's immediate left. On 20 March General Eisenhower agreed and informed the Combined Chiefs that a single assault in south-eastern Sicily was the most feasible approach for Husky.[61] Six days later the British Chiefs of Staff agreed with the proposed change.[62]

In the final plan the British 8th and US 7th Army would land on a front of about 100 miles. The British would send ashore four divisions and an independent brigade while Americans landed three divisions. Prior to the main seaborne assault two airborne divisions would drop behind Axis coastal defenses. Naval forces included two fleet and eight escort carriers, four battleships, fourteen cruisers, fifty destroyers and 124 smaller combatants. Landing craft included 100 LSTs, 370 LCMs, 120 LCIs and forty transports; Anglo-American air power consisted of 1,376 combat and 312 transport aircraft.[63]

After the initial landings, the 8th Army was to advance on Syracuse, Augusta and Catania and then push toward Messina. The 7th Army would also move forward guarding the 8th Army's left flank. Beyond the initial advances there were no detailed plans. Decisions were left to commanders in the field.[64] Flexibility was of course necessary, but the 7th Army was assigned no specific objectives after the initial assault thus raising the possibility of friction between the two army commanders.

The landing date was set for 10 July, little more than two months after the capture of Tunisia. Allied planners continued to worry that the Germans would reinforce Sicily and force a cancellation of Husky.[65] Fortunately, the island's garrison contained only two German divisions and four Italian infantry and six coastal divisions. The Italian troops were poorly equipped and despite the fact that they were defending their homeland, Italian morale was generally poor. The coastal divisions were not mobile, and German and Italian mobile formations were scattered in order to cover likely landing areas. Axis air power included 300 German and 300 Italian combat aircraft in Sicily plus an additional 100 German planes on the Italian mainland. The Italian fleet was large and modern but unlikely to risk a major encounter with the Allied fleet.[66]

The concern that the presence of a larger German force in Sicily would render Husky unfeasible was, judging by the difficulties encountered by the landing forces, well founded. On the night of 9–10 July the preliminary airborne assaults were nearly disastrous. High winds, an excessively complex flight plan and inexperienced flight crews produced a wide scattering of parachutists. In the British sector, of 144 gliders supposed to land near Syracuse only twelve arrived at their assigned location, sixty-nine crashed in the sea, and the rest landed over a widely dispersed area. Of 3,400 American paratroopers most landed in a random pattern thus jeopardizing the 7th Army's landings by weakening the force that was supposed to control access to one of the main assault beaches.[67]

The assault landing of 10 July involved over seven divisions, the largest single force put ashore during the entire war. Allied forces quickly overcame the resistance offered by Italian coastal units. Sporadic German counter-attacks failed to dislodge the Allies although the Germans did manage to overrun a US infantry battalion, capturing the commander and many of his men. Meanwhile, despite the use of new types of landing craft unloading went very slowly, and by mid-morning of 10 July, over 150 were stranded on the shoreline. The beaches were clogged with heavy equipment waiting to move inland and Axis air and artillery attacks were inflicting substantial losses.[68]

On 11 July a German and an Italian division mounted a major counter-attack against the American beachhead. Congestion on the beaches prevented the employment of artillery and armor. Consequently, Axis forces advanced to within 200 yards of the shore before ground and naval gunfire repelled them. Throughout the day Allied close air support was ineffective because the air control system required that requests for air sorties be relayed back to North Africa thus imposing substantial delays. Finally, an effort to reinforce the American sector via an air drop was a near catastrophe. The parachute drop near Gela on the night of 11 July was met with heavy anti-aircraft fire from Allied ships which brought down thirty-seven of the 144 transport planes.[69]

The Americans eventually forced their way inland and along with British forces began to advance north along Sicily's eastern coast. The arrival of German reinforcements, however, led to stiffening resistance against the 8th Army. To avoid heavy losses in frontal assaults General Montgomery requested and General Alexander approved an extension of the British front to the central part of the island.[70] The Americans consequently had to sidestep the new British front thereby reducing the momentum of the whole Allied drive.

The Americans, facing little opposition, moved quickly to take the western portion of the island. The 7th Army entered Palermo on 23 July. The Germans, however, brought in more reinforcements from the Italian mainland and created a firm position in the north around Mount Etna. General Alexander then ordered the 7th Army to advance on Messina along the east coast while the 8th Army moved north on the other side of the island. Excellent defensive terrain and hard fighting by four German divisions led to a slow, costly advance. The Germans conducted a well organized retreat unhindered by several amphibious flanking operations mounted by the 7th Army.

On 11 August 1943, the Germans began to evacuate their men and equipment from Sicily back to the Italian mainland. Extensive minefields and expert demolition of bridges along the limited highway network continued to impose delays on the Allied advance. US troops entered Messina on 17 August, but the Germans had evacuated over 100,000 men and more than 10,000 vehicles by the time the city was occupied.

SEEKING A STRATEGY – 1943

In slightly more than a month the Allies had captured Sicily thus easing shipping and communications in the Mediterranean by eliminating the threat of aerial attacks from the island's bases. Nevertheless, the campaign was in many ways a disappointment. The Allies took large numbers of Italian prisoners, but few Germans fell into their hands. The insistence that the invasion take place within the range of land-based air cover precluded bolder strategic strokes including a direct strike at the Catania area. The loss of momentum due to the shifting of fronts also demonstrated an excess of caution and probably lengthened the campaign.

Sicily was also a lost opportunity for the Axis. Earlier reinforcement of the garrison by German troops might have led to Husky's cancellation or to the defeat of the landings. The consequences of a setback would have produced a serious strategic dilemma for the Anglo-American coalition. Since the conquest of Sicily did not produce an immediate Italian collapse, Allied planners began to examine closely operations against the Italian mainland which they had been discussing for several months.

Even before the launch of Husky, strategists were contemplating the best means of rapidly exploiting a successful invasion of Sicily. In late April, Allied intelligence predicted that in the wake of an Italian collapse the Germans with only a few divisions in Italy would in the face of an Allied invasion of the mainland rapidly withdraw their forces northward to secure Venetia and South Tyrol.[71] The Germans might also attempt delaying actions along the Pisa–Rimini line or along the Adige River.[72] German forces would not, however, offer a sustained defense of south or central Italy.[73]

An American intelligence assessment of 1 July was also optimistic. The Germans, the report noted, would attempt to hold a line from Genoa to the Adige or from Pisa to Ravenna if the Allies landed in Italy.[74] There would be no major effort to hold south or central Italy.[75] On 19 July as the Allies were advancing in Sicily the JCS War Planning Committee recommended a bold Mediterranean strategy in general, but became very cautious when suggesting a particular operation. The Committee suggested an amphibious landing in Southern Italy in order to be sure of land-based air cover.[76] After the initial landings, the planners called for a rapid advance to Naples and Rome. They expected minimal German resistance.[77]

In North Africa, General Eisenhower's staff was also involved in examining post-Husky operations including invasions of Sardinia and the Italian mainland. On 20 July the Combined Chiefs of Staff directed Eisenhower to invade Italy striking as far north as shore-based aircraft would allow.[78] An intelligence report four days later indicated that in Italy, including Sardinia and Sicily, the Germans had a total of seven divisions which in case of invasion would withdraw to a line from Pisa to Ravenna.[79] Mussolini's removal from office on 25 July and subsequent secret negotiations with the Italians added to the general optimism surrounding concepts for the invasion of Italy.

A US planning staff study of future operations in Italy, sent to the JCS on 7 August, also predicted a rapid German retreat to the north in face of an Allied invasion. After the landings the Allies would move quickly to exploit captured Italian air bases for the Combined Bomber Offensive and prepare American and Free French forces for entry into southern France either overland via northern Italy or by sea.[80] The implicit assumption in the appraisal was that the Germans would not offer an extended defense of either central or north-western Italy thereby rendering feasible an invasion of southern France via the Maritime Alps. On 11 August the British Chiefs of Staff informed the Joint Chiefs of Staff that if the Allies invaded Italy the Germans would retreat north. They would not seek to protect the Milan–Turin area. Instead they would establish defensive positions designed to cover Venetia and the Tyrol.[81]

Optimistic estimates concerning the prospects of an Italian campaign also dominated the highest levels of the Allied governments. At the Quadrant Conference held in Quebec City in August, the British advocated a major campaign in Italy in order to tie down German strength there, so making a cross-Channel offensive – Overlord – more feasible. An advance into north-western Italy would also enable the Allies to obtain air bases for the strategic bomber offensive.[82] The Americans agreed that an invasion of Italy was the logical outcome of Husky, but were reluctant to tie down in Italy resources that might otherwise be used for Overlord.[83] The JCS wanted to advance only as far as the Florence area. The final Quadrant decisions included a renewed pledge to execute a cross-Channel attack in May 1944 plus a simultaneous invasion of southern France. In 1943 the Allies would invade Italy in order to capture Rome and air bases in the area. After the fall of Rome, Anglo-

American forces would move as far north as conditions warranted.[84]

In Algiers in late August Allied planners produced a plan – Operation Avalanche – for the invasion of the Italian mainland. Despite the strategic optimism radiating from Washington and London the actual plan was very cautious. The planners presumed that Allied forces had three possible landing sites – north of Naples, the Gulf of Naples and the Gulf of Salerno some twenty-five miles south of Naples. The first alternative was rejected because it lay outside of the range of land-based fighter cover; strong coastal defenses eliminated the second. The planners therefore chose Salerno which was located within range of fighter cover and had unmined beaches with acceptable gradients for landing craft. The mountainous bottlenecks north of Salerno were accepted as a problem that the Allies could surmount with relative ease. A parachute drop at the Volturno River crossings would block German reinforcements and assist a rapid Allied thrust towards Naples.[85] The airborne assault, however, was abandoned; considering the problems encountered by airborne and glider assaults in Sicily, the planners decided upon prudence.

The Avalanche Plan called for a British and an American corps under the control of the US 5th Army, a formation created expressly for the Italian operation, to land in the Gulf of Salerno on 9 September. Once ashore the 5th Army was to seize the port of Naples and surrounding air bases and prepare for further operations.[86] Prior to the landings the 8th Army would invade Calabria and move on Naples, thus threatening the German flank.

The most significant problem with Allied plans and projections was that the Germans had a very different view of Italy's future role in the war. Far from intending to retreat to the Adige or the Piave when the Allies came ashore, the Germans decided to offer a serious defense of the Italian peninsula well south of Rome. Expecting the defection of the post-Mussolini regime, the Germans moved substantial reinforcements into the peninsula building their forces in the southern part of the country to eight divisions. Thus, the formal announcement of an armistice between Italy and the Allies had little impact on the Reich's ability to respond violently to the Allied landings.

The British invasion of Calabria on 3 September met little opposition, but Calabria was a strategic dead end. The few German units in the toe of Italy used the excellent defensive terrain to execute

63

extensive demolitions and slow the British advance to a crawl. The 8th Army's slow advance in turn placed the Salerno landings in great jeopardy. Rather than being a serious threat to the German flank, the British invasion became little more than a minor irritant to the defenders and offered no real assistance to the 5th Army. The Allies in effect mounted two separate unco-ordinated operations that permitted the Germans to shift forces to counter the more dangerous threat.

The Salerno assault met violent resistance. Initially surprised, the Germans reacted swiftly. Moreover, the 5th Army's decision to forgo a preliminary naval bombardment in order to achieve surprise left German artillery intact, and the landing forces faced heavy fire even before the troops disembarked. Attacks by elements of five German divisions launched between 12 and 13 September came close to splitting and shattering the lengthy but shallow Allied bridgehead.

After heavy losses, the Allies managed to repulse the counter-attacks, reinforced the landing area and began to advance on Naples. Naples, however, did not fall until 1 October, and it took several weeks for the Allies to repair the damage done by their own bombs and German demolitions. Subsequent advances were slow, met as they were by continued stiff resistance. By mid-November it had become clear that the Italian campaign would not involve a rapid advance into northern Italy. Allied forces were in fact quickly bogged down well south of Rome.

By the end of 1943 the Allies had made significant advances in both the Pacific and the Mediterranean but were still a long way from achieving their overall political and military objectives. Nor did the Allies have specific plans for the next steps required to defeat the Axis powers. Internal debates over campaign plans had imposed a number of delays on particular operations, and enemy resistance, often unexpectedly violent, had transformed a number of campaigns from swift decisive strokes into lengthy battles of attrition.

The Second World War was in large measure a war of production and attrition; the latter ultimately favored the Allies. In the Pacific the slow advance in the Solomons and New Guinea held the Allies back but also led to a serious weakening of the Japanese naval air arm. The Americans were therefore able to increase the scope and tempo of future operations directed at the heart of Japan's empire. In the Mediterranean, the Allies had driven Italy from the war, but Germany remained a powerful, dangerous and resourceful foe. The Italian campaign forced Berlin to divert many divisions from other fronts. The true striking power of the Third Reich, however, lay in its armored divisions, and few of these formations fought in Italy. Moreover, the war in Italy absorbed substantial Allied resources. After the fall of Tunisia the Allies had to do something, but it remained an open question as to whether Germany or the Anglo-American coalition gained more from operations in Italy.

NOTES

1. JCS Minutes of Conference, January 15, 1943 at 10 a.m.
2. JCS Minutes of Conference, January 16, 1943 at 9:30 and JCS Minutes of Conference, January 16, 1943 at 5 p.m.
3. Minutes 9:30 and Minutes 5 p.m.
4. Ibid.
5. CCS 155/1 January 19, 1943 Conduct of the War in 1943.
6. Ibid.
7. Ibid.
8. Ibid.
9. Ibid.
10. CCS 170/1 Report to the President and Prime Minister, January 23, 1943.
11. Ibid.
12. Ibid.
13. CCS 166 January 20, 1943 Bomber Offensive from the United Kingdom.
14. CCS 170/1 op. cit., and C J M Goulter, *A Forgotten Offensive Royal Air Force Coastal Command's Anti-Shipping Campaign, 1940–1945*, London, Frank Cass, 1995.
15. Ibid.
16. Ibid.
17. CCS 83rd Meeting (Trident), 13 May 1943.
18. Ibid.
19. Ibid.
20. Ibid.
21. Joint Staff Planners Minutes of Meeting 18 May 1943.
22. CCS 242, 21 May 1943, Draft of Agreed Decisions and CCS 242/6, 25 May 1943, Final Report to the President and Prime Minister.
23. CCS 242/6 op. cit.
24. CCS 242 op. cit.
25. CCS 242/6 op. cit.
26. Ibid.
27. Ibid.
28. Ibid.
29. Timothy J. Runyan and Jan M. Copes, eds., *To Die Gallantly. The Battle of the Atlantic.* Boulder, Westview Press, 1994, p. 226.
30. George W. Baer, *The U.S. Navy, 1890–1990 One Hundred Years of Sea Power*, Stanford, Stanford University Press, 1994, p. 201.
31. Ibid.

32. Ibid., pp. 199–200.
33. Ibid., p. 203. As the Allies gradually turned the tide in the Battle of the Atlantic American submarines in the Pacific were becoming more effective. Inadequate torpedoes hampered the Americans in 1942 and 1943. The problem was resolved by 1944, and by 1945 U.S. submarines had destroyed about 80 percent of Japan's prewar merchant navy. Ibid, p. 235.
34. JPS 67/3 February 15, 1943 Operations in the South and Southwest Pacific areas during 1943.
35. Archives of the Department of the Army, Military Archives Division, Record Group 165, Box 1793, 'Elkton' February 28, 1943.
36. Ibid.
37. Ibid. and Record Group 165 Elkton, 24 February 1943, Box 1793.
38. Record Group 165 ABC File Box 1781 Cartwheel.
39. JCS 238/5/D 28 March 1943.
40. Ibid.
41. Record Group 165 ABC File Box 1781 Cartwheel.
42. Ibid.
43. Ibid.
44. HQ US Army Japan Japanese Monograph no. 37, 18th Army Operations, Vol. I, Tokyo OCMH 1957.
45. Phibsopac (TF61) OpPlan A4-43 Serial 00113, Cleanslate, February 15, 1943. See also Comsopac OpPlan 5-43 Cleanslate, February 12, 1943.
46. OpPlan 5–43 op. cit.
47. Comsopac Serial 00800 May 6, 1943 and Comsopac Serial 0859, 17 May 1943.
48. Comsopac Serial 0859 op. cit.
49. TF31 Serial 00274 OpPlan A8–43 Toenails.
50. Ibid.
51. Comsopac Serial 006613 OpOrder A12-43, 11 August 1943 and Comsopac Serial 001476 OpPlan 14A–43, 11 August 1943.
52. Comsopac Serial 001901 Warning Order, 22 September 1943.
53. Ibid.
54. Ibid.
55. Ibid.
56. Saburo Sakai, *Samurai*, New York, E.P. Dutton and Co., p. 267.
57. CCS171/2/D Operation Husky Directive to Commander-in-Chief Allied Expeditionary Force in North Africa, 23 January 1943.
58. Ibid.
59. CCS Memorandum for Information, No. 47, March 2, 1943.
60. Ibid.
61. CCS 161/2 Operation 'Husky' March 20, 1943.
62. CCS 161/5 Operation 'Husky' March 26, 1943.
63. Archives of the Department of the Army, Military Archives Division, ABC File Box 18.
64. Ibid.
65. CCS 161/2 op. cit.
66. CDR 8th Fleet Serial 00218 Op-Plan 2–43, 26 May 1943.
67. A. J. Birtie, The U.S. Army Campaigns of World War II, *Sicily*, Washington, DC, GPO nd. p. 9.
68. Ibid., pp. 14–15.
69. Ibid.
70. Viscount Montgomery, *El Alamein to the River Sangro*, New York, E.P. Dutton and Co, 1949, pp. 122–3.

SEEKING A STRATEGY – 1943

71. JIC(43) (86CO) (Final) Mediterranean Strategy – Possible Developments if Italy Collapses, 23rd April 1943.
72. Ibid.
73. Ibid.
74. Joint Intelligence Subcommittee, The Situation in Italy, 1 July 1943.
75. Ibid.
76. J.C.S. 417, 19 July 1943.
77. Ibid.
78. C.C.S. 268/5 FAN169, 20 July 1943.
79. Joint Intelligence Subcommittee, Collapse of Italy, July 24, 1943.
80. JPS 247 606-1 Plans for Occupation of Italy and Her Possessions, 7 August 1943.
81. J.I.C. (43) 324 (Final) 3rd August 1943 and JCS 614-2, 11 August 1943.
82. Combined Chiefs of Staff 108th Meeting Quadrant Conference, 15 August 1943.
83. Ibid.
84. Combined Chiefs of Staff 319/5 Final Report to the President and Prime Minister, 24 August 1943.
85. W-8788/8549 NAF345, 31 August 1943.
86. Ibid. and Task Force 81, Serial 00200 Operation Order No. K-43, 30 August 1943.

4

Strategic Alternatives – 1943–44

By late 1943 American and British forces were on the offensive in both the Pacific and the Mediterranean. In neither portion of the globe, however, did the Allies have a clear strategic plan. After each campaign, there was usually an extensive and occasionally acrimonious debate over what to do next. Thus, the Allies had won a number of major victories only to discover that planning subsequent steps was a very difficult process.

In the Pacific there was constant discussion and debate concerning strategic options. Differing service points of view often clashed, and the views of theater commanders frequently differed from the plans devised by the JCS in Washington. To complicate matters further the results of concurrent operations often influenced subsequent strategic appraisals.

In the spring of 1943 the JCS approved an outline plan for the defeat of Japan. The Combined Chiefs accepted it on 19 May during the Trident Conference.[1] *The Strategic Plan for the Defeat of Japan* called for advances by forces in the Southwest and Central Pacific with the main effort concentrated in the Central Pacific. Allied forces would seek to recapture the Philippines and drive to the coast of China where they would retake Hong Kong.[2] The Allies would then establish air power in China and unleash a strategic bombardment campaign against the Japanese home islands followed, if necessary, by an amphibious invasion.[3]

The plan offered no timing guidelines for specific operations, nor did it allocate forces for the Southwest and Central Pacific thrusts. The plan did endorse a dual offensive against the Japanese perimeter, but shipping constraints and the number of available amphibiously trained divisions meant that operations within the two theaters would have to be sequential rather than simultaneous. Finally, General MacArthur whose forces were about to launch Cartwheel felt that operations in the Central Pacific might deny him forces necessary to complete his campaign.

JCS planners next began to examine specific operations to achieve the objectives of the Strategic Plan. On 17 June the planning staff submitted a concept of operations for an attack on the Marshall Islands calling for a direct thrust into the center of the island group in December 1943. Two amphibiously trained divisions, eight carriers, four battleships, fifty LSTs and forty-two transports would assault Kusaire and Eniwetok Islands. After seizing the two positions, the Americans would construct air bases and begin the interdiction of Truk – the main base of Japan's Combined Fleet – by long-range bombing.[4] Shortage of amphibious divisions led the planners to suggest that necessary forces be taken from the Southwest Pacific Command which would lead to a severe limitation or possibly the elimination of operations in the Southwest Pacific.[5] Moreover, the plan required a deep advance into Japanese territory without the benefit of land-based air cover and the possibility of a counter-attack by the weakened but still dangerous Japanese fleet. Finally, the planners lacked detailed intelligence concerning Japanese strength in the Marshalls, and Admiral Nimitz's staff was reluctant to move into the Marshalls without first neutralizing the Gilbert Islands and establishing land-based air facilities.

The planners therefore revised their proposals and on 10 July presented a new scheme of operations calling for the seizure of Tarawa, Makin, and Naru in the Gilberts. The target date was 1 December 1943.[6] As in the June plan, an attack on the Gilberts still required troops from the Southwest Pacific Command. In their absence a Central Pacific drive would have to be postponed until some time in the following year.[7]

The planning staff, therefore, recommended a modification of Cartwheel to eliminate the capture of Rabaul. Instead, forces from the Southwest and South Pacific would seek to control rather than occupy the Bismarck Archipelago by continuing to advance along the New Guinea coast and by seizing Manus Island. From the new positions US forces would neutralize Rabaul and the Bismarcks with a naval and aerial blockade. The isolation of the Bismarcks would in turn free two Marine divisions for operations in the Gilberts and Marshalls.[8]

In examining post-Cartwheel operations the JCS planners recommended on 5 August 1943 that the conduct of subsequent operations fall into three phases – the seizure and activation of airfields on Wewak, New Guinea, amphibious assaults on Kavieng and New Ireland coupled with an invasion of the Admiralty Islands, and the neutralization of Rabaul.[9] The first phase would begin in February 1944. The seizure of Rabaul, the planners argued, would prove to be an intolerable drain on resources and manpower whereas neutralization could be achieved in a shorter time and at a much lower cost.[10]

The following day the planners presented to the Joint Chiefs a complete outline of Pacific operations for the second half of 1943 and 1944. The basic objective remained the invasion of Japan following a massive aerial assault from bases in China.[11] In the Southwest Pacific, after neutralizing Rabaul, MacArthur's forces would continue to move along the north coast of New Guinea to the Vogelkop peninsula at the western end of the island.[12] The British would attack into Burma in order to open land routes to China that would enable the Allies to supply Chinese forces and sustain an air offensive against Japan from Chinese bases.[13] In the Central Pacific American forces would seize the Gilberts, the Marshalls and Truk in the Caroline Islands. Finally, Central Pacific forces would invade the Palau Islands.[14] Thus, by the end of 1944 the Americans would have reached a line stretching from the Palaus to western New Guinea.

The 6 August plan continued to adhere to the dual offensive in the Pacific but said nothing about operations in 1945. Nor did the plan specify how the Allies would sustain China's war effort and create and sustain a large American air force in central China. Furthermore, after the capture of Truk the plan did not delineate the direction of subsequent advances. Finally, the planners faced an adverse reaction from General MacArthur, who was unwilling to see the Southwest Pacific command reduced to the role of flank guard for Central Pacific forces.

In early August 1943 MacArthur presented the JCS with his own plan for post-Cartwheel operations. Codenamed Reno II, the plan emphasized a single major thrust aimed at the southern Philippines.[15]

The Allies should in 1944 concentrate all available resources on a single line of advance. Cutting the sea lanes between Japan and her Southeast Asian resources would fatally weaken Japan. The Allies could most effectively sever Japanese sea lines by establishing ground and air power in the Philippines. Therefore, MacArthur argued, Mindanao was the logical initial objective. From Mindanao the Americans could develop air bases making possible a further advance to Luzon, and from Luzon American forces would be in a favorable position to cut Japan's sea communications to Malaya and the East Indies.[16]

A Central Pacific offensive, MacArthur argued, would not attain a decisive objective until it reached the Philippines. Any advance across the Central Pacific would suffer from logistical problems and the lack of land-based air cover. An advance from New Guinea and the Solomons on the other hand could take full advantage of both sea and land-based air power. Therefore, the Reno II Plan concluded that operations in 1944 should be focused on the occupation of Mindanao by successive moves along the Bismarck Archipelago–New Guinea axis supported by the Pacific Fleet.[17] Specific operations included the seizure of Rabaul and the Vogelkop, the occupation of the Ambon Islands in the East Indies to protect the Southwest Pacific's left flank, and the invasion of the Palaus by the Central Pacific to guard the right flank of the main drive. With the flanks secured the Southwest Pacific forces would invade Mindanao in the spring of 1945.[18]

The Navy, especially Admiral King, disagreed with Reno's strategic approach. The waters of the Solomons and Bismarcks were unsuited to the operation of large fleets based on carriers. A Central Pacific advance by contrast would allow the Navy to employ effectively its rapidly growing fleet and would require fewer troops. Furthermore, a drive into the Western Pacific promised to force the Japanese fleet into a major engagement. A Central Pacific offensive would also offer protection to the advances by Southwestern Pacific forces by forcing the Japanese to divide their resources to cope with two threats. Finally, islands in the Gilberts, Marshalls and especially the Marianas could sustain large land-based air assets, a factor of growing importance to the Army Air Force.

Initially, the Air Force intended to begin a bomber offensive against Japan in October 1944 from bases located in China, in which twenty-eight groups of long-range B-29s with twenty-eight planes each would be supplied from Calcutta. About 2,000 B-24 bombers, converted to transports, would move supplies from Calcutta to China.[19] Late in 1943 a report indicated that bombers could strike targets in Manchuria, Korea and Kyushu from bases in Chengtu in China. By September 1944 air elements operating from China would be able to launch three raids a month, each of 100 planes, against the Japanese coke industry.[20] In early December, however, planners noted that the establishment of air bases in China would place logistical constraints on other theaters and that a wider range of targets was required in order to produce a significant impact on Japan's war economy.[21]

As doubts grew about the utility of a bombing campaign from China, planners began to examine the possibility of using islands in the Marianas as bases from which to mount long-range bombing operations. In early March 1944 the JCS staff recommended that the development of bases in China – Project Matterhorn – for eight groups continue and that twelve air groups should operate out of the Marianas.[22] Later in the month planners recommended the reduction of Matterhorn deployments to four groups and the expansion of forces scheduled to operate from the Marianas to sixteen with subsequent expansion as rapidly as possible.[23]

The growing interest in using the Marianas as a base for long-range bombers placed additional emphasis on the importance of a Central Pacific offensive. The JCS preference for a dual offensive in the Pacific with major emphasis placed on the Central Pacific drive was accepted by the British at the Quadrant Conference. On 24 August the Combined Chiefs gave final approval to Pacific operations for 1943 and 1944.

Forces in the Central Pacific were to seize the Gilberts as preparation for an invasion of the Marshalls.[24] The Americans would then move into the Carolines, take Truk and establish a fleet base. The Central Pacific command would next invade the Palaus followed by operations designed to take the Marianas. South-western Pacific forces were to continue to advance along the north coast of New Guinea and also seize the Admiralty Islands, thereby isolating Rabaul which was to be neutralized rather than captured.[25]

Both the Joint and Combined Chiefs agreed upon a dual advance in the Pacific with priority going to the Central Pacific thrust. The ultimate destination of the offensives remained unclear, but the emphasis placed upon the Central Pacific seemed to be confirmed by the success of the invasion of Tarawa – Operation Galvanic.

Pacific Ocean Area forces had in May and August cleared the Japanese out of Attu and Kiska in the Aleutians, but a shortage of ships and manpower had precluded major offensive operations until late 1943. Naval construction programs had by the second half of the year delivered sufficient numbers of warships, transports and landing craft to enable commanders to risk attacking Japanese positions without support from land-based aircraft.

Operation Galvanic's objectives in the Gilberts were to seize Betio Island in the Tarawa atoll and Makin Island further north. Betio contained a large airstrip essential for subsequent advances into the Marshalls. A Marine division staging out of New Zealand was to attack Tarawa, and an Army division from Hawaii was to invade Makin. The newly designated 5th Fleet, commanded by Admiral Spruance, was to escort and support the invasion. The fleet included four fleet, four light and four escort carriers, thirteen battleships, fifty-six destroyers, thirty-eight LSTs and over 100 amphibious tractors.[26]

Operations in the Central Pacific were very different from the campaigns in the Solomons and New Guinea. The Gilbert Islands were small and often well fortified. American troops would experience immediate resistance to amphibious assaults in contrast to the largely unopposed landings in the South and Southwest Pacific theaters. Moreover, Central Pacific operations were at least initially conducted in the absence of land-based air support, thereby risking the possibility of a Japanese naval riposte against an invasion armada which had to sacrifice mobility in order to support the ground forces. Consequently, a rapid assault and conquest of island objectives was vital. Landing forces, therefore, faced the problem of attacking small islands; Tarawa, for example, was only two and a half miles long and at most 800 yards wide, with little room to maneuver. American planners hoped that preliminary air and naval bombardment would materially ease the tasks of the assault troops.

Planning staffs expected Operation Galvanic to be difficult, but they had in fact underestimated the ferocity of Japanese resistance. Despite the expenditure of over 3,000 tons of shells and bombs many Japanese positions on Tarawa were not destroyed. Consequently, on 20 November 1943 Marines stormed ashore amidst a hail of small arms fire. Hydrographic information was inadequate with the result that most landing craft were halted on submerged coral reefs, and the troops had to wade some 700 yards to reach the shore. Gunfire support and air cover was slow and cumbersome and of the first 5,000 Marines ashore, 1,500 were killed or wounded.[27]

Despite heavy losses the Marines continued to press forward and after three days of bitter fighting secured Betio. Army troops took Makin with relatively light losses, but a Japanese submarine sank a light carrier with heavy loss of life. On Betio the Marines lost 1,085 men killed and 2,248 wounded; the Army at Makin lost sixty-four killed and 187 wounded, while the Navy suffered about 850 killed and 1,500 wounded. The Japanese garrison, about 4,900 strong, died almost to the last man.[28]

The Americans quickly built airfields on Tarawa and by the beginning of 1944 were flying reconnaissance missions over the Marshalls. As the Central Pacific Command prepared to attack the Marshalls, high level arguments concerning the future of America's strategy against Japan continued unabated.

On 2 December 1943 the Combined Chiefs of Staff meeting in Cairo at the Sextant Conference approved an American-inspired overall plan for the defeat of Japan. The plan called for the South-western Pacific Command to continue to advance along the coast of New Guinea while Central Pacific forces moved into the Marianas and prepared to conduct a long-range bomber offensive against the Japanese home islands.[29] In theory both offensives were to be mutually supporting, and both theaters were to be in positions from which to launch a major assault into the Formosa–Luzon–China triangle in the spring of 1945.[30]

The plan also noted that when conflicts of timing or resource allocation existed between theaters, due weight was to be accorded to the fact that Central Pacific operations promised a more rapid advance into the heart of the Japanese Empire plus the prospect of acquiring bases for long-range bomber operations. The Central Pacific advance was also likely to force the Japanese fleet to seek a major battle.[31]

The following day, JCS planners issued a paper dealing with specific operations for 1944. The paper called for the Southwest Pacific Command to continue to advance in New Guinea while Central Pacific forces moved into the Marshalls and Marianas. Once

Guam, Saipan and Tinian had fallen, long-range bombers would, in conjunction with forces in China, begin aerial operations against the Japanese home islands.[32] A schedule of operations called for MacArthur's forces to reach western New Guinea by mid-August 1944. The Central Pacific Command was to capture the Marianas in October and begin the bombing campaign at the end of the year. British forces would move into upper Burma to improve communications with China and provide an enhanced supply line to American air elements stationed in China.[33]

At this juncture General MacArthur re-entered the strategic debate by submitting the new plan, Reno III, calling for his forces to invade the Southern Philippines and from there to recapture Luzon.[34] Admiral Nimitz had meanwhile submitted on 27 December the Granite Plan calling for drives into the Marshalls, Carolines and Marianas. After taking the Marianas, American forces would invade the Philippines and then strike for the China Coast.[35]

On 13 January 1944, Admiral Nimitz submitted a more detailed Granite Plan. The goal of individual campaigns in 1944 was to obtain positions from which both Central and Southwest Pacific forces could strike into the Luzon–Formosa–China area in the spring of 1945.[36] The plan also raised the possibility of invading the Palaus in November to assist MacArthur's forces and suggested bypassing Truk in order to accelerate operations.[37]

JCS planners examined both the Reno III and Granite plans and issued a report on 16 February 1944. The planners assumed that, barring a sudden collapse, the Allies would ultimately have to attack the Japanese home islands. Air and amphibious assaults on Japan would in turn require ports and bases in China and in Formosa or Luzon. Of the two, Formosa was strategically the most valuable since its capture would enable the United States to establish additional air bases and open a sea route to China.[38] China, however, was growing steadily weaker thus increasing the importance of reaching the Formosa, Luzon, and China coast areas as soon as possible.[39]

The planners rejected MacArthur's Reno III Plan because they believed that an advance to Mindanao required the seizure of a series of land masses which required large ground forces to challenge the Japanese in the field of manpower where they had relatively greater advantages.[40] The Reno Plan would not make the most effective use of American naval power yet would require a level of naval support of such magnitude as to prevent full-scale operations in the Central Pacific. The capture of Mindanao would not open sea communications to China, would require additional campaigns in the central and northern Philippines, and B-29s could not strike at Japan from Mindanao.[41]

The Granite Plan by contrast involved fewer and longer steps. It emphasized American advantages in sea and air power, and an advance into the Marianas would assist MacArthur's drives. From the Marianas, American forces could begin an aerial assault on Japan and prepare for moves into the Formosa, Luzon, and China areas.[42]

The planning staff recommended that the JCS make the Central Pacific Offensive the primary effort against Japan. The main strategic objective would be the Formosa, Luzon, and China Coast area. Specific objectives included the capture of the Marianas, the isolation or seizure of the Carolines, an invasion of the Palaus, and an advance to Formosa either directly or, if necessary, via Luzon.[43] JCS planners thus raised the possibility of by-passing Luzon and striking directly at Formosa.

Unwilling to see his theater reduced to a secondary role, General MacArthur submitted another plan in early March – Reno IV – advocating concentration on the Southwest Pacific theater. It called for a continued advance along the New Guinea coast culminating with the invasion of Mindanao.[44] From Mindanao American forces would move north and invade Luzon.[45] Having taken Luzon, MacArthur's forces would then establish bases for an offensive into the Formosa–China area while the Air Force would begin the long-range bomber offensive against Japan from Luzon.[46]

On 19 March 1944, JCS planners rejected Reno IV asserting that a campaign against Luzon would require an unacceptable diversion of resources from operations directed at Formosa and the China coast.[47] The seizure of Formosa would split Japan's empire in half and permit further offensives in any direction. Logical intermediate steps, therefore, included the Marianas and Palaus in order to isolate Truk, provide long-range bomber bases at an early date and set the stage for a campaign to take Formosa. The capture of Luzon would provide air bases for the attack on Formosa and a fleet anchorage, but a campaign on Luzon would be long and costly and would require forces that could be better employed elsewhere.[48] The capture of Mindanao was a better option, since American forces could establish air bases on Mindanao. The bases could assist in suppressing Japanese air power on Luzon thereby assisting the advance to Formosa via the Central Pacific.[49] Thus the planning staff concluded that Southwest Pacific forces should occupy Hollandia in New Guinea and invade Mindanao in November while Central Pacific forces invaded the Marianas and Palaus followed by a move on Formosa early in 1945.[50]

Before the JCS made its final decision on future operations they had to take into account the results of operations in both theaters. Central and Southwestern Pacific forces had in fact been advancing swiftly against Japanese positions in the Marshalls and the New Guinea area.

Having taken Tarawa in November, the Central Pacific Command quickly prepared to invade the Marshalls, a region of some 400,000 square miles with thirty-two separate island groups. Initial plans called for the simultaneous seizure of Kwajalein, Wotje and Maloelap using two divisions supported by twenty-three carriers, thirteen battleships, fourteen cruisers, fifty-four destroyers, sixty-four LSTs, and forty-two LCIs.[51]

Admiral Nimitz, however, decided to strike at a single target – Kwajalein Atoll. He had learned from intelligence decryptions of Japanese signals that the Japanese, anticipating an attack on the periphery of the Marshalls, had shifted the bulk of their forces to the outer islands. Moreover, he had shipping for only two assaults. A strike directly at Kwajalein would give him the advantage of surprise, and once captured, he could establish air bases on Kwajalein and neutralize the other island groups.[52] The revised plan for Operation Flintlock called for the employment of two divisions plus two separate regiments escorted by a fleet even larger than in the original plan, a measure of growing American naval strength. D-Day was set for 31 January 1944.[53]

The Japanese had 5,000 men on Kwajalein which also contained a large air strip. There were 4,000 troops on nearby Roi Namur. Prepared defenses were extensive, but the absence of air and sea power in the Marshalls meant that any garrison attacked by the Americans was doomed. All that Japanese ground troops could do was to fight on without hope of rescue and sell their lives as dearly as possible.

Having absorbed the lessons of Tarawa, the Americans delivered much heavier preliminary fires than they had done in November. On 31 January 1944, Army units took several small islands off the coast of Kwajalein and emplaced artillery to supplement the naval bombardment. The main landings took place on 1 February, and by 4 February the island was secured. Casualties were light – 177 killed and 1,000 wounded. Almost all the defenders perished.[54] Heavy gunfire and air support also eased the task of the assaulting troops at Roi Namur which fell on 2 February, again with light American casualties and the destruction of almost all of the defenders.

The rapid success of Flintlock enabled the Americans to hasten the pace of operations. Admiral Spruance advanced the date of Catchpole, the assault on Eniwetok in the western Marshalls, from 1 May to 17 February.[55] To support the invasion the 5th Fleet mounted Operation Hailstone, a preliminary move involving fifteen carriers undertaking a massive raid on Truk.[56] The raid was a complete success destroying over 250 Japanese aircraft, mostly on the ground, and sinking or damaging over thirty ships.[57]

While the 5th Fleet was bombing Truk, American forces came ashore on a series of small islands near Engebi, the main island in the Eniwetok chain. As in Flintlock, artillery on the small islands added additional firepower to the initial shore bombardment. The next day ground forces secured Engebi in about six hours. On 19 February Army and Marine forces landed on Eniwetok clearing the island by the 21st. The next day the Americans seized Parry Island. American casualties were again light – fewer than 1,000 killed and wounded whilst almost all 2,000 Japanese defenders died. Remaining Japanese garrisons in the Marshalls were bypassed.

The rapid seizure of the Marshalls and the light casualties involved enabled American planners to contemplate advancing the dates of future operations. Moreover, the campaign and the raid on Truk provided important assistance to the operations waged by forces in the Southwest Pacific.

In New Guinea on 17 December 1943 General MacArthur ordered his forces to capture Saidor so as to divide Japanese forces and establish a new base for further attacks. US Army troops came ashore on 2 January 1944 with almost no losses, and a few weeks later American forces had linked up with Australians who had been moving along the coast. By 11 January engineers had a captured airfield in operation.

To obtain additional bases New Zealand forces were ordered to seize Green Island on 15 February.[58] Met by only scattered opposition, the New Zealanders secured the island within five days. By 5 March an airfield was operational.[59] While preparations to complete Cartwheel continued, General MacArthur received information that enabled him to increase dramatically the pace of his operations.

On 1 April allied troops were to invade the Admiralties, but pilots reported that there was no significant activity in the islands and that the airfield in the area appeared to be abandoned. MacArthur's intelligence officer insisted that there were some 4,000 Japanese troops on Manus and Los Negros, the largest islands in the Admiralties, but MacArthur decided to believe the pilots. On 21 February he ordered a reconnaissance in force to land on Los Negros on 29 February.

A hastily assembled force of about 1,000 men landed on the island against minimal opposition. Operations in the Marshalls had virtually eliminated the possibility of Japanese air and naval counterblows. Opposition on the ground, however, was heavier than expected. A series of counter-attacks momentarily threatened the American foothold but were beaten back as reinforcements strengthened the defense perimeter. The Americans then advanced and secured the island by 18 March. US troops landed on Manus on 15 March, and by mid-April Manus and other islands were securely in American hands. On Bougainville, the Japanese launched unsuccessful counter-attacks on 8 March and again on 23 March. Thus, by early April Cartwheel was finally completed. Rabaul was isolated and Southwest Pacific forces were poised for further advances.

The Los Negros operation was a high-risk venture. Better co-ordinated Japanese counter-attacks might have crushed the initial landing force. Many of MacArthur's officers questioned the wisdom of the operation both before and after the event.[60] The operation, however, worked, and victory in the Admiralties compelled the Japanese to retreat from Madang on New Guinea back to Hansa Bay, Wewak and Aitape.[61] General MacArthur, for his part, was already contemplating bypassing these positions and executing a 580-mile amphibious advance to Hollandia.

The successes achieved by the Central and Southwest Pacific Commands also influenced the strategic decisions made by the Joint Chiefs of Staff. On 12 March 1944, a JCS directive declared that the Formosa–China–Luzon triangle was the basic objective of operations during 1944. The Marianas, Carolines and Palaus were essential preliminary goals along with Mindanao.[62]

The JCS, therefore, increased the tempo of operations and instructed the Southwest Pacific command to complete the conquest of the Admiralties and the isolation of Rabaul and to seize Hollandia by 15 April. MacArthur was to invade Mindanao by mid-November.[63] Admiral Nimitz's forces were to neutralize Truk and invade the Marianas by 15 June. They were to invade the Palaus by mid-September and attack Formosa by mid-February 1945.[64]

Although the JCS seemed to rely most heavily on the Granite Plan approach, the 12 March directive provided no conclusive decision as to which theater was the most crucial. The Joint Chiefs, in fact, left a large loophole in the directive when they stated that although Formosa was the most important objective, Luzon would be assaulted if such an operation were necessary to assist the Formosa landings.[65] Thus, the lengthy and often heated discussions among the JCS, theater commands and service staffs produced little in the way of long-term strategic guidance. The dual offensive approach was retained, but its goals after mid-1944 remained unclear.

Having been directed to capture Hollandia, MacArthur was quick to comply, setting a landing date of 22 April. Taken by surprise, the Japanese offered virtually no opposition to American landings on both sides of Hollandia. The ground forces moved rapidly and seized three airfields near Lake Sentani by 26 April. Another surprise attack drove off the Japanese garrison at Aitape seizing still another airfield. By the end of April all the fields were operational.[66]

Thus, by the late spring of 1944 Allied forces in the Pacific had scored a number of significant victories and increased the tempo of operations. Both the Southwest and Central Pacific forces were making major strides forward. On the other hand, despite the operational flexibility provided by the dual offensives, the United States still lacked a co-ordinated Pacific strategy which remained in a constant state of flux as planners and decision makers reacted constantly to operational developments.

In the Mediterranean and European theaters strategic decisions hinged primarily on coalition politics. American and British views concerning campaigns in Italy and the eastern Mediterranean and the timing of the cross-Channel attack differed substantially, and by the end of 1943 Washington and London had reached such an impasse that both powers placed the future of Allied strategy in the hands of a third party – Marshal Stalin.

As Anglo-American armies in Italy ground to a halt in front of the German Gustav Line, British and American political and military leaders met at the Sextant Conference in Cairo to discuss future strategy and to prepare for a meeting in Teheran with Stalin. At Cairo the British reopened the whole question of the relationship between the invasion of France and campaigns in the Mediterranean.

At the Trident and Quadrant Conferences the British had agreed to launch Overlord in May 1944 along with a supporting invasion of southern France. On 24 November, however, Churchill suggested that the timing of Overlord should not be such a tyrant as to rule out every other activity in the Mediterranean.[67]

The next day the British Chiefs of Staff presented a formal proposal calling for continued offensive operations in Italy up to the Pisa–Rimini line, an intensification of aid to Greek and Yugoslav partisans, and measures to bring Turkey into the war. Finally, the British advocated operations in the Aegean to assist the Turks and force the Germans to scatter further their forces. If such measures required forces assigned to Overlord, the date of the cross-Channel invasion should be put back.[68]

The British proposals clashed directly with the American strategic approach which emphasized concentration of force. President Roosevelt was anxious to land in France as soon as possible since the presence of a large American army in Western Europe would enhance his position at any subsequent peace conference. Moreover, he was determined to have American forces in Berlin at the end of hostilities.[69] When the British presented the Rankin Plan for the occupation of Western Europe and Germany in case of a sudden collapse of the Nazi regime, the British planners for logistical reasons assigned American forces an occupation zone in southern Germany.[70] Roosevelt insisted, however, that Rankin be changed to give the Americans an occupation zone stretching from the Low Countries to Northern Germany including at least a portion of Berlin.[71] Although preliminary plans for Overlord placed American armies on the Allied right, the Americans insisted that despite any logistical problems involved, the US zone would be located in Northern Germany and Berlin.[72]

The President and the Joint Chiefs also realized that in the absence of Rankin conditions American forces would have to strike as soon as possible to achieve their territorial goals. Finally, the Americans sought a rapid defeat of Germany in order to transfer military assets to the Pacific and hasten the defeat of Japan.[73] With logistical preparations for Overlord stretching back to the Rocky Mountains, American leaders feared that expanded campaigns in the Mediterranean might render Overlord unfeasible in 1944.[74] A two or three month delay of Overlord would push the invasion date back to mid- or late summer. Deteriorating weather conditions in the Channel in the summer and fall would then increase drastically the risks of any assault and perhaps render the attack unfeasible in 1944.

The Americans rejected the British view that additional operations in the Mediterranean would wear down German power and facilitate Overlord at a later date, and the Sextant Conference reached an impasse. At this juncture the issue of campaigns in Southeast Asia threatened to render unfeasible any compromise.

President Roosevelt, concerned with keeping China in the war, promised Chiang Kai-shek an amphibious assault in the Bay of Bengal in early 1944. There were not enough landing craft for operations in northwestern Europe, the eastern Mediterranean and the Bay of Bengal. Fearing that the Americans would devote additional assets to the war in Asia and the Pacific, the British suggested delaying the Bay of Bengal operation and focusing Allied efforts on Overlord and the Mediterranean.[75] The Joint Chiefs replied that both Roosevelt and Churchill had agreed to the Bay of Bengal operation, and only they could delay or cancel it.[76] The British pointed out that if the Allies undertook operations in the Mediterranean and the Bay of Bengal, Overlord would have to be postponed. The Joint Chiefs replied that they understood the problem but for political reasons could accept no delay of the Bengal operation.[77]

On 26 November the Combined Chiefs reluctantly agreed to a series of strategic proposals for the Teheran Conference. Allied forces in Italy would advance to the Pisa–Rimini line; increased aid would go to Yugoslav partisans; Turkey would be brought into the war, and Allied forces would capture Rhodes to secure access to the Dardanelles. There would be an operation in the Bay of Bengal, and Overlord would be delayed.[78]

Neither the British nor the Americans were satisfied with the Sextant strategy, but by accident or design American insistence on the Bay of Bengal campaign forced a choice between Overlord and the Mediterranean since there were not enough landing craft for all three operations. The Americans insisted that the choice be left to Stalin in order to break the deadlock, and the British agreed.[79] Both the United States and Great Britain recognized that the Soviet Union was playing a crucial role in the European conflict. Furthermore, the British and Americans were willing to do all in their power to assist the Soviets in their gigantic struggle against Germany. It was, nevertheless, a measure of the deep Anglo-American division over strategy in Western Europe and the Mediterranean that fundamental political and strategic choices were placed in the hands of a third party.

The British and American delegations arrived in Teheran each hoping that Stalin would side with them. On 28 November 1943, the first day of the Eureka Conference, President Roosevelt informed Stalin that Anglo-American forces had two basic options – Overlord or the Mediterranean – and asked the Soviet leader which approach would be of most assistance to the Russian war effort.[80]

Stalin's response began with a promise to enter the war against Japan after the defeat of Germany.[81] He went on to note that Red Army operations were slowing down because of logistical problems and German counter-offensives in the Ukraine and that the western powers could best assist Soviet forces by launching Overlord. Mediterranean operations had been useful in opening the area to shipping, but operations in Italy were of no further use. Even a successful Italian campaign would be unlikely to penetrate the Alps and open the way into Austria and Southern Germany.[82] In the unlikely event that Turkey entered the war the Allies could abandon the cross-Channel assault and launch their major offensive from Italy and the Balkans, but barring Turkish entry into the war, the Soviets believed that northern France was the best location for an Anglo-American offensive in 1944.[83]

Churchill continued to advocate continued operations in Italy and the eastern Mediterranean. There were adequate forces in the region aside from the Overlord build-up, and Mediterranean campaigns would be of direct assistance to the Soviets even if they required a few months delay in launching Overlord.[84] Stalin replied that the Allies were scattering their forces in non-supporting offensives and that it would be more effective if they focused their efforts on the cross-Channel attack.[85] Stalin added that after the fall of Rome the

Allies should invade southern France to support Overlord. He also noted that the Allies might even forgo the capture of Rome and invade southern France prior to Overlord, but Churchill insisted that Rome's capture was of transcendent importance to the British public and that the failure to do so would bring down his government.[86]

Thus, on the first day of the Eureka Conference, the American strategic view had prevailed. Stalin had chosen Overlord in preference to immediate assistance in the form of Mediterranean operations. The British continued to advocate the pursuit of Mediterranean options, but the cross-Channel invasion had again come to dominate Allied strategic thinking.

In military discussions the following morning, Marshall, Brooke, and Voroshilov reiterated their individual national positions. Marshall emphasized the primacy of Overlord, Brooke called for additional Mediterranean thrusts, and Voroshilov stated that the USSR viewed Overlord as the most important Allied operation for 1944. An invasion of southern France was not in the Soviet view absolutely necessary. Voroshilov added that Stalin did not insist on it, but did insist on the execution of Overlord in May 1944.[87]

In a plenary session the same day Churchill assured Stalin that Britain had no political designs on the Balkans but did wish to carry out a number of operations in the region. Stalin replied that he had no objection to the diversion of two or three divisions to aid partisans or take Rhodes but that Overlord remained the most decisive Anglo-American operation. A landing in southern France would, he added, contribute to the success of Overlord.[88] Roosevelt objected to the commitment of forces to the eastern Mediterranean fearing that operations in the region would require the use of landing craft needed for Overlord. Any ventures in the eastern Mediterranean, the President insisted, should be done on a scale that would not require assets taken from Overlord.[89] Churchill admitted that if Turkey remained neutral, operations in the Aegean were pointless but continued to argue that Mediterranean operations were essential to prevent the Germans from sending reinforcements to France. Roosevelt insisted that nothing delay Overlord, and Churchill finally agreed that England had the obligation to cross the Channel with all available strength.[90]

On 30 November the Combined Chiefs of Staff agreed to recommend to the President and Prime Minister that they inform

Stalin that Anglo-American forces would launch Overlord in May in conjunction with an invasion of southern France. Stalin, at a plenary session, promised to launch a concurrent offensive to contain the maximum number of German divisions on the Eastern Front.[91]

On 1 December Roosevelt, Stalin and Churchill agreed to a series of strategic undertakings. The Allies would provide increased assistance to Yugoslav partisans and encourage Turkey to enter the war. If Turkey joined the Allies, and as a result Bulgaria attacked the Turks, Stalin would immediately declare war on Bulgaria. The British and Americans would launch Overlord in May 1944 in conjunction with an operation against southern France, and Soviet forces would launch an offensive at about the same time.[92]

Thus, if the Teheran Conference did not end Anglo-American strategic debates, it did reaffirm the Trident and Quadrant decisions to launch Overlord in the spring of 1944. Because of the Soviet participation in the decision, the Eureka Conference made Overlord a virtually unbreakable commitment. Moreover, the provision of a specific date for the invasion placed severe restraints on other operations that might impose delays on the assault.

Back in Cairo, the Anglo-American political and military leaders agreed on 5 December to reduce the size of the Bay of Bengal operation in order to provide additional assault shipping for Overlord and Anvil (landing in southern France).[93] The next day the Combined Chiefs agreed to a general strategy for 1944. Overlord and Anvil were to be the supreme operations. Both invasions would be launched in May and nothing was to be undertaken in other areas that would deprive the assaults of necessary assets. In Italy, Allied forces would advance to the Pisa–Rimini line, and the Mediterranean theater could retain sixty-eight LSTs, due to return to the British Isles, until mid-January. Amphibious operations in the Bay of Bengal were finally cancelled, and landing craft assigned to Southeast Asia would be reassigned to Overlord and Anvil.[94]

The Sextant Conference reaffirmed the decisions arrived at in Teheran. Overlord and Anvil were officially accepted as the major Anglo-American operations for 1944. The Americans had finally established the primacy of the strategic approach they had been advocating since 1942. In return, the Americans agreed to the cancellation of major operations in Southeast Asia and to the continuation of the Italian Campaign. Operations in Italy, however, were to have a significant impact not only in the Mediterranean but also on the Overlord–Anvil operations.

In Italy, Allied commanders realized that the logical solution to the stalemate along the Gustav Line was an amphibious turning movement. In late October a series of discussions involving Generals Eisenhower, Alexander and Clark concluded that an amphibious operation was the best way to break the stalemate, but a turning movement was not feasible because projected landing areas were too far from the battle line thereby rendering a link-up at best problematic.[95]

Additional conferences decided that if the Allies launched an amphibious attack Anzio was the best site because of adequate beaches and the port itself. By mid-November planners called for a drive by the 5th Army to a point midway between Rome and Cassino at which time a reinforced division would land at Anzio to threaten German supply lines. The planners assumed that the landing force and the 5th Army would link up in about six days.[96] An outline plan approved by General Mark Clark, commander of the 5th Army, in late November assumed that an Anzio landing, Operation Shingle, coupled with an advance by the 5th Army would force the Germans to retreat.[97] The 5th Army, however, failed to crack the Gothic Line. Consequently Clark began to contemplate a larger landing, but lack of landing craft subsequently convinced him to recommend the cancellation of Shingle.[98]

The British, however, were still interested in breaking the Italian stalemate and capturing Rome. On 26 December Churchill informed Roosevelt that a two-division Shingle could force the Germans to abandon Cassino and the Gothic Line. To execute Shingle, landing craft designated to return to the British Isles would have to stay longer in the Mediterranean. Roosevelt agreed. The Combined Chiefs then reassigned LSTs – twenty would leave the Mediterranean for England and three assigned to Southeast Asia would go to the Mediterranean. A total of eighty-seven LSTs would participate in Shingle. In March thirty-three of them would proceed to England and fifteen would participate in Anvil.[99]

The Americans agreed to assign LSTs designated for Overlord to Italy for a limited period on the presumption that Shingle would produce a rapid victory. There was, however, a considerable difference of opinion between the 15th Army Group and the 5th Army concerning the role of Shingle. General Alexander's Army group staff was far more optimistic about Shingle than the 5th Army planners.[100]

On 2 January 1944, the 15th Army Group directed the 5th Army to mount a two-division assault at Anzio with the object of cutting enemy supply lines and threatening the rear of German forces at Cassino and in the Liri Valley. The 5th Army was to attack Cassino before the seaborne assault, force a breach in the German front, and link up rapidly with forces at Anzio.[101] On 12 January Army Group Headquarters issued more detailed orders. The 5th Army was to launch a series of attacks against Cassino culminating with an advance across the Rapido river on 20 January in order to force the Germans to commit reserves to the Gustav Line thus easing the tasks of the Anzio landing on 22 January.[102] Troops at Anzio would then advance into the Alban Hills to cut the communications lines of German forces on the Gustav Line. The two forces would link up rapidly and push the Germans north of Rome.[103]

American planners were less optimistic. On 3 January, General Eisenhower reported to the JCS that Shingle forces would land with only eight days' worth of supplies and that within three days after D-Day the Germans could concentrate more than three divisions against a beachhead. If the 5th Army failed to break through to Anzio by D+8, the landing force would have to be withdrawn. Thus, Shingle was a risky venture, but, Eisenhower concluded, the hazards were probably worth the risks.[104]

The 5th Army's orders for Shingle issued on 12 January were quite cautious. The invasion force of an American and a British division under the command of a US corps were to secure a bridgehead at Anzio and advance on the Alban Hills.[105] There was no mention of taking Rome or even a timetable for advancing into the Alban Hills. Naval escort forces issued orders the same day noting that January was an unfavorable period for amphibious operations because of adverse weather conditions. Consequently, troops would land with seven days of supplies and resupply by sea was a very remote possibility.[106]

The goals of Shingle were in fact unclear. The 15th Army Group regarded Shingle as a major thrust that would unhinge the Gustav Line and lead quickly to the capture of Rome. The 5th Army viewed Shingle as a supporting attack for the main thrusts at Cassino and the Liri Valley. In either case a single reinforced corps was probably too small to accomplish either mission. An immediate post-landing advance to the Alban Hills would stretch the corps to a point where German counter-attacks could threaten the beachhead, whereas pushing cautiously inland would not place sufficient pressure on the Germans to force them to retreat from the Cassino position. Moreover, once ashore the Single force and the rest of the 5th Army were not within mutual supporting distance. Consequently, to succeed Shingle had to be part of a victorious 5th Army offensive since it was not strong enough to break the stalemate by itself.

The 5th Army offensive began on 20 January but was a singular failure. Troops struck across the Rapido river south of Cassino, and the Germans drove them back with heavy casualties. The attack had forced the Germans to commit reserves, but the line remained intact. At this point the Allies should perhaps have delayed or cancelled Shingle, but instead the 5th Army planned new attacks and allowed the amphibious assault to go ahead as originally planned.

The landings at Anzio on 22 January met virtually no resistance. Although expecting an amphibious turning movement, the Germans had nonetheless failed to detect either the massing of naval forces at Naples or the convoys at sea. By the afternoon of D-Day Allied troops had taken Anzio and the nearby port of Nettuno, and by midnight 36,000 men and over 3,000 vehicles had come ashore. Debarkations continued during the days following while troops ashore moved inland. By 24 January the Allies had reached positions seven miles inland.[107]

Though taken by surprise, the German response was rapid and violent. By 24 January elements of three divisions were facing the beachhead with more units on the way from Italy, Yugoslavia and France. As more troops arrived the Germans began to shift their thinking from containing Shingle to destroying it.[108]

Realizing that two divisions were insufficient, the Allies reinforced the beachhead with an infantry and an armored division and on 25 January began to move on the Alban Hills. It was, however, too late. Aided by bad weather which severely limited the effectiveness of Allied air power, the Germans halted the advance, and by the end of the month had 95,000 men around Anzio ready to launch their own attacks.[109] The Allied high command soon realized the precarious position of the Shingle forces. On 2 February the 15th Army Group ordered forces in Anzio to begin constructing defensive positions. Five days later the 5th Army ordered forces in the bridge-head to build defenses in depth.[110] Survival rather than a victorious march on Rome had become the essential objective of Shingle.

On 3 February the Germans launched the first of three major attacks against the Anzio positions. Severe fighting lasted until March. Allied attacks around Cassino made small gains with heavy losses and failed to divert German strength from Anzio. By late February the Allied situation was desperate. The JCS noted that Allied forces in Italy were located in two groups more than fifty miles apart. They had lost the initiative, and the Germans were mounting heavy assaults on the Anzio position. A defeat at Anzio would have catastrophic repercussions including the probable cancellation of Overlord, and even if Overlord went forward, Anvil could not be launched simultaneously because of the situation in Italy. Finally, large air corps elements would have to be diverted from strategic missions to help alleviate the situation around Anzio.[111]

Hard fighting plus extensive air support finally halted the German attacks though at a heavy cost in lives. By early March, a stalemate existed both at Anzio and along the Gustav Line. Consequently, on 24 March the JCS concluded that because of the situation in Italy, Anvil would have to be delayed at least until 10 July 1944.[112]

In Italy the Allies prepared new offensives. Between March and May the Anzio bridgehead was reinforced reaching a strength of two British and five American divisions. The 5th Army received two new divisions from the United States, and the 8th Army shifted forces to the 5th Army's right. By April, the 5th Army had concentrated four corps against the southern portion of the Gustav Line while Allied air forces launched a massive bombardment to hinder the flow of reinforcements and supplies from northern Italy to forces south of Rome.

On 5 May General Alexander issued orders for a general offensive. The 5th and 8th Army would break through the southern portion of the Gustav Line while forces at Anzio attacked north to cut the major road link between the Gustav Line and Rome.[113] The following day the 5th Army ordered two corps to attack in the Liri valley while forces at Anzio prepared to advance north. D-Day was to be 11 May.[114]

In the forthcoming offensive the Allies were much stronger than the Germans. Each side had twenty-two divisions in Italy, but the

Allies enjoyed a vast superiority in artillery, armor and air power. The Germans held strong defensive positions and despite all their disadvantages were prepared to offer stiff resistance.

The offensive began on schedule and by 16 May, after heavy fighting, American troops broke through the southern part of the Gustav Line while the French pushed forward to unhinge German positions in the Liri valley. Further north, Polish and British troops finally captured Cassino. On 23 May forces at Anzio began to attack to the north and on 25 May elements of the 5th Army, advancing along the coast, linked up with troops from Anzio.

On 26 May, however, General Clark altered the mission of the forces moving out of Anzio from attempting to cut the highway between Rome and the main Italian front to a drive to the north-west, which was the most direct route to Rome.[115] The shift of the main weight of attack from the north to northwest forced the Americans to fight their way through the Alban Hills and weakened the drive on the crucial highway along which the Germans were withdrawing their forces from the shattered Gustav position. Consequently, the Germans were able to delay the advance against the highway while thousands of troops escaped the Allied clutches.

The Americans did manage to batter their way through the excellent defensive terrain in the Alban Hills while other forces pursued retreating German formations along the highway. On 4 June American forces began to enter Rome, but the anticipated publicity due the 5th Army was short-lived when two days later Allied forces began the invasion of France.

The Anzio campaign was largely devoid of significant strategic results. It had also been very costly. From 1 January to 4 June the 5th Army lost 15,700 killed, 65,000 wounded and 13,600 missing. German losses were about 78,000.[116] Allied operations did tie down a number of German divisions which might have been used elsewhere, but an equivalent number of Allied divisions served in Italy. The Anzio landings were initially too weak to threaten serious German defensive positions along the Gustav Line, and, far from threatening the Germans, Shingle forces were soon waging a desperate struggle for survival. The need to sustain the Anzio bridgehead in turn imposed serious delays on the projected Anvil operation, thereby rendering the forthcoming Overlord assault all the more risky and difficult.

The period from late 1943 to June 1944 witnessed a growing Allied superiority. The Japanese were unable to retain control of any position directly attacked by the Allies, and the Germans finally had to retreat north of Rome. The Allies, however, had still not devised a comprehensive strategy either in the Pacific or in Europe. In the Pacific, American service and field commanders had and would continue to debate the course of future operations. In Europe American and British strategic differences had grown so divisive that heads of state had to leave the future of Anglo-American strategy to a third party. The Americans finally obtained a firm commitment for a cross-Channel attack in the spring of 1944, but the problems encountered in the Italian campaign forced a delay in the invasion of southern France, and the ultimate fate of Anvil was destined to roil Anglo-American relations once again.

NOTES

1. Joint Chiefs of Staff Memorandum: Strategic Plan for the Defeat of Japan Approved by the Combined Chiefs of Staff, 19 May 1943 (JCS 287/1 and CCS 220).
2. Ibid.
3. Ibid.
4. JPS 205/1 17 June 1943 Operations against the Marshall Islands.
5. Ibid.
6. JPS 205/3 10 July 1943 Operations against the Marshalls–Gilberts.
7. Ibid.
8. Ibid.
9. JPS 243 5 August 1943, Operations in the New Guinea–Bismarck Archipelago–Admiralty Islands area, subsequent to Cartwheel.
10. Ibid.
11. JCS 446 603-2 JPS 245 Specific Operations in the Pacific and Far East, 1943–44, 6 August 1943.
12. Ibid.
13. Ibid.
14. Ibid.
15. Archives of the Department of the Army Military Archives Division Record Group 165, Box 1852 Reno II.
16. Ibid.
17. Ibid.
18. Ibid.
19. CCS 323 Air Plan for the Defeat of Japan, 20 August 1943.
20. JPS 320 Early Sustained Bombing of Japan, 9 November 1943.
21. JPS 3201/1 3 December 1943.
22. JCS 742 2 March 1944 871-16, Optimum Use, Timing and Deployment of V.L.R. Bombers in the War against Japan.

23. JCS 742/4 27 March 1944.
24. CCS 319/5 Final Report to the President and Prime Minister, 24 August 1943.
25. Ibid.
26. HQ Pacific Fleet Serial 00207 OpPlan No. 13-43, 5 October 1943.
27. Ronald Spector, *Eagle against the Sun*, New York, The Free Press, 1993, pp. 312–13.
28. Michael B. Graham *Mantle of Heroism Tarawa and the Struggle for the Gilberts, November 1943*. Novato, Presidio Press, 1993, pp. 312–13.
29. CCS417, 2 December 1943, Over-All Plan for the Defeat of Japan.
30. Ibid.
31. Ibid.
32. JCS 581/2 Specific Operations for the Defeat of Japan, 1944, 3 December 1943.
33. Ibid.
34. Military Archives Division Record Group 165, Box 1852, Reno III.
35. Campaign Plan Granite Cincpac, 27 December 1943.
36. Cincpac Fleet Granite Serial 0004, 13 January 1944.
37. Ibid.
38. JCS 713 Strategy in the Pacific, 16 February 1944.
39. Ibid.
40. Ibid.
41. Ibid.
42. Ibid.
43. Ibid.
44. Military Archives Record Group 165 Box 1852 OPD, General Records, Reno IV, 6 March 1944.
45. Ibid.
46. Ibid.
47. JCS 713/1 Future Operations in the Pacific, 10 March 1944.
48. Ibid.
49. Ibid.
50. Ibid.
51. Military Archives Record Group 165 OPD Box 1835 and Cincpac Serial 00218 OpPlan no. 16–43, 12 October 1943.
52. Cincpac Serial 001689, 14 December 1943.
53. Ibid. and Military Archives Division Record Group 165 Box 1870, 6 January 1944.
54. Burton Wright, *Eastern Mandates*, Washington, DC, nd., pp. 14–19.
55. Cincpac File Serial 00233 Catchpole, 29 November 1943.
56. Cincpac File 00010 Hailstone Staff Study, 18 January 1944.
57. Wright, op. cit., p. 14.
58. Comsopac Serial 0036, 3 January 1944.
59. Comsopac Serial 00280 Op-Plan 5–44, 24 January 1944.
60. Daniel Barbey, *MacArthur's Amphibious Navy Seventh Amphibious Force Operations 1943–1945*, Annapolis, U.S. Naval Institute, 1969, pp. 154–7.
61. Ibid., pp. 286–7.
62. JCS 713/4, 12 March 1944, Future Operations in the Pacific.
63. Ibid.
64. Ibid.
65. Ibid.
66. Spector, op. cit., pp. 284–7.
67. Sextant Conference Minutes of the Second Plenary Meeting, 24 November 1943.
68. CCS 409 Overlord and the Mediterranean, 25 November 1943.
69. Mark Stoler, *The Politics of the Second Front*, Westport, Greenwood Press, 1977, p. 138.

70. JCS 577, 8 November 1943, Europe-Wide Rankin.
71. CCS 320/4 Operation Rankin Memorandum from the United States Chiefs of Staff, 4 December 1943.
72. Ibid.
73. Ibid.
74. Stoler, op. cit., p. 137.
75. CCS 131st Meeting, Sextant Conference, 26 November 1943.
76. Ibid.
77. Ibid.
78. Ibid.
79. Stoler, op. cit., p. 142.
80. Eureka Conference Minutes of Plenary Session, 28 November 1943.
81. Ibid.
82. Ibid.
83. Ibid.
84. Ibid.
85. Ibid.
86. Ibid.
87. CCS Eureka Conference Minutes of Military Conference, 29 November 1943.
88. CCS Eureka Conference Minutes of Plenary Session, 29 November 1943.
89. Ibid.
90. Ibid.
91. CCS Eureka Conference Minutes of Plenary Session, 30 November 1943.
92. CCS Memorandum for Information, No. 165, Military Conclusions of the Eureka Conference, 2 December 1943.
93. CCS Sextant Conference Minutes for the Fourth Plenary Meeting, 5 December 1943.
94. CCS 426/1, 6 December 1943, Report to the President and Prime Minister.
95. Carlo d'Este, *Fatal Decision Anzio and the Battle for Rome*, New York, Harper Collins, 1991, p. 70.
96. Chester G. Starr, *From Salerno to the Alps, A History of the 5th Army 1943–1945*, Washington, Infantry Journal Press, 1948, pp. 123–4.
97. d'Este, op. cit., p. 74.
98. Ibid.
99. CCS 455, 3 January 1944, LST's for Operation 'Shingle'.
100. Ibid.
101. Headquarters 15th Army Group, 2 January 1944, Operations Instruction No. 32.
102. Headquarters 15th Army Group, 12 January 1944, Operations Instruction No. 34.
103. Ibid.
104. Military Archives Division Record Group 165 ABC 1 File Box 440, 3 January 1944.
105. Headquarters 5th Army, 12 January 1944, Field Order Number 5.
106. Op Plan 147-43 Serial 00409 (OP), 12 January 1944.
107. d'Este, op. cit., Chapter 8, *passim.*
108. Ibid.
109. Ibid., Chapter 9, *passim.*
110. Headquarters ACMF, 2 February 1944, Operations Instruction No. 37 and Headquarters Fifth Army Operations Instruction No. 15, 7 February 1944.
111. Military Archives Division Record Group 165 ABC File Box 441.
112. CCS 465/13, 24 March 1944.
113. Headquarters Allied Armies in Italy, 5 May 1944.
114. VI Corps Field Order No. 26, 6 May 1944.
115. Headquarters 5th Army Operations instruction No. 24, 26 May 1944.
116. d'Este, op. cit., p. 414.

5

Assaulting the Citadels – 1944

By the end of 1943 the Anglo-American coalition had agreed that the invasion of northern France would be the supreme Allied effort in 1944. Earlier high level conferences – Trident and Quadrant – had called for an invasion in the spring of 1944, but Britain's insistence on conducting operations in the Mediterranean even at the price of delaying Overlord clashed with America's emphasis on concentration of forces for an early assault. Not until the Sextant and Eureka Conferences did Washington and London agree to direct their full efforts towards invading north-western Europe.

Despite high level disagreements Anglo-American military planners had worked together since 1943 to devise an invasion plan. By the end of the year they had provided a basic framework for Overlord. At the Casablanca Conference the Combined Chiefs of Staff had agreed to continue the Bolero build-up of American forces in England and set a goal of fifteen divisions and 938,000 men by the end of the year. The Combined Chiefs also decided to establish a combined staff to prepare plans for an emergency return to the Continent and for a full-scale invasion in 1944. COSSAC (Chief of Staff to the Supreme Allied Commander) would be headed by a British general on the assumption that the Overlord commander would be an American.[1]

On 5 March 1943, the British Chiefs of Staff recommended that Lieutenant General Frederick E. Morgan assume the COSSAC post, and on 23 April the Combined Chiefs issued a directive to General Morgan to prepare a series of plans including a deception plan to convince the Germans that the Allies would invade France in 1943, plans for an emergency return to the Continent in the event of a sudden German collapse, and plans for a full-scale assault in the spring of 1944.[2]

While the COSSAC staff was at work, the Joint Chiefs of Staff was independently examining prospects for an invasion of France. On 8 May 1943 the Joint Chiefs approved a paper written by the War Plans Committee dealing with a 1944 invasion of northern France. The planners estimated that by April 1944 thirty-six Allied divisions would be available for a cross-Channel operation. They would face thirty-two German divisions in France, seven of which were armored.[3] Reinforcements from Germany and the Eastern Front would swell the numbers to sixty within three weeks. German ground formations would be supported by 1,254 aircraft initially, with the numbers increasing quickly to 1,766.[4]

The Allies would therefore have to establish in France a lodgement area that included port facilities in order to bring in forces stationed in the British Isles plus up to fifty-three divisions being organized in the United States.[5] To meet German counter-attacks, ports had to be captured very quickly to permit a rapid Allied build-up. The two most promising areas for assault operations were the Caen area and the Cotentin peninsula which would afford port capacities for a build-up of 912,000 men within twelve months. By extending the lodgement to include Le Havre and Rouen the build-up would increase to over four million men and a hundred divisions.[6] The JCS submitted their appraisal to the British at the Trident Conference.

JCS planners had established two basic principles. Allied forces would not strike at the Pas de Calais which was the shortest route across the Channel but was heavily defended. Rather, they preferred to land in Normandy which contained beaches adequate for the amphibious assault as well as a number of ports. After a successful landing, the Allies would undertake an extensive build-up of forces and create a logistics structure before advancing further. Both concepts – a landing in Normandy and a major reinforcement phase – were to characterize all subsequent invasion plans.

At the Trident Conference on 18 May American and British planners agreed that Allied forces would establish a lodgement in the north of France, undertake a build-up within the bridgehead and then launch an offensive to the east. Air superiority would delay the arrival of German reinforcements and was, therefore, an essential factor in any invasion and post-invasion operation.[7] The next day the Combined Chiefs agreed that the Allies would attempt to land on the

Continent in May 1944. The initial assault phase would comprise nine divisions, and the reinforcement phase would consist of three to five divisions per month.[8] The British added that as a condition for launching the invasion German mobile reserves should not exceed twelve full strength divisions.[9] The final report of the Trident Conference of 24 May accepted the results of the strategic discussions. The Allies agreed to establish a force of twenty-nine divisions in the United Kingdom and to invade France on 1 May 1944.[10]

The COSSAC staff meanwhile completed a preliminary Overlord plan and presented it to the British Chiefs of Staff on 27 July. On 5 August the JCS received a copy.[11] The COSSAC Overlord plan included many of the strategic assumptions of earlier studies.

The plan noted that the Pas de Calais offered many obvious advantages as an area for the initial landings. It represented the most direct route between the British Isles and the French coast thus facilitating air support and quick turnaround time for shipping. Beaches in the Pas de Calais had a high capacity for passing vehicles and supplies inland. On the other hand, the Calais region was the focal point for German fighter aircraft and was the most heavily defended portion of the whole French coast.[12] Finally, the area offered limited opportunities for subsequent operations. Development of a lodgement would in fact require the capture of Belgian ports as far north as Antwerp or the seizure of Le Havre and Rouen. An advance on Antwerp would have to traverse numerous water obstacles and the capture of the Seine ports involved a 120-mile flank march.[13]

A landing on the Cotentin peninsula had the advantage of ensuring the early capture of Cherbourg, but there were few airfields in the region and the terrain precluded the rapid construction of new airstrips. Finally, the narrow neck of the peninsula would enable the Germans to seal the bridgehead thereby rendering very difficult subsequent attempts to advance to the east.[14]

The Caen area offered better prospects. The sector was weakly held, had beaches of high capacity and the inland terrain was suitable for airfield development. Moreover, the terrain was suitable for defense against German armored counter-attacks. There was a limited number of enemy airfields within range of the Caen area. The major disadvantage of Caen was that the projected landing beaches were relatively distant from any major port.[15]

Landing forces partly in Caen and partly in Cotentin was very dangerous. Such landings would entail a division of the assault forces and separating them by the low-lying marshy ground and intricate river system at the neck of the peninsula. Such a landing would risk defeat in detail.[16]

The COSSAC staff, therefore, concluded that the Caen beaches despite the fact that there would be a considerable lapse of time between the landings and the capture of a major port, offered the best prospects for a successful landing and subsequent exploitation. After the landings, the Allied forces would seek to capture first Cherbourg and then the Brittany ports.[17]

Prior to any assault the Allies would have to reduce the strength of the German fighter force by the destruction of the aircraft production industry coupled with major air battles. COSSAC estimated that a campaign for air superiority beginning in 1943 would face 1,740 German aircraft in France. The Americans would have 7,300 aircraft including 2,448 heavy bombers and 2,500 fighters, and the RAF would possess 4,075 aircraft including 1,600 heavy bombers and 792 fighters.[18]

Dominance in the air would enable the Allies to slow the arrival of German reserves which in any case could not exceed a dozen full strength mobile divisions if the landings were to have a reasonable chance of success. Moreover, if the Germans were able to move nine divisions to the Caen area by D+8 and transfer more than fifteen first-class divisions from the Eastern Front during the first two months after the landings, the Allied assault would face serious and perhaps insurmountable problems.[19]

The Allies would launch their invasion with twenty-six to thirty divisions available in the British Isles. Three divisions would land simultaneously on the Caen beaches followed by reinforcements consisting of three brigades. Airborne troops would seize the town of Caen, and by the following day the Allies would hold a bridgehead some thirty-five miles long and seven miles deep stretching from Caen to the southern part of the Cotentin peninsula.[20] Subsequent action would involve a thrust south in order to acquire airfield sites and to gain depth for a turning movement into the Cotentin peninsula directed at Cherbourg. By D+14 Cherbourg would be in Allied hands, fourteen airfields would be in operation, and eighteen divisions would be ashore in France.[21]

The COSSAC staff assumed that at this juncture the Germans would withdraw to the line of the Seine where they could obtain air cover from fields in north-eastern France and Belgium. The Germans would also bring in forces from the Russian Front. The Germans would, however, continue to hold Brittany and southern France. The Allies would secure their left flank by advancing to a line along the Eure river to Rouen and from Rouen along the Seine to the Channel. At the same time, the Allies would take Chartres, Orléans and Tours. Under cover of these operations the Allies would send forces to capture the Brittany ports of Nantes, St Nazaire and Brest as well as other small Breton harbors.[22]

By D+50 the Allies would have at least thirty divisions in France. The next step would be to build up resources in the lodgement area in order to execute operations designed to force the line of the Seine and capture Paris and the Seine ports. The Allied armies would then advance towards northern France and Belgium while other forces pushed due east from Paris. In both the invasion and exploitation phases American forces would serve on the right of the Allied line and the British and Canadian units on the left.[23]

On 15 August at the Quadrant Conference, the Combined Chiefs accepted General Morgan's initial plan and authorized him to proceed with detailed preparations.[24] Two days later the Combined Chiefs approved the concept of Overlord as the primary Allied effort in Europe in 1944 and agreed on a landing date of 1 May. After securing adequate ports in France, subsequent operations would secure a major lodgement area. Following the establishment of strong Allied forces in France, operations would then strike at the heart of Germany.[25] The final report of the Quadrant Conference noted that the CCS approved General Morgan's plan and again authorized him to begin detailed planning for Overlord. Along with Overlord the Allies as a diversion would land in southern France and take Toulon and Marseilles.[26]

As a result of the Sextant and Eureka Conferences the Combined Chiefs again agreed that Overlord would be the main Allied effort in 1944. The Combined Chiefs appointed General Eisenhower as the Supreme Commander and General Montgomery as the Commander of the 21st Army Group which would execute the initial assault on the French coast. General Montgomery would initially command the British 2nd and US 1st Army. He would retain control of ground operations until the Americans had sufficient forces ashore to establish their own army group. In early February 1944 the Combined Chiefs formally defined Eisenhower's mission in one of the most famous directives of the war, 'you will enter the Continent of Europe, and in conjunction with other United Nations, undertake operations aimed at the heart of Germany and the destruction of her armed forces'.[27]

Meanwhile, the Combined Chiefs had examined the availability of forces for Overlord in the light of global commitments. By 1 May 1944 planners estimated that American, British and Canadian ground strength in the United Kingdom would consist of thirty-one and two-thirds operationally available divisions. After the landings, an additional twenty-eight US divisions would be available and, beginning in August 1944, could reach the Continent through captured ports at a rate of four per month. In the Mediterranean the Allies had thirty-one divisions, ten of which would participate in Anvil.[28] In England and the Mediterranean the Allies possessed 3,783 heavy and over 1,000 medium bombers and about 4,200 fighters. Landing craft shortages continued to be a problem, but the Combined Chiefs concluded that there would be sufficient numbers to carry out the operations agreed upon at Sextant. The Combined Chiefs concluded that Overlord was feasible although it was planned on a very narrow margin and should, if possible, be strengthened.[29]

Thus, by the first months of 1944, the British and American Chiefs of Staff were committed to launching Overlord in May. Furthermore, there was general agreement that the Allies would not strike at the Pas de Calais but rather would seek to land in Normandy. There was also agreement that after establishing lodgement the next step would be the seizure of Cherbourg followed by the capture of the Brittany ports. The Allies would then establish a firm base in France, bring in additional supplies and reinforcements and advance to the Seine and from there move east into the Low Countries and Germany. The preliminary plans called for a phased approach moving from assault landings to the creation of a lodgement area and finally to major campaigns in northwest Europe. Additional planning would alter a number of significant details but the broad outline would be retained.

The first significant change came as a result of a Supreme Commander's conference held in England on 21 January 1944. General

Montgomery examined the COSSAC plan and asserted that the three-division initial assault was inadequate. The assault provided too narrow a front to assure success and made it too easy for the Germans to concentrate forces against the bridgehead.[30] Operation Neptune (the official code word, since Overlord was a more general name used when the target area and date were not specifically mentioned) required a more extended landing frontage and additional assault troops in order to establish a beachhead and provide for a rapid drive on Cherbourg. Montgomery therefore called for a first wave of five divisions and an extension of the invasion beaches to the base of the Cotentin peninsula. He also called for an airborne operation as part of the initial attack.[31]

Admiral Ramsay, RN, Commander of the naval forces pointed out that an increase in the assault force required more landing craft and obtaining them would force a postponement of the 1 May landing date. General Eisenhower, however, agreed with Montgomery on the need for a larger assault and a wider landing area.[32]

On 24 January General Eisenhower informed the Combined Chiefs that it was essential to mount a five-division assault as nothing less would provide an adequate margin of success. He therefore proposed adding to the one American and two British divisions assaulting the Caen beaches an American and a British division to extend the landing frontage. He also called for two more divisions to land on the second D-Day tide.[33]

Eisenhower and Montgomery also believed that it was vital to Neptune's success to attain air supremacy over northern France. To this end the objectives of the Combined Bomber Offensive (CBO) were altered to concentrate on the reduction in strength of the German air force especially the fighter arm. The CBO would therefore focus its attacks on fighter airframe and component production factories as well as the installations of the air defense forces.[34]

In the last week of February 1944, the US 8th Air Force resumed long-range daylight raids into Germany. Bomber strength had grown to 165 heavy bomber squadrons with about 1,900 aircraft. Fighter escort strength grew to forty-five squadrons all equipped with drop tanks, thereby giving the escorts the range to accompany the bombers all the way to their targets. The 9th Air Force's sixty-three fighter squadrons and the RAF's fifty-nine would also contribute assets to escort and air suppression missions.[35]

Starting with 'Big Week' in February 1944, the 8th Air Force began a bitter aerial battle of attrition with the Luftwaffe. The presence of long-range escort fighters gave the bomber squadrons an advantage they lacked in the previous year. The bombing itself did substantial damage to the German aircraft industry but did not deliver a death blow. German fighter production actually increased in 1944, but in the absence of the raids, production would have grown much faster than it did.

The raids did, however, force the German air force to redeploy many squadrons back to Germany leaving few aircraft to guard the coast of France and the Low Countries. The raids also forced the Luftwaffe to draw resources from some Eastern Front sectors as well. In the air battles, RAF Fighter Command would engage the forward elements of the German fighter force thus enabling the long-range escorts to penetrate German air space where they inflicted heavy losses on the defenders. The *Luftwaffe* in turn had to commit pilots to battle with progressively less training, thereby further increasing losses. Consequently, the ensuing months of the air war saw the gradual destruction of the German fighter defense force.

The missions of the strategic bomber forces became a subject of debate among Allied commanders in early 1944. British and American air commanders wanted to continue missions against the German war economy, while ground force commanders called for missions in direct support of Neptune. There were also debates among air commanders over the right targets to attack within Germany. Finally, on 27 March the Combined Chiefs decided that Neptune had priority over Pointblank and gave General Eisenhower control over air operations to support the forthcoming invasion. Eisenhower then directed the 8th Air Force and Bomber Command to concentrate on disrupting the French rail network to hamper German efforts to move reinforcements to Normandy after the landings.[36]

As the air battles raged over the skies of Europe, planning for Neptune progressed rapidly. Planning worked its way from the highest levels of command to subordinate echelons which created their own specific plans to fulfill the roles allotted to them.[37] Combat service support elements – engineers, logistics, medical and construction commands – also produced their own plans.

The 21st Army Group issued an *Initial Joint Plan* for Neptune on 1 February 1944. The intention of the plan was to invade Normandy between the Carentan estuary and the river Orne.[38] Assault forces would comprise elements of the US 1st Army and the British 2nd Army. On D-Day the Americans would capture Ste Mère-Eglise and Carentan and then move on St Lô and Cherbourg. British and Canadian forces would take Bayeux and Caen on D-Day and then move south and east to gain territory for airbase construction while protecting the 1st Army's flank as it moved on Cherbourg.[39] Airborne divisions would be dropped on either flank to seal off the main routes to the invasion beaches.[40] A cover plan would attempt to deceive the Germans as to the time and place of the invasion. After the landings, the deception operation would attempt to convince the Germans that Neptune was a diversion and that the Allies would deliver their main assault at the Pas de Calais.[41]

Subsequent changes to the initial plan included the addition of a second airborne division in the American sector to seal off the western portion of the Cotentin peninsula.[42] Because of the extension of the landing beaches the number of LSTs was increased from 149 to 168 American plus sixty-one British vessels.[43]

By early May planning echelons had completed their work. Under the command of the 21st Army Group, Neptune would deploy the 2nd British Army on the left and the American 1st Army on the right. The British would make their assault with two British and one Canadian division on three beaches and capture Bayeux and Caen on D-Day. The Americans would land elements of three divisions on two beaches.[44] The Allies intended to bring reinforcements ashore as soon as possible. By the end of D-Day the Americans planned to have two and two-thirds divisions and 6,800 vehicles plus the airborne divisions in the beachhead, and the British expected to have three divisions and 8,900 vehicles on shore.[45]

To support the assault, the Allies would employ over 800 medium bombers and 2,500 fighters. Airborne operations would involve 1,300 transports and about 2,000 gliders. The 8th Air Force and RAF Bomber Command would also provide support for the landings.[46] Naval forces included seven battleships, a monitor, twenty-three cruisers, eighty large and thirty-nine small destroyers, ninety-eight minesweepers, sixty-three frigates, seventy-one corvettes, 495 coastal patrol craft and other light elements for a total of 1,213 warships. The American Navy even reduced substantially its Atlantic convoy escorts in order to amass sufficient vessels for the invasion.

The United States and the Royal Navies also committed 229 LSTs and 3,372 landing craft of other types to the Neptune assault.[47]

Rapid reinforcement of the landings was vital to Neptune's success. Allied intelligence estimated that the Germans had between fifty-five and sixty divisions in Western Europe, including nine or ten armored units. Many of the infantry divisions were static formations, but between seventeen and twenty-two of them were fully capable of mobile field operations. Some twelve divisions from other fronts could move to France soon after the invasion. Eisenhower's headquarters estimated that by D+25 the Germans would be able to concentrate ten panzer and twenty-seven mobile infantry divisions against the Allied bridgehead.[48] Consequently, in addition to the delays and attrition on German reinforcements imposed by air power, rapid reinforcement was critical to blunt German counter-attacks and to continue the projected advance.

The Neptune plan therefore called for a total of eight and two-thirds divisions to land in Normandy by the end of D-Day. By D+1 the Allies were to have ten and one-third divisions ashore and fifteen and a third by D+6. By D+12 the build-up was to comprise twenty-six to thirty divisions and by D+40 the 1st Army intended to have 457,732 men and 92,700 vehicles in France.[49]

Logistics requirements to sustain the ground forces ashore were immense. Up to D+10 the British forces required 13,500 and the Americans 16,000 long tons per day, not including bulk fuel. Between D+25 and D+40 requirements would grow to 18,000 tons per day for the British and 24,000 tons for the Americans.[50] Fuel requirements were also large. By D+15 the 1st Army would need 474 tons of fuel per day and 1,800 tons daily by D+32.[51] A substantial percentage of Allied logistics requirements would come via undersea pipelines, the Mulburry and other artificial harbors, and over the beaches, but as the number of troops in Normandy rose, it would become imperative to capture a number of functioning ports.

Logistic requirements and strategic prudence thus defined Allied plans for operations after the assault landings. Phase 1 involved the amphibious and airborne landings, the establishment of a beachhead and the capture of Cherbourg. By D+17 Neptune called for the Allied front line to run from Granville to a point east of Caen. The US 1st Army reinforced by elements of the US 3rd Army, would next drive south to the Loire to cut off the Brittany peninsula and take the

Brittany ports. The forward echelon of the communications zone would organize the area behind the 1st Army while the tactical air force repaired captured aerodromes and built new airfields to provide direct support for the ground forces. Phase 1 was to be complete by D+50.[52]

Phase 2 called for the 1st Army to swing northeast to the line of the Upper Seine abreast of British and Canadian forces to the north. The 3rd Army would deploy into France and operate between the south flank of the 1st Army and the Loire by D+90. While the field armies advanced to the Seine, the communications zone would organize Brittany to accept forces directly from the United States at a rate of four divisions per month.[53] Having built up a logistics network, the 21st Army Group and the US 12th Army Group, which would become operational upon the conquest of Brittany and the arrival of the bulk of the 3rd Army's forces, would advance towards the German border. General Eisenhower expected that the battle for the Siegfried Line would begin by D+330.[54]

In examining post-Overlord strategy General Eisenhower informed the JCS in April and again in May that to achieve the objectives of the CCS – the conduct of operations aimed at the heart of Germany and the destruction of the German armed forces – the Ruhr was the optimum objective. Occupation of the Ruhr would effectively destroy Germany's capacity to carry on the war for any length of time. Moreover, the Germans would have to place the defense of the Ruhr industries among their highest strategic priorities. An Allied attack on the Ruhr would, therefore, force the German army to stand and fight, thus providing the Allied forces with an opportunity to bring the German army to battle and destroy it.[55]

There were four possible avenues of advance to the Ruhr. The first was a move southeast from the lodgement area to cut off German forces in the south of France and defeat them in detail. General Eisenhower rejected this approach, for even if successful, it would threaten nothing vital to Germany. Moreover, an advance to the southeast required a major movement away from Allied air bases and such an advance would also produce serious logistical problems.[56]

The second option was a move east with the main axis of advance directed south of the Ardennes on Metz and the Saar. Eisenhower also rejected this option since it would entail operations on a narrow front with little opportunity for surprise or maneuver. Moreover, the terrain was highly defensible, and the route did not lead directly to objectives vital to Germany.[57]

A third alternative involved an advance north of the Ardennes. The projected route had the advantages of close proximity to air bases in the United Kingdom and to ports in the Low Countries. The advance would directly threaten the Ruhr. On the other hand, the terrain was very defensible, and a single axis of advance would involve a frontal assault against the main enemy forces.[58]

A fourth approach called for a combination of the second and third alternatives. A dual advance weighted most heavily on the northern axis would enable the Allies to employ surprise and deception, unbalance enemy dispositions, and gain adequate superiority for the main thrust north of the Ardennes. Therefore, Eisenhower recommended a major thrust on a line Amiens–Maubeuge–Liège–Ruhr and a subsidiary advance from Verdun to Metz. The double thrust would give the Allies flexibility of maneuver over terrain suitable for armored warfare. The dual advances could be supported logistically, and the northern drive could receive air support from bases in Britain.[59]

The lengthy planning process produced a number of basic assumptions. COSSAC identified as early as 1943 the initial target for the amphibious landings. Montgomery, backed by Eisenhower, demanded and received a larger initial assault. Once ashore planners called for a phased, almost methodical, advance from the beachhead to Cherbourg, to Brittany, and the line of the Seine and from there to the western border of the Reich. Logistical considerations led Allied planners to think in terms of advancing in stages in order to permit the development of lines of supply needed to sustain a massive Allied force that would ultimately reach a strength of more than sixty divisions.

By the beginning of June the Allies were ready. Waiting in England, the United States had 1,537,000 men, sixteen million tons of supplies, 4,200 tanks, 13,700 wheeled vehicles and 3,500 artillery pieces.[60] The Allied air forces dominated the skies over France and had seriously damaged the rail network between Germany and the French coast to impede the movement of German reserves and reinforcements. German air strength in France had been reduced to about 300 aircraft. The deception plan had succeeded in convincing the Germans that a non-existent army group was poised to strike at the Pas de Calais, and that if the Allies launched other attacks, they would be mere diversions.

On the other hand, the Germans had built numerous well fortified positions along the French coast. Moreover, they had ten panzer and forty-eight infantry divisions in France. The number of fully mobile divisions vastly outnumbered the initial Allied invasion force. Thus the invasion would in a sense measure the ability of the Allies to breach the Atlantic Wall and reinforce the landings faster than the Germans could move forces to the invasion beaches and mount full scale counter-attacks.

As the day of the invasion approached the weather in the English Channel became stormy, forcing SHAEF (Supreme Headquarters Allied Expeditionary Force) to postpone the assault from 5 to 6 June. Weather conditions remained poor, but forecasters predicted a break sufficient to permit the launching of the invasion. The Supreme Commander decided to take the risk of attacking on 6 June rather than waiting three weeks for the next favorable period of moon and tide. The stormy weather actually worked to the advantage of the Allies. The Germans assumed that the foul weather precluded an invasion during the first week of June, and many senior commanders went to Brittany for an anti-invasion war game while the Army group commander went back to Germany to celebrate his wife's birthday.[61]

Shortly after midnight on 6 June 1944, airborne units began the invasion of France. British paratroopers successfully took their objectives, seizing the bridges over the river Orne and the Caen canal to anchor the 21st Army Group's left flank. American airborne operations were not quite so successful, in part because the airborne troops of both divisions landed in widely scattered small groups. One battalion did seize the important crossroads town of Ste Mère-Eglise. Other small groups sowed a certain amount of confusion in the minds of German commanders, but on the whole the airborne attacks had a limited impact on the subsequent seaborne landings.

Shortly before dawn, Allied bombers launched what would amount to a daily total of more than 11,000 sorties, and at 5:50 a.m. over 700 warships began an intensive bombardment of the assault beaches. The naval and air bombardment destroyed or silenced numerous enemy artillery and infantry emplacements and detonated many minefields. German naval resistance was minimal. Torpedo boats sank a Norwegian destroyer but did no further damage. The Luftwaffe was virtually absent.

Between 6:30 and 7:00 a.m. landing craft began their run to the beaches. On the Allied left the British 2nd Army landed on three beaches – Sword, a British objective, Juno, a Canadian objective, and Gold, a British target. All three landings met stiff initial resistance, but 2nd Army troops overcame it quickly and began to move inland. The Germans, however, moved local armored reserves into and around Caen. The British and Canadian troops moved forward cautiously and reinforcements and supplies experienced serious difficulties in moving off the beaches. Consequently, the Germans won the race for Caen. Although the 2nd Army successfully established a position ashore, it failed to take the D-Day objective of Caen, a failure that was to cost the Allies dearly in the weeks to come.

The American landing on Omaha Beach on the British right was a near disaster. Regiments from two US divisions encountered a first-class German infantry division that had recently moved to the Normandy coastal defenses. Allied intelligence had not located it prior to D-Day. High seas swamped many landing craft and sank fifty-seven of ninety-six amphibian tanks. Wind and currents pushed many landing craft away from designated sites and into areas where there was no supporting naval gunfire. To make matters worse gunfire and bombing support was inaccurate, landing well behind the defenders leaving most beach obstacles intact. Most radios for artillery forwarded observers had gone down with sunken landing craft leaving the infantry to attack well emplaced defenders with little armor, artillery or air support.

The initial assault waves at Omaha Beach were pinned down at the water's edge. Many landing craft became entangled in obstacles. Troops had to wade ashore under fire from machine guns and mortars. Little more than a third of the first wave reached the shore, and lacking heavy weapons, the survivors could do little more than seek cover behind sand dunes and a small seawall. As casualties mounted the 1st Army Commander debated whether or not to cancel the assault and move the remaining forces to another beach.

On shore, however, order gradually reasserted itself. In some places smoke from exploding munitions blinded German gunners, and small groups of infantry seized the opportunity to move inland. A few surviving tanks provided fire support, and Allied destroyers moved close to the shore to bombard German positions. Despite the fact that the beach was a shambles of burning vehicles and crippled landing craft, the Americans managed to take the bluffs above the

107

beach and move into flatter terrain. By nightfall Omaha Beach was secure and some 34,000 men were ashore to stay.

At Utah Beach on the Allied right the landings encountered minimal resistance. Although German artillery did sink an Allied destroyer, the landing craft, carried by swift currents to a point several miles south of their intended objectives found the beach lightly defended. Commanders on the scene therefore decided to continue disembarking on the new beach, and within three hours American forces had crushed light resistance and were moving inland. By evening more than 23,000 men were ashore at a cost of fewer than 200 casualties among the ground troops.

By the evening of 6 June over 100,000 Allied soldiers had come ashore. Losses had been heavy – about 9,000 men, one-third of whom were killed – but not as severe as planners had predicted. The British and Canadians had not taken Caen, nor were individual beachheads linked together to form a solid front. Furthermore, their shallow depth enabled German artillery to hit almost the entire landing zone. The defenders, however, lacked the forces to launch a decisive counter-stroke. Allied fighter bombers delayed the movement of reserves, and a Byzantine command structure precluded a rapid and effective response to the invasion. The continued success of the Allied deception plan convinced the Germans not to move significant forces from the Calais area. Consequently, local reserves in Normandy could do little more than shore up threatened points along the German perimeter around the landing zones. The Allies were then firmly ashore although the initial post-landing advances fell short of planned D-Day objectives.

After D-Day, the German High Command responded to the invasion in a manner not expected by Allied planners. Instead of falling back from coastal areas and amassing forces for a counterblow, the defenders received orders to hold their forward positions at all costs. Around Caen the terrain was suitable for armored warfare while the city itself and a number of surrounding villages were transformed into strong points thereby creating a dense defensive network. On the right, the Normandy 'bocage' country with sunken lanes and hedgerows four to five feet high and several feet thick, provided the defenders with excellent terrain and made any forward movement a genuine nightmare.

After linking the various bridgeheads, the Allies began to move further inland. The British 2nd Army sought to fight its way into and beyond Caen, but by the end of the month three full-scale efforts to take the city had failed. The attacks did, however, force the Germans to commit most of their armor and mechanized divisions against the 21st Army Group's left where they halted British and Canadian attacks but suffered in the process heavy losses.

The German concentration against the British 2nd Army eased somewhat the task of the US 1st Army, but advances were nonetheless slow and costly. By 18 June the Americans had fought their way across the Cotentin peninsula and began to advance on Cherbourg. The German garrison offered stubborn resistance until 27 June. The Allies thus had a major port, but German engineers had thoroughly demolished the docking facilities, and it would take three weeks before Cherbourg was open to minimal shipping and months before the port could handle cargo in significant quantities. Storms between 19 and 21 June had ruined the American and seriously damaged the British artificial harbors. The Allies, however, quickly learned to move adequate supplies across open beaches, but still had not gained the use of a major harbor.

By 1 July the Allies had a million men and over 17,000 vehicles ashore in a beachhead seventy miles long and from five to twenty-five miles deep. The Germans for their part showed no intention of retreating from Normandy and thereby denied the Allies the opportunity to break out into open country. The Allied High Command, therefore, had no choice but to continue the murderous and costly conflict of attrition.

The ensuing weeks witnessed more heavy fighting. On 9 July the British 2nd Army finally took Caen but was unable to break the German lines which recoiled slightly but still held firm. The American advance was also slow and costly. Poor weather limited close air support, and US casualties became alarming. Nevertheless, the US 1st Army reached the outskirts of St Lô by 15 July and in three days of house-to-house combat secured the town.

By late July the Allies had a firm foothold in France but had failed to break out into open country or capture a major operational port. The Germans had used the excellent defensive terrain of Normandy to good advantage, forced the Allies into a war of attrition, and given up limited amounts of territory. Attrition, however, worked both ways. The Allies suffered severe losses but so did the Germans who lost over 100,000 men killed or wounded in the weeks after D-Day. The Germans had also been unable to amass forces for a major counter-attack. Ultimately, attrition would work against the Germans who simply could not match Allied human and material resources.

Meanwhile, the pace of the Pacific war was accelerating. Despite numerous unpleasant tactical surprises the strategic initiative in the Pacific remained with the Americans. Although distant goals remained unclear, both the Southwest and Central Pacific forces continued and accelerated their advance into the center of the Japanese Empire.

Following the JCS Directive of 12 March 1944 MacArthur's forces had successfully taken Hollandia and Aitape in late April. Japanese forces on New Guinea mounted a series of counter-attacks against Aitape in July. The Americans, however, had through reconnaissance, radio intercepts and captured documents learned of the Japanese preparations and reinforced the defenses around Aitape. Although fighting raged for nearly a month, the Japanese failed to dislodge the Americans, lost about 9,000 men and ceased to be a significant threat to further American advances in New Guinea.[62]

Even while the Japanese were preparing for their attack at Aitape, American forces executed another amphibious leap to Arare on the New Guinea mainland on 17 May. The following day US troops invaded the nearby island of Wakde in order to capture airfields and push the air umbrella further north. In two days of fighting the Americans captured the airfield and cleared the island. A few days later the field was in use by US aircraft.

Southwest Pacific forces then moved on the town of Sarmi on the New Guinea coast. The Japanese, however, were well entrenched in the area, and the Americans encountered ferocious resistance. Small gains were made at a high cost, and the Japanese held out in the Sarmi area until the end of the war. Despite their successful resistance they could not halt the inexorable advance of MacArthur's forces.

As part of the drive to gain control of the New Guinea coast and extend land-based air power to the Philippines, Southwest Pacific forces invaded Biak Island on 27 May. American troops encountered little opposition at the beaches, but upon moving inland the invaders were met with vigorous Japanese counter-attacks. The Japanese, using light tanks, pushed the advancing forces back, and one American battalion to avoid destruction had to be evacuated from the island.

Another week of hard fighting left the Americans in possession of Biak's main airfield, but from overlooking ridges, the Japanese kept the field under constant mortar and small arms fire. Consequently, it took several weeks of hard fighting to secure the main airfield and several smaller ones and additional weeks of intense combat were necessary to secure the entire island. Fighting continued to the end of June and might have gone on longer had the Japanese been willing to risk transports and escorts in an effort to reinforce the defenders. Growing threats in the Central Pacific, however, forced the Japanese to focus their efforts on the defense of the Marianas.

In three months, forces of the Southwest Pacific Theater had advanced 1,400 miles from the Admiralties to Biak. Superior sea and air power had made possible long distance moves and the isolation of several major Japanese garrisons in New Guinea. On several occasions Japanese resistance had been tactically much more effective than expected, but tactical proficiency could not compensate for the strategic disadvantages under which the Japanese fought.

While MacArthur's forces were advancing, the Central Pacific Command was preparing Operation Forager – the invasion of the Marianas. Operation Forager called for the occupation of Saipan, Tinian and Guam in order to use the islands as bases for further advances and to provide facilities for the Air Force to execute long-range bombing attacks on the Japanese home islands.[63] Plans called for twelve groups of B-29s to operate from the Marianas.[64]

For the Marianas Campaign, the Central Pacific command deployed massive forces. Naval assets included fourteen battleships, seven fleet, eight light and fourteen escort carriers, 136 destroyers, and eighty-seven LSTs and 109 other landing craft. Land forces consisted of two amphibious corps with a total of three Marine and two Army divisions plus an additional Marine brigade.[65] Saipan was the first objective followed by Tinian and Guam. D-Day for Saipan was 15 June.[66]

Saipan is located 1,000 miles from Eniwetok and 1,200 miles from Tokyo. The Japanese regarded the Marianas as an indispensable part of their Empire's inner defense ring and bolstered the Saipan garrison to about 32,000 men. Moreover, the Japanese Navy was willing to risk a major fleet engagement in order to save the Marianas and perhaps reverse the entire course of the war by waging a single Mahanian decisive battle at sea.

111

On 11 June, five days after the Normandy landings, American aircraft began to attack the Marianas destroying over 150 Japanese aircraft in the process. On 13 June the naval shore bombardment began, and on 15 June two Marine divisions began to assault the island. The Marines suffered a rude surprise. The Japanese forces on Saipan were about twice as large as American intelligence had predicted. Shore defenses, though incomplete, were very formidable, and the preliminary bombardment had been both inadequate and inaccurate. The Marines came ashore in lightly armored amphtracs which were supposed to dash rapidly inland, but the Japanese halted them virtually at the water's edge. Consequently, the Marines had to fight their way ashore which they did with heavy losses. Nevertheless, by nightfall over 20,000 men were ashore holding a bridgehead 1,000 yards deep.

Saipan, unlike the atolls in the Gilberts and Marshalls, was a fairly large island with a variety of terrain features – coral reefs, jungle, mountains and steep ravines – all of which favored the defense. An Army and two Marine divisions therefore had to undertake a series of bloody engagements to root the Japanese out of a maze of bunkers and caves. Each move forward was paid for in blood.

News of the American invasion of Saipan led to a sortie by the Japanese Combined Fleet from Philippine waters. This fleet included six large and three smaller carriers with 222 fighters and 200 dive and torpedo bombers. The US 5th Fleet with fifteen carriers deployed almost 500 fighters and 400 dive and torpedo bombers. The Japanese aircraft had longer range and lighter armor than their American equivalent, but their fighter planes lacked self-sealing fuel tanks. Japanese pilots were not as well trained as US Naval and Marine pilots. The Japanese intended to strike at long range and obtain support from aircraft on Guam and Tinian. They also intended to rearm and refuel carrier aircraft on air bases in the Marianas thereby increasing range and sortie rates. The Americans had no nearby airfields and had the dual tasks of supporting the land battle on Saipan and combating the enemy fleet.

The apparent Japanese advantages were largely negated, however, by the fact that prior to the Saipan landings the 5th Fleet had virtually destroyed Japanese airpower in the Marianas and rendered the air bases unusable. Japanese carrier pilots, hastily trained after the losses sustained in the air battles in the northern Solomons, would, therefore, have to face American airmen with two years' training including three hundred hours of pre-combat flying.

The outcome of the air battles of 19 June was disastrous for the Japanese. At the start of the Battle of the Philippine Sea the Japanese launched a series of massive air attacks against the 5th Fleet. Of the 373 planes involved in the attacks, fewer than 100 returned to the carriers; the Americans lost twenty-nine planes. Furthermore, US submarines sank two Japanese fleet carriers. The next day the Americans located the Japanese fleet and ordered attacks at the extreme range of carrier aircraft. At dusk the Americans sank a carrier and damaged three others. About eighty planes ran out of fuel and had to ditch on the return journey, but most of the pilots and crewmen were rescued.

There was a good deal of regret at the time and later that the remaining Japanese carriers escaped, but these were in fact less critical than the pilots and aircrewmen. The Japanese naval air arm had been largely destroyed in the Solomons and was reconstituted in time to fight in the Marianas where it was again crushed even more quickly than in the previous year. In fact, Japanese carrier air power was never again to play a major offensive role in the war. The Japanese had lost the battles of production and training and attrition. Poorly trained pilots flying inferior aircraft could not, despite all their personal courage, turn the tide of battle. Moreover, the defeat of the Combined Fleet doomed the garrisons in the Marianas.

On Saipan bitter fighting continued throughout the month of June and into July. By 9 July the Americans had crushed the last resistance at a cost of 14,000 men killed and wounded. The Japanese lost about 30,000 killed plus a number of civilians who chose suicide in preference to capture. On 21 July Marine and Army forces landed on Guam, and three days later Marines invaded Tinian. Fighting was intense but not as prolonged as the battle for Saipan. The Americans secured Tinian by 1 August and Guam nine days later.

Central Pacific forces had made an advance of a thousand miles in a single bound and crippled the Japanese fleet in the process. The victory in the Battle of the Philippine Sea was in turn of significant assistance to the Southwest Pacific theater where General MacArthur decided to continue his advance even before mopping up operations on Biak were completed.

MacArthur's next target was Noemfoor Island sixty miles west of

Biak. Heavy aerial bombardments began on 20 June, and American forces went ashore on 1 July against minimal opposition. By the end of the month airfields on the island were in full operation, and American forces had landed at Sansapor on the Vogelkop peninsula thus completing the campaign on New Guinea.

By the summer of 1944 the Allies were advancing in both Europe and the Pacific. Individual plans had not been completely successful, and military operations had frequently been more expensive and difficult than predicted. Anzio had forced the Allies to delay Anvil. Overlord met unexpected resistance, and by July the 21st Army Group had not yet broken through German defenses and reached open country. Fighting on Biak and Saipan was brutal and costly.

On the other hand the Allies had gained a firm foothold in France, and if the subsequent advance was much slower than originally expected, the lodgement was secure, and the Germans had no hope of driving the Allies into the sea. In the Pacific the American advance was actually moving ahead of schedule, and Japanese naval air power was a spent force. Japanese defenders of island bastions fought without hope of reinforcement or rescue. They could and did sell their lives dearly but were unable to alter the war's strategic direction.

The Allies still had to contemplate the means and methods needed to achieve final victory. Anglo-American differences over the course of future operations in France and Italy were destined to produce additional debates. Inter-service and intra-theater debates concerning strategy in the Pacific also led to serious disputes. If the Allies retained the strategic initiative in Europe and the Pacific, they had yet to agree on the shape and objectives for subsequent campaigns.

NOTES

1. CCS 170/1 January 23, 1943, Report to the President and Prime Minister.
2. CCS 169/30 5 March 1943 and CCS 169-8-D April 23, 1943 in Military Archives Division RG331 SHAEF Minutes of SHAEF Conferences and Briefings, Box 122.
3. JCS 291/1, May 8, 1943 Invasion of the European Continent from the United Kingdom in 1943–1944.
4. Ibid.
5. Ibid.
6. Ibid.
7. CCS 235, 18 May 1943 Defeat of Axis Powers in Europe.
8. CCS 237 19 May 1943 Draft Resolutions by the Combined Chiefs of Staff.
9. Ibid.

10. CCS 242/3 24 May 1943 Final Report to the President and Prime Minister.
11. Military Archives Record Group 331 SHAEF 381, Box 76 C.O.S. (43) 416 (O).
12. Ibid.
13. Ibid.
14. Ibid. See also JCS 442 5 August 1943 Operation 'Overlord'.
15. Ibid.
16. Ibid.
17. Ibid.
18. Ibid.
19. Ibid.
20. Ibid.
21. Military Archives Record Group 331 SHAEF 381/9 Overlord, Box 79, COSSAC (43) 28.
22. Ibid.
23. Ibid.
24. CCS 304 15 August 1943 Operation 'Overlord' – Outline Plan.
25. CCS 303/3 17 August 1943 Strategic Concept for the Defeat of the Axis in Europe.
26. CCS 319/5 24 August 1943 Final Report to the President and Prime Minister.
27. 12 February 1944 CCS 304/12 Directive to Supreme Commander Allied Expeditionary Force.
28. CCS 428 (Revised) 15 December 1943 Relation of Available Resources to Agreed Operations.
29. Ibid.
30. Military Archives Record Group 331, HQ 12th AG Box 86.
31. Ibid.
32. Ibid.
33. Military Archives Record Group 165 ABC1 File Box 415.
34. CCS 166/11 13 February 1944 Revised Directive for Combined Bomber Offensive.
35. Military Archives Record Group 331 SHAEF 381 Box 76.
36. Ibid. and Record Group 331 SHAEF G-3 Box 17, Entry 23.
37. Ibid.
38. Military Archives Record Group 331, 12th Army Group AG 370.2, 'Neptune' Initial Joint Plan, 21st Army Group.
39. Ibid.
40. Ibid.
41. Ibid. and C.O.S. (43) 779(0) Revised Plan 'Bodyguard' 25 December 1943.
42. Military Archives Record Group 331, Box 119 SHAEF Operations A, Section 17100/1 – 17105, 31 March 1944.
43. Task Force 122, 18 March 1944, Serial 00164 Op Plan 1–44.
44. Headquarters First United States Army, 20 May 1944 381(C) Operation 'Neptune'.
45. Military Archives Record Group 331 SHAEF 381, Box 76.
46. CCS 428 (Revised) op. cit. and CCS 304/12, 12 January 1944.
47. CCS 486 Provision of Naval Forces for 'Overlord' 10 February 1944 and Cdr TF 122 Serial 0093, 25 May 1944.
48. J.I.C. (44) 198 (0) Final, 13 May 1944 and Military Archives Record Group 331, HQ 12th Army Group, Box 86.
49. Military Archives Record Group 331 SHAEF Operations A, Section 17100/1 – 17105, Box 119 and TG331 HQ 12th Army Group, Box 86.
50. Military Archives Record Group 331, HQ 12th Army Group, Box 86 and Box 123.
51. Ibid.
52. Military Archives Record Group 331 Hq 12th Army Group, Box 85 and Record Group 331 SHAEF 17100/1-17105, 21 Army Group 100/741/391/G (Plans) Box 119.

53. R.G. 331, Box 85, op. cit.
54. Military Archives Record Group 331, SHAEF G-3 Division, Decimal File Box 74.
55. Ibid. and SHAEF/18008/ Ops Ref. No. 551470.
56. RG 331 SHAEF, Box 74, op. cit.
57. Ibid.
58. Ibid.
59. Ibid.
60. Military Archives Record Group 331 SHAEF, Overlord 381/2, Box 78.
61. The literature on D-Day is vast. A useful brief study is William M. Hammond, *Normandy*, Washington, DC, G.P.O., n.d., published under the auspices of the U.S. Army's Center of Military History. Hammond supplies a brief account of the landings and subsequent operations. See also Military Archives Record Group 331, 21 Army Group 00/477/OPS(B) for a daily account of the landings and subsequent operations.
62. For an excellent account of the Pacific war see Ronald H. Spector, *Eagle against the Sun*, New York, The Free Press, 1985, *passim.*
63. JCS 712/6 VLR Bombers in the War against Japan, 6 April 1944.
64. Ibid.
65. Serial 00275 Op Plan 3-44, 23 April 1944.
66. Ibid.

6

Strategies in the Balance

Having seized the strategic initiative in both Europe and the Pacific, the Allies continued to move forward in the second half of 1944. In both areas differing views on the course of operations and logistical problems led to acrimonious debates within the Allied ranks.

In France by late July, though well short of planned objectives, the Allies had deployed eighteen American, thirteen British and three Canadian divisions in Normandy. The 21st Army Group had activated an additional field army – the 1st Canadian – and the Americans would soon activate a new army of their own – the 3rd. Fifteen air bases were operational in France with seven more under construction and, despite the failure to capture a major port, supplies entering Normandy over the beaches were adequate to sustain operations.

Fighting continued to be difficult; advances were small and costly. British and Canadian attacks made little progress but had attracted most available German armor to the eastern part of the front, and the deception plan continued to convince the Germans to retain substantial forces in the Pas de Calais. The American sector on the bridgehead's western flank therefore presented the best opportunity to break the stalemate.

On 25 July the Americans launched a major attack using saturation bombing to carve an opening in the German defenses in the area around St Lô. Some 1,500 heavy and 400 medium bombers plus 550 fighter-bombers struck an area 7,000 yards wide and 3,000 deep just south of St Lô. A portion of the 4,700 tons of bombs struck American positions causing considerable casualties, but most bombs hit the Germans with devastating effects. Three divisions sustained by fourteen artillery battalions then moved forward and despite stubborn resistance by survivors advanced nearly two miles by the end of the day.

In the days following, the German divisions facing the Americans began to disintegrate as the latter pushed additional divisions through the gap. By late July two full corps began to drive on Avranches, a town located at the junction of the Cotentin and Brittany peninsulas. On 30 July US forces entered Avranches and the next day armored units moved beyond the town and were prepared to advance further south. The Germans had meanwhile held off a Canadian assault on 25 July and halted a British attack a few days later. Thus at the start of August the German right wing continued to offer stout resistance while the left collapsed.

The German situation presented the Americans with an opportunity not foreseen in the original Neptune plan. On 29 July General Bradley emphasized that the capture of Brittany ports remained the highest priority for US forces. The 3rd Army, which was to become operational on 1 August, would therefore move into Brittany and capture Brest, St Malo, Quiberon Bay and other ports in the region.[1] On 6 August, noting that German resistance was weakening, General Bradley ordered the 1st Army to advance to the east in order to widen the corridor between St Lô and Avranches. The 3rd Army was now to divide its forces sending only one corps into Brittany, placing several divisions to protect the American flank along the Loire and moving additional forces eastward to Alençon and Le Mans where they were to prepare for further advances towards the Paris–Orléans Gap.[2]

At this juncture the Germans made a decision that played into the Allies' hands. With the left flank collapsing the logical move would have been to withdraw to a new more secure line – perhaps the Seine. Instead, Hitler ordered a major counter-attack at Mortain with the objective of striking west to the sea and isolating and destroying the American forces which had advanced south of Avranches. By 6 August elements of six panzer divisions were ready to strike, but on the same day the Americans, having learned of German intentions from Ultra decrypts, warned army commanders of the forthcoming attack.[3]

The attack began on 7 August. In three days of desperate fighting the Americans halted the German thrust, and the 12th Army Group ordered an immediate counterblow even while fighting raged around Mortain. On 8 August General Bradley halted the 3rd Army advance to the east and instructed it to strike north at Argentan.[4] Forces from the 21st Army Groups were to thrust south towards the town of Falaise in order to surround and destroy the entire German force.[5]

The results of the Allied offensive were mixed. The Americans rapidly reached their objective taking Argentan on 13 August. They halted to await the southward advance of the Canadian Army but, despite the fact that much of their armor had been shifted to the American sector, the Germans resisted the Canadian and British attacks quite effectively. The Canadians took Falaise on 16 August, but there still remained a fifteen-mile gap between the 21st and 12th Army Group. Through this narrowing gap, known as the corridor of death, the Germans sought to retreat under violent attack from both ground and air. The British and Canadians pressed south and the Americans, while continuing to hold Argentan, sent forces to the east, entering Chartres on 15 August and throwing forces across the Seine four days later.[6]

As the Americans were crossing the Seine, the Canadians linked up with US forces at Argentan to close the Falaise gap. The German defeat was spectacular. Of the nearly 80,000 Germans in the Falaise pocket, about 10,000 died and 50,000 became prisoners. The Allies destroyed over 500 tanks and self-propelled guns, 700 artillery pieces and 7,000 other vehicles. The 5th Panzer Army and the 7th Army ceased to exist as effective fighting formations. Although more than 30,000 German troops escaped the trap, they did so as scattered remnants incapable for the moment of sustaining organized resistance.

The Germans had suffered a near catastrophic defeat. The Seine, the next logical line of resistance, had been breached. If the Allies had been behind schedule in July, by mid-August they were several weeks ahead of pre-invasion projections with little to stop them from executing additional dramatic advances. Finally, as German armies struggled to extricate themselves from the Falaise pocket another threat appeared in the south – a major invasion of the French Riviera.

Launching Anvil, however, produced another heated series of arguments between American and British strategists. The British had agreed to Anvil on several occasions in 1943. In late August 1943 the Combined Chiefs informed General Eisenhower that there would be an invasion of southern France to create a diversion for Overlord.[7] On 5 December the Combined Chiefs agreed that Anvil would approximately coincide with Overlord and would consist of two assault divisions drawn from the Mediterranean area.[8] On 28 December Eisenhower's staff drew up a preliminary plan and submitted it to the Combined Chiefs on 7 January 1944. The plan called for a two-division assault and a subsequent build-up to ten divisions.[9] Exploitation northward required the capture of Toulon and Marseille, and the combination of the range of land-based air cover, proximity of ports, beach conditions and shore defenses dictated a landing east of Toulon on the Riviera coast.[10] Terrain north of the Riviera offered limited opportunities for armored operations. Consequently the Anvil force when fully deployed would consist of eight infantry and two armored divisions drawn from the Italian front.[11]

The preliminary plans hinged on the erroneous assumption that the Allies would be able to execute a rapid advance in Italy up to the Pisa–Rimini line, thereby freeing troops and landing craft for Anvil. The difficult fighting at the Gothic Line coupled with the near disastrous situation at Anzio had forced the Allies to delay Anvil until after Neptune, and the subsequent fall of Rome in turn led the British to question the value of Anvil.

The British claimed that the breaking of the Italian stalemate presented a great strategic opportunity for a continued advance into northern Italy and from there into Yugoslavia. The British Chiefs of Staff therefore called for the cancellation of Anvil and a continuation and intensification of the Italian campaign. They contended that advances in Italy would be of greater assistance to Neptune than Anvil since Italian operations would pin down German divisions in the Italian Peninsula and prevent their transfer to France.[12]

Commanders in the Mediterranean, including General Clark and General Juin, commander of French forces in Italy, agreed with the British position. The American Joint Chiefs of Staff, however, vehemently opposed the alteration of the original strategy. The JCS insisted upon the need for Anvil even if the operation was launched after D-Day. In a memorandum of 24 June the JCS maintained that the defeat of Germany required the Allies to concentrate maximum forces against the Germans in France. Such concentration in turn required the seizure of another major port. The best use of forces in the Mediterranean was therefore an invasion of southern France as soon as possible. Anvil would provide support for Overlord, place at least two major ports in Allied hands and permit French forces to engage in the liberation of their homeland.[13] Anvil would in short allow for the concentration of forces and their employment in the decisive theater of war.[14]

Three days later the JCS stated bluntly that the British proposal to scrap Anvil in favor of Italian operations was completely unacceptable.[15] The JCS noted that there was complete disagreement between the American and British strategic proposals. The JCS totally rejected additional major operations in Italy and again insisted that Anvil was the best way to deploy and sustain the largest possible American force in France.[16]

The impasse in turn led the President and Prime Minister to take a direct role in the strategic debate with an exchange of memos written by their respective Chiefs of Staff. Churchill argued for a continued push through northern Italy, through the Ljubljana Gap and into the plains of Hungary. Landings in the south of France would, he asserted, produce no decisive results since the Rhône valley provided limited scope for maneuver, and the Germans could offer formidable resistance. Thus troops landed in southern France could offer little if any assistance to forces in Normandy since it was about 600 miles from Marseille to the Normandy front. The Allies would do better to exploit the favorable situation in Italy while reinforcing the Normandy bridgehead by seizing Bordeaux and sending other forces to France via the Gulf of Lions.[17]

The President replied on 29 June that Anvil was vital to Overlord and that the operation had been agreed upon with Stalin at Teheran. France was the decisive theater and required maximum support. Moreover, even if troops for Anvil were taken from Italy, there would remain forces adequate to mount a vigorous campaign.[18] An advance to Istria and beyond would be very difficult because of the terrain and even if successful logistical constraints would prevent putting more than six divisions into Yugoslavia and Hungary. Even if feasible, such an operation would render little if any help to Overlord. Despite its limitations the Rhône corridor was a better operating area than the Alps.[19] Roosevelt then stated that he would not agree to the use of American forces against Istria, and that even after withdrawing forces for Anvil, the Allies would have twenty-one divisions and about 5,500 aircraft in Italy. Thus, the Allies could still maintain a vigorous campaign in Italy, but Anvil remained transcendently important. If the British government continued to reject Anvil, the only choice would be to hold further discussions with Stalin and the French as soon as possible.[20]

American insistence finally forced Churchill to agree to Anvil which at his insistence was renamed Dragoon. On 2 July the Combined Chiefs of Staff informed the Commander of the Mediterranean theater to launch Anvil–Dragoon at the earliest possible date with every effort made to land by 15 August.[21] The initial assault would consist of an airborne contingent, commandos and three divisions. Reinforcements would increase the Anvil force to ten divisions.[22]

The assault was scheduled for 15 August. An airborne force of more than eleven battalions was to drop inland prior to the main landings in order to block or delay the arrival of enemy reinforcements. Four commando groups were to silence coastal artillery batteries on two small islands overlooking the left flank of the landing area along the Riviera. Other commando units on the Allied right were to block the roads from Cannes to the invasion beaches. Three American divisions of the US 7th Army would then land simultaneously followed closely by a French armored regiment.[23] Additional forces would come ashore over the original invasion beaches.[24]

Shipping for each division in the initial landings included six transports, twenty-two LSTs, thirty-eight LCTs and thirty-eight LCIs.[25] Naval fire support forces included four battleships, seventy-nine destroyers and nine escort carriers.[26] Some 900 heavy bombers and 1100 medium bombers were to attack German defenses and cut vital communications to the invasion area. The air campaign also tried to deceive the Germans as to the precise time and location of the invasion. Allied aircraft therefore attacked targets from Genoa to Marseille. Only during the hours just before the assault would the Allies attack massively the beach defenses in the landing zones.[27]

Operation Anvil–Dragoon bore a number of similarities to the Neptune plan. The operation was to unfold in phases. The first phase called for securing a beachhead and capturing an airfield. After the arrival of reinforcements, French forces would capture Toulon by D+25. The French would next move against Marseille while other forces moved up the Rhône valley on Lyon and Vichy.[28] Until the capture of major ports Franco-American forces would be supplied over open beaches.[29]

The build-up phase was not expected to last as long as the Neptune build-up because planners expected to face substantially less German resistance. Allied intelligence expected to encounter seven

German divisions, only one of which was armored and about 300 combat aircraft.[30] In fact, because of the strain of operations in northern France, German forces in the southern coastal area amounted to seven understrength divisions and an armored unit. Coastal defenses were reasonably strong, but operational reserves were virtually non-existent. German air strength was negligible. Consequently, the invasion forces sailing from Italy, Corsica and North Africa would face stiff initial resistance, but the Germans simply lacked the forces to contain the Allies as they had done in Normandy.

The pre-invasion airborne and commando assaults launched on the night of 14–15 August were, on the whole, quite successful. A small French team was wiped out west of Cannes, and a parachute artillery battalion landed in the wrong place, but other preliminary operations were successful. At 8:00 a.m. on 15 August the amphibious landings overcame German opposition with light losses – fewer than 200 killed. By the evening of D-Day all three assault divisions were ashore. Over 2,000 Germans had surrendered, and there were no significant counter-attacks. By the evening of 17 August the Allies had landed over 86,000 men, 12,000 vehicles and 46,000 tons of supplies.

The unexpected success of the assault offered field commanders two alternative lines of action. They could continue the operations as planned with emphasis on the capture of Marseille and Toulon, or they could seek to exploit the success and attempt to trap the enemy in the Rhône Valley. The American corps commander decided on the bolder course: he ordered a two pronged attack. One force on the left would move west to the Rhône and then advance north along the river. A second force would move northwest and then swing west and shut the trap further north along the river.

Leaving the French to capture Marseille and Toulon while airborne units secured the Allied right, the US 7th Army began to advance on Grenoble.[31] At virtually the same moment, the Germans left forces to hold the major ports and began a full-scale retreat northwards. By 20 August the Americans in an attempt to cut them off were about to enter the Rhône valley.[32] By 25 August the Americans had entered Grenoble and were within artillery range of the river.[33]

Desperate to keep their escape route open the Germans launched persistent counter-attacks against the American spearheads. The

Americans at this time were suffering severe supply shortages, especially of artillery ammunition. German garrisons still held Marseille and Toulon, and the 7th Army had to continue to obtain supplies over open beaches. The long distance from the beaches to the rapidly moving advance elements reduced and delayed the arrival of reinforcements and vital supplies. The Americans were, therefore, unable to close the trap. The Germans lost 15,000 men in prisoners alone plus some 4,000 vehicles, tanks and guns, but by 28 August they had managed to withdraw the bulk of their forces beyond the 7th Army's grasp.

The Americans nonetheless continued to pursue. French forces meanwhile took Marseille and Toulon by 28 August while other French divisions occupied Lyon on 3 September. The Americans moved on Belfort while the French took Dijon on 10 September. The following day French advanced units made contact with the US 3rd Army, and on 14 September firm contact was established between the 7th and 3rd Armies.

Logistical problems had slowed the advance of the 7th Army which had nevertheless advanced far more rapidly than originally anticipated. To the north logistical constraints were also beginning to hamper the Allied advance which had been moving far more rapidly than projected in the original Neptune plan. Thus, by the first weeks of September logistical problems were becoming progressively more serious for Allied forces throughout France.

The victory at Falaise in early August had produced the conditions for rapid advances by the 21st and 12th Army Groups. Abandoning plans to halt at the Seine in order to regroup and organize a communications and supply system, Allied Commanders decided to seize the opportunity provided by the German collapse in Normandy to pursue the defeated foe without pause and perhaps bring the war to a successful conclusion by the autumn of 1944. American and French forces liberated Paris on 25 August and virtually without delay continued to move east. The 21st Army Group moved to clear the Havre peninsula and pressed on to the line of the Somme while the 12th Army Group crossed the Seine on the flank of the British and Canadian forces.[34] Following General Eisenhower's pre-invasion decision to place the main emphasis of the Allied offensive north of the Ardennes, the 21st Army Group was to move to envelop the Ruhr from the north while the 12th Army Group would support the attack by protecting the right flank of Montgomery's forces. After assuring the success of the main thrust, Bradley's forces would then advance on Cologne.[35]

The Allied advance initially made spectacular gains as a result of the German catastrophe at Falaise. On 30 August the US 3rd Army crossed the river Meuse, and the next day the British 2nd Army entered Amiens. Brussels fell to the British on 3 September. On 4 September British troops captured Antwerp, Europe's largest port. The Allies had captured Antwerp undamaged, but the Germans continued to hold the mouth of the river Scheldt thus rendering the port useless to the Allied armies.

Denying the use of Antwerp to the Allies was part of a broader German effort to gain time to reinforce and regroup their forces by creating logistical problems for the Allied armies. The German High Command ordered garrisons to remain in French ports and to destroy the harbors if attacked and forced to capitulate. Consequently, the Allies did not take Dieppe until 3 September, Le Havre on 11 September, Brest on 18 September, Boulogne on 22 September, and Calais on 30 September. Garrisons at Lorient, St Nazaire, Dunkirk and La Rochelle held out until the end of the war. The Allies also had to devote large resources to counter potential attacks on channel supply lines by E-boats and submarines. Coupled with holding the mouth of the Scheldt, the Germans managed to place severe constraints on Allied logistics.

The core of the Allied logistical problem was not getting supplies to the Continent. Adequate tonnage reached France via Cherbourg, minor Normandy ports, and the original invasion beaches. In August, for example, the Americans discharged over 260,000 long tons of material at Cherbourg and more than 536,000 tons via Utah and Omaha beaches. The real problem was in delivering supplies to the rapidly advancing armies. Before D-Day, planners expected to support twelve divisions across the Seine by D+120, but by D+90 there were already sixteen divisions up to 150 miles beyond the Seine.[36] Motor transport was in short supply. Vehicles and tanks with the field armies were wearing out, and no forward supply or maintenance facilities existed beyond Normandy. Moreover, French bridges and railway lines so heavily bombed in the spring were not easily repaired. Desperate expedients, including the Red Ball Express and air delivery of supplies, could not provide permanent solutions to the growing supply problem.

The solution was of course the capture of undamaged working ports closer to the Allied lines of advance, but German defensive measures precluded the rapid capture and utilization of Channel ports north of Normandy. Toulon and Marseille were severely damaged and in September 1944 could only with difficulty support the forces in southern France and the Rhône valley. The use of Antwerp would have solved the Allied supply problems, but the failure to clear the approaches precluded its use for the immediate future.

The Allied high command in early September faced a serious dilemma. Planners believed that the German army was shattered and that the Allies should breach the Rhine as quickly as possible. Supply problems, however, reduced the number of divisions that could pursue the beaten foe.[37] General Montgomery suggested that General Eisenhower give the 21st Army Group supplies sufficient to break into Germany and lunge across the Rhine, while halting in place all or most of the 12th Army Group. Alternatively, General Eisenhower had the option of adhering to the original approach of emphasizing operations north of the Ardennes while still maintaining attacks further south.

Eisenhower believed that a single thrust approach was unwise both politically and strategically. The American public would not, he believed, accept the halting of American advances while allowing the British to win what most assumed would be the last campaign of the war. Strategically, the 21st Army Group, which was still drawing most of its supplies over the D-Day beaches, was unlikely to reach the Rhine in strength even if it received virtually all available logistics support. If the 21st did reach the Rhine, it would have to mount an assault crossing of the river. Since the Germans would probably demolish existing bridges, the British would have to build new ones thereby imposing further strains on an already overburdened logistical system. Bad weather in autumn would reduce tactical air support and airlift sorties, and halting the American forces, which would, nevertheless, still require some logistical support, would permit the Germans to concentrate against any single thrust further north. Thus, if the shock of a single advance over the Rhine did not produce an immediate German collapse, the 21st Army Group would find itself in a difficult situation – short of supplies and facing German resistance unencumbered by serious threats from the American forces to the south.

On 9 September Eisenhower informed the Combined Chiefs of Staff that he would adhere to the original strategic concept. Operating northwest of the Ardennes, the Allied forces would advance to seize the Ruhr while armies south of the Ardennes advanced on Frankfurt. Priority of support would still go to forces in the north.[38] Eisenhower also emphasized the need to open Antwerp's approaches and the simultaneous intent to employ airborne forces to gain control of Rhine crossings at Arnhem. The logistical situation was, he noted, strained to the breaking point, but he would take risks to get into the heart of Germany.[39] On 13 September Eisenhower informed Montgomery that he would give the 21st Army Group an additional 1,000 tons of supplies per day which would enable the British and Canadian forces both to cross the Rhine with Operation Market-Garden and capture the approaches to Antwerp.[40]

Operation Market-Garden, designed to gain a foothold across the Rhine, fell into two phases. Market involved dropping three airborne divisions, two American and one British, along an axis stretching from Eindhoven to Nijmegen and then to Arnhem. Garden called for a ground attack by a British corps which would link up with the airborne forces which would have seized bridges across the Maas, Waal and Lek rivers which constituted the mouth of the Rhine. The 21st Army Group would then exploit the capture of the Rhine bridges to turn east, outflank the Westwall defenses and advance on the Ruhr.[41]

There were a number of problems inherent in the Market-Garden plan. Most seriously it required the British 2nd Army to advance more than 35 miles to the north before turning east to cross still another river – the Ijssel – in order to gain access to the area north of the Ruhr. Paratroopers had to seize several important bridges, while the ground forces had to advance along a single road since the terrain in southern Holland was unsuited for mechanized operations. Moreover, the British parachute division had to land outside Arnhem and fight its way into the town. Any organized resistance could pose severe problems for either aspect of the operations.

Allied planners presumed that the Germans were still in a state of collapse and near disintegration. On 12 September the 21st Army Group Intelligence Summary noted that two SS Panzer divisions were unlocated but were probably in Holland. The Summary asserted that the divisions were probably very weak.[42] Field orders for Market were equally optimistic noting the presence of elements of eleven divisions including three armored units but claiming that the units were not located in the target zones. The report asserted that there were no organized troop concentrations in the Arnhem–Nijmegen area but noted the presence of strong flak concentrations.[43] The report failed to note that many German anti-aircraft guns were dual purpose weapons, and did not include the two missing SS armored divisions in the enemy order of battle. Allied intelligence underestimated German defensive capabilities and the ability of the German army to recover from a severe defeat. The Allies also failed to locate a major armored force.

Finally, Operation Market-Garden in effect reduced the importance of opening the Scheldt and gaining the use of Antwerp. Essentially, the Allies were still seeking to end the war in 1944 and were willing to run a significant risk to achieve an early victory. Making Arnhem more important than Antwerp meant that SHAEF was willing to postpone solving the logistical problems facing the Allied Armies in order to keep the momentum of the summer's advance going.

The gamble failed. Launched on 17 September, the 21st Army Group's advance was stopped short of Arnhem where the British airborne division was virtually destroyed by German counter-attacks. Remnants of the division withdrew across the Lek on the night of 25–26 September. The land drive had managed to link up with the American airborne units, but the advance along a single road facilitated the German efforts to contain the attack. Ironically, the two unlocated SS armored divisions played a major part in defeating the Market Garden forces.

In the midst of the Market-Garden battles the Allied High Command held a major meeting at Versailles. Over twenty general officers including American army group and field army commanders, representatives from the British and Canadian forces and air force and naval commanders were in attendance at the 22 September meeting. The gathering was supposed to clarify Allied strategy and establish priorities for future operations.

At the conference, General Eisenhower emphasized the urgency of opening Antwerp to shipping since even if Market-Garden were successful, the possession of a functioning deep-water port was an indispensable prerequisite for subsequent operations directed at the

Ruhr and Berlin.[44] Therefore, the most important immediate 21st Army Group mission was to clear the Scheldt. After opening access to Antwerp, Montgomery's forces supported by the US 1st Army, part of the 12th Army Group, would advance to and cross the Rhine and envelop the Ruhr from the north. Additionally, the 12th Army Group would extend its front northward to relieve a British corps while continuing to push into the Rhineland towards Cologne. Forces not directly involved in these operations, primarily the US 3rd Army, were to undertake no further aggressive actions until the requirements of the main effort had been met.[45] The 6th Army Group, containing the US 7th and French 1st Army, moving from the south of France was to advance on Strasbourg to contain German forces in Alsace.[46]

However, efforts to sustain the offensive failed. British and Canadian forces were unable to clear the mouth of the Scheldt until the last days of November, by which time the Germans had succeeded in establishing a coherent front. From Holland to Alsace the Allied advance met stiffening resistance. From late October to mid-December Allied advances were measured in yards rather than miles. Fighting on their own frontiers with shortened lines of communication and aided by increasingly bad weather which reduced the effectiveness of Allied air power, the Germans stabilized their front and achieved, at least for the moment, a stalemate in the West.

The Allies had tried to sustain the momentum of the summer offensive beyond the capabilities of the supply system. During the Second World War armies had great difficulty sustaining advances of more than 200 to 300 miles without halting or at least slowing the pace of operations to allow the logistics system to displace forward. By the fall of 1944, the Allied armies had moved about as far as they could within the constraints of the logistical system. The early capture of Antwerp and its approaches might have solved the logistics problem but the 21st Army Group commander, sustained by the Supreme Commander, chose to try crossing the Rhine rather than clearing the Scheldt. Market-Garden was a gamble which did not pay off. Consequently, there would be no victory in Europe in 1944, and the Allies would have to fight on into 1945. The necessity of mounting additional major operations in Europe in turn had a direct impact on strategic decisions in the Pacific.

Successful campaigns in the Marianas and New Guinea enabled strategic planners to contemplate increasing the pace of operations.

Planners in both the Pacific and Washington still did not have an overall strategic plan for the defeat of Japan or even for the next phase of operations. Consequently, strategy in the Pacific again became a matter of extended discord and debate.

On 12 March 1944 the JCS had directed General MacArthur to prepare plans for a return to Mindanao. On 15 June MacArthur issued Plan Reno V, an updated version of earlier plans. Reno 5 called for an invasion of Mindanao in October 1944 followed by an invasion of Leyte in mid-November.[47] On Mindanao and Leyte the Americans would establish air bases from which they could suppress Japanese air power in the rest of the Philippines and support future advances.[48] Reno V also presumed that an advance on Formosa would require the prior invasion and occupation of Luzon and the employment of the full resources of the Pacific Fleet in a campaign in the Philippines.[49]

Although there were serious doubts concerning the proposed date of the Leyte invasion, all parties agreed on the utility of the Mindanao and Leyte operations. There was, however, substantial disagreement over the next step. In late July, General MacArthur and Admiral Nimitz met President Roosevelt at Pearl Harbor. MacArthur made an impassioned plea for an invasion of the Philippines. Little was decided. Nimitz and MacArthur agreed upon the Leyte invasion while MacArthur continued to push for an invasion of Luzon after Leyte.

Planners in Washington rejected the General's strategic approach and on 29 July informed the Joint Chiefs that the Reno V plan, if adopted, would unduly delay operations against Formosa. After Leyte, the planners favored an advance directly on Formosa.[50] Pacific forces would occupy Formosa in February 1945, the Bonins in April and the Ryukyus in May. American forces would then invade Kyushu in October and the Tokyo plain at the end of the year. Formosa was, according to the planners, the essential stepping stone for the ultimate invasion of Japan.[51]

On 4 August the JCS Staff Planners noted that the occupation of Formosa should precede any major operation against Luzon. Leyte and Mindanao should be taken in order to establish air power to reduce Japanese air strength in the northern Philippines which might otherwise hinder the advance on Formosa.[52] The invasion of Leyte and Mindanao should occur on 1 December. Formosa should be invaded on 15 February 1945.[53] From Formosa the Americans would institute an air and sea blockade of the Japanese home islands and prepare for the final invasion.[54]

In late August General MacArthur proposed landings on Mindanao on 15 November and an assault on Leyte on 20 December. The Central Pacific would co-ordinate its actions with the Southwest Pacific by invading the Palau Islands on 15 September taking Peleliu, Anguar, Yap and Ulithi.[55] The Palaus were, the Pacific command believed, important strong points in the outer defenses of the Philippines: their capture was essential to provide a fleet base and land-based air cover for the Leyte operation.[56]

On 2 September the JCS issued instructions for forthcoming operations. General MacArthur and Admiral Nimitz were to conduct necessary preliminary operations. MacArthur's forces were to seize Morotai Island, north of New Guinea, while Nimitz's command was to invade the Palaus. On 20 December the Southwest and Central Pacific Commands were to invade Leyte.[57] The Joint Chiefs avoided the question of Luzon or Formosa by stating that they would choose the next objective after the seizure of Leyte. Commanders in the Pacific were to draw up plans for an invasion of Luzon on 20 February 1945 and an invasion of Formosa on 1 March, and the JCS would decide which operation to approve according to conditions prevailing after the occupation of Leyte.[58]

Events in the Pacific then intervened to accelerate the American timetable. On 7 and 8 September the 3rd Fleet launched a series of air raids against the Palaus and for the next two days bombed Mindanao. On 12 and 14 September the fleet attacked the Central Philippines. Admiral Halsey, the 3rd Fleet Commander, informed Admiral Nimitz that his forces had virtually destroyed Japanese air power and oil stocks in the Philippines and that American forces could accelerate the pace of operations, eliminate intermediate objectives, and strike directly at Leyte. Admiral Nimitz agreed and offered to transfer to MacArthur an army corps scheduled to invade Yap. The JCS then at the Quebec Conference for an Anglo-American meeting received Nimitz's proposal and passed it to MacArthur whose Chief of Staff accepted it in his commander's name. On 15 September the JCS ordered MacArthur to cancel the southern Mindanao invasion and to move directly from Morotai to Leyte on 20 October. The JCS also ordered Nimitz to cancel the Palaus invasions and move directly on Leyte. Nimitz, however, insisted on attacking Peleliu for use as a forward base for the Leyte invasion. The Morotai and Peleliu operations were scheduled for 15 September, and the Leyte invasion was advanced by two months.[59]

Both landings were expected to be easy; that on Morotai was unopposed. However, the attack on Peleliu encountered fierce resistance. The Japanese garrison numbered over 11,000 men who had created strong defensive positions in a series of caves on the north end of the island. The Americans had inadequate information abut the terrain or defensive installations, and preliminary bombardments did little damage to fighting positions which were dug into a series of coral ridges. Consequently, Army and Marine troops had to fight a series of bitter costly engagements until 30 September when the island was officially declared secure although fighting went on for an additional two months in order to destroy isolated pockets of resistance.

Taking Peleliu cost US forces nearly 2,000 killed and more than 6,000 wounded. Virtually all the Japanese defenders died. Ironically, the island was at best of marginal utility as an air and naval base for the forthcoming invasion of Leyte. Ulithi, on the other hand, rapidly became a major fleet operating base and it had been taken without opposition.

Japanese resistance had been unable to delay the American timetable for the Leyte invasion, but the course of the war in Europe had a major impact on the issue of whether to invade Formosa or Luzon. On 4 September, in a memorandum to his colleagues on the JCS, Admiral King called for an immediate decision on the Luzon–Formosa issue. King favored Formosa since its seizure would cut the Japanese Empire in half, deprive Japan of the resources of the East Indies and Malaya, give the United States access to the China coast and enable America to provide assistance to China and support a long-range bomber force on the Chinese mainland.[60]

The long-range planning group agreed and on 7 September informed the JCS that it was not necessary to invade Luzon as a preliminary operation for the attack on Formosa. Rather, US forces should move directly to Formosa. Once established in Formosa, American forces could limit Japanese support of Luzon, but the reverse was not true.[61] In fact, by invading Luzon before Formosa the duration of the war might be extended by six months.[62] The planners therefore recommended an invasion of Formosa on 1 March 1945.[63]

An invasion of Formosa – Operation Causeway – required six divisions supported by eight battleships, eleven fleet and thirty-two escort carriers, 171 destroyers and 200 LSTs.[64] Assault forces were available in the Pacific, but there was a serious shortage of service troops. The probable collapse of Germany or at least a substantial reduction of German capabilities in the autumn, however, would free service units in Europe for redeployment to the Pacific. Moreover, service units based in the United States and scheduled to go to Europe could be redirected to the Pacific.[65]

Later in the month, however, planners came to realize that the Causeway operation was not feasible primarily because of the military situation in Europe. The failure of Operation Market-Garden and the ensuing stalemate along the German border meant that the rapid redeployment of service troops to the Pacific could not take place in time to meet the target date for Causeway.[66] Planners noted that an invasion of Luzon was logistically feasible in late 1944 using forces currently available in the Pacific.[67] Although Formosa was preferable since it would provide better long-range bomber-base facilities than Luzon or the Marianas and allow B29s to carry larger bomb loads, logistical shortages resulting from the inability to transfer support units from Europe and the United States to the Pacific would unduly delay Causeway. Luzon was consequently the logical target after Leyte, and Formosa might even be bypassed if Japanese air and naval strength were weakened further and the shortage of service personnel remained acute.[68] If the United States decided to bypass Formosa, American forces should strike at the Bonins after the conquest of Luzon, followed by a drive into the Ryukyus.[69]

On 2 October 1944 Admiral King accepted the inevitable and abandoned his support of a Formosa invasion. He told his fellow members of the JCS that Pacific strategy should henceforth focus on the sequential post-Leyte invasions of Luzon, Iwo Jima and Okinawa. The Formosa operation would be relegated to an opportunistic move at an unspecified date.[70] On 3 October the JCS issued a new directive concerning future operations in the Pacific. After the occupation of Leyte, Southwest Pacific forces would invade Luzon on or about 20 December. Central Pacific forces would cover the landings and provide initial air support. Next, Nimitz's forces would invade Iwo Jima on 20 January and Okinawa on 1 March

1945.[71] The Formosa–China coast operation was finally abandoned, and the Joint Chiefs devised another version of the dual offensive involving a campaign in the Philippines and one into the island chains on the approaches to Japan.

Meanwhile, General MacArthur's staff was preparing plans for the forthcoming Philippine operations. Musketeer was a logical extension of the Reno V plan and included a series of operations, each with a separate code name, for the progressive reconquest of the Philippines. Musketeer II written in late August dealt with the capture of Luzon as the first step in retaking the entire archipelago.[72] The seizure of Leyte and part of neighboring Samar, an essential preliminary step, was known as Operation King-Two.[73]

On 21 September MacArthur's headquarters issued orders for Operation King-Two. The basic objective was to occupy Leyte and western Samar and establish naval, air and logistic facilities for the support of subsequent operations. Four divisions with an additional two in reserve would carry out the assault supported by six battleships and eighteen escort carriers. The 3rd Fleet would provide additional naval support.[74] The Musketeer plan assumed that the Japanese would have only one division on Leyte and that the invasion forces could accomplish their tasks on schedule.[75]

Events elsewhere in the Pacific were to force the Americans to revise their estimates and timetables. While preparing for King-Two, Admiral Halsey's 3rd Fleet launched a series of air raids to pave the way for the invasion. Between 10 and 14 October the 3rd Fleet struck Luzon, Okinawa and Formosa. The Japanese on Formosa struck back massively. The standard of Japanese pilot training which had been in decline since 1942 was at a low ebb by 1944 and the Japanese suffered huge losses. The Americans downed over 500 aircraft for a loss of less than a hundred. Japanese pilots sank no US ships and damaged only a few vessels. Inaccurate pilot reports, however, convinced Japan's High Command that they had scored a major victory and seriously hurt the American fleet. The Japanese therefore decided to wage a major ground campaign on Leyte and to commit the Combined Fleet to a major naval engagement. Thus, as the US invasion fleet of more than 400 vessels carrying 160,000 troops approached Leyte on 20 October 1944, they were unaware that instead of a virtually unopposed landing they were facing a major campaign on both land and sea.

After a massive shore bombardment, four divisions went ashore at

10:00 a.m. on 20 October. A few days before, rangers had occupied four small islands guarding the entrance to Leyte Gulf, and the main landing faced only sporadic resistance. During the next two days the Americans steadily expanded their beachhead seizing several Japanese dirt airstrips. The Americans continued to push inland against gradually stiffening resistance as the Japanese fed reinforcements into Leyte to bring the original 20,000-man garrison to 55,000 by November.

The Japanese fleet, meanwhile, prepared to launch its last major offensive of the war. The Combined Fleets' 'Victory' plan was typically very complex, but the essential aim was to use the remaining carriers, which were virtually depleted of aircraft, as decoys to lure the US 3rd Fleet north and away from Leyte Gulf. As the Americans moved north, two large surface ship task forces would thread their way through the narrow passages of the Philippines. One force would approach Leyte Gulf from the south, the other from the north. Both would converge and attack the transports, supply ships and escorts, thereby isolating the American forces ashore.

On the evening of 24 October the 7th Fleet, which usually escorted Southwest Pacific forces and consisted primarily of old battleships and escort carriers, met and defeated the southern arm of the Japanese pincer in a night engagement. Earlier in the day the 3rd Fleet had driven back the northern force and then headed north to engage the carriers. The commander of the Japanese northern force, however, turned about, made his way through the strait and shortly after midnight on 25 October entered the Philippine Sea and moved down the coast of Samar toward Leyte Gulf. The US 3rd Fleet had departed north while the 7th Fleet was still concentrated in the south. Nothing seemed to stand in the way of the Japanese approach to the Gulf except a few escort carriers and destroyers.

There ensued a running battle as the carriers and destroyers sought to delay the Japanese approach to the Gulf until reinforcements arrived. As the 3rd Fleet destroyed the Japanese carriers, the 7th Fleet continued its desperate efforts to stave off disaster losing two escort carriers, two destroyers, a destroyer escort and a patrol boat. Numerous other warships were damaged.

On the verge of success the Japanese fleet suddenly turned around and withdrew. Disconcerted by the 7th Fleet's attacks and fearing the arrival of American reinforcements, the Japanese Commander had broken off the action. Admiral Halsey's decision to take the 3rd Fleet, including the surface component, north had almost led to disaster, but the 7th Fleet and the invasion force survived. The Battle of Leyte Gulf involved over 250 ships and was the biggest naval engagement of the war. The Japanese lost four carriers, three battleships, six heavy and three light cruisers and eight destroyers. The Americans lost a light and three escort carriers plus a number of smaller warships. The Japanese fleet was finished and never again came out in force to engage the Americans.

Defeated at sea, the Japanese were nevertheless determined to continue the struggle on land. As reinforcements moved to Leyte the Americans found themselves facing growing problems. The reason for invading Leyte was to establish air bases to project power over Luzon, but this task was beyond American capabilities. The soil of the island was completely unsuitable for airfield construction, and the captured dirt strip was soon rendered inoperable by heavy rains. Having ruled the islands for more than forty years, the Americans should have been aware of the soil and climatic conditions. Engineers did manage to open a small field at the end of October but for the most part had to rely on carrier aircraft for support. The Japanese committed major air elements brought from Luzon, Formosa and the home islands to contest the skies over Leyte. The Japanese lost heavily but managed to prevent the Americans from cutting the flow of supplies and men to Leyte. The Americans gradually gained air supremacy over Leyte but were unable to seal off the island from the rest of the Philippines.

By November 1944 American forces were locked in positional warfare against a well entrenched Japanese force which even managed to mount several counter-attacks including an airborne assault. On 7 December an additional American division made an amphibious landing behind the main Japanese positions. The troops landed near the port that the Japanese used as a major supply base and entry point for reinforcements. Three days later the Americans took the port thereby splitting the defenders and cutting off the flow of reinforcements.

Fighting continued for several more months until the island was secure. Continuing problems with airfield construction on Leyte led to a decision to take Mindoro for airfield sites. Troops seized the island on 15 December. There was virtually no opposition on the ground. The invasion fleet, however, encountered heavy attacks by suicide planes – the kamikazes. First encountered at the end of the Leyte Gulf battle, the kamikazes began to appear in ever larger numbers. At Mindoro they inflicted severe damage on a cruiser and two LSTs and were destined to become a growing menace.[76]

The battles on and around Leyte had a significant impact on both belligerents. Japanese naval power had been fatally weakened. Ground and air elements committed on Leyte substantially reduced available combat power on Luzon thus limiting the possibility of offering an effective defense of the island. For the Americans, the Leyte campaign had been far more difficult than expected, and because of intelligence failures the Americans were unable to emplace substantial air power assets on the island. Finally, the extended duration of Japanese resistance on Leyte forced the Americans to postpone the Luzon invasion until January 1945. As in Europe, the war would continue well into the following year.

Throughout the summer of 1944, American and Allied forces in both Europe and the Pacific had made great strides forward. In Europe at least some commanders began to believe that the war might be won by late 1944. Pacific strategic planners began to contemplate an invasion of the southernmost Japanese home island in the spring of 1945. Logistical problems coupled with the resilience and ferocity of German and Japanese resistance put an end to any thoughts of an early victory. The Allied drive in Europe stalled, and Pacific campaigns were delayed. By mid-December 1944 American forces in the Pacific were preparing to invade Luzon while in Europe the Germans were preparing to upset SHAEF's plans by launching a massive attack of their own.

NOTES

1. Headquarters Twelfth Army Group, Letter of Instructions, Number 1, 29 July 1944, and Military Archives Record Group 331 TacHq 21 Army Group Jul 44 for descriptions of the Normandy fighting and the St Lô breakthrough.
2. Ibid., Letter of Instructions, Number 3, 6 August 1944.
3. Ibid.
4. Ibid., Letter of Instructions, Number 4, 8 August 1944.
5. Ibid.
6. Ibid., Letter of Instructions, Number 5, 17 August 1944.
7. CCS 319/5, 24 August 1943.

8. CCS 424, 5 December 1943, Amphibious Operation against the South of France.
9. CCS 424/1, 7 January 1944, Operation 'Anvil'.
10. Ibid.
11. Ibid.
12. CCS 465/21, 17 April 1944.
13. CCS 603, 24 June 1944, Operations to Assist 'Overlord'.
14. Ibid.
15. Operations to Assist 'Overlord' Memorandum by the United States Chiefs of Staff, 27 June 1944.
16. Ibid.
17. U.S. Military Attaché, London, England to the President of the United States, Number 718, 28 June 1944, Prime Minister to President Roosevelt.
18. JCS 925, 29 June 1944, Operations to Assist Overlord.
19. Ibid.
20. Ibid.
21. CCS 603/5, COSMED 139, 2 July 1944.
22. Ibid.
23. Military Archives Record Group 165 370.2 Vol I, Box 63 SHAEF/17107/Ops (A), 1 August 1944, Operation 'Dragoon'.
24. Ibid.
25. Cdr. 8th Fleet, Serial 00495, 15 April 1944.
26. Ibid., and TF8M Serial 00267 Op Plan 2-44, 5 August 1944.
27. Military Archives Record Group 165 SHAEF 370.2, Vol. I, Box 63, 1 August 1944, SHAEF 17101/OPS (A).
28. Ibid. and Record Group 331 SHAEF Decimal File, May 1943 – Aug 1945, Box 72.
29. Ibid.
30. 8th Fleet, Serial 00987, Op Plan 4–44, 24 July 1944.
31. 7th Army No. 2 (Dragoon) 1200B, 19 August 1944.
32. Ibid.
33. 7th Army No. 3 1800B, 25 August 1944.
34. 12th Army Group Letter of Instructions Number 6, 25 August 1944.
35. 12th Army Group Letter of Instructions Number 9, 25 September 1944 and Military Archives Record Group 331 SHAEF G-3 Future Plans Section Decimal File 1943–45, Box 76.
36. Stephen E. Ambrose, *The Supreme Commander: The War Years of General Dwight D. Eisenhower*, New York, Doubleday Co., 1970, pp. 493–4.
37. Military Archives Record Group 331 SHAEF G-3 Future Plans Section Decimal File 1943–45 Box 76.
38. Military Archives Record Group 331, SHAEF Decimal File Box 74.
39. Ibid.
40. Military Archives Record Group 331 SHAEF Office of the Chief of Staff Decimal File, May 1943–Aug 1945, Box No. 91.
41. Military Archives Record Group 331 G3 Division, Numeric File 1944–45, Box 150, SHAEF 14 Sep 1944, 21st Army Group Intentions and Record Group 331 12th Army Group, TS Decimal File 1943–45, Box No. 68, 11 September 1944 Task Force for Operation Market.
42. Military Archives Record Group 331 SHAEF, G-3 General Records Summary 159, 12 Sep 44, Box 17, Entry 23.
43. Military Archives Record Group 331 SHAEF 381 Market, Box 75, 13 September 1944, Field Order No. 4.
44. Military Archives Record Group 331 Headquarters 12th Army Group, Box 77 SHAEF Special Meeting, 22 September 1944.

45. Ibid.
46. Ibid.
47. Military Archives Record Group 165, OPD General Records Box 1852, Reno V, June 15, 1944.
48. Ibid.
49. Ibid.
50. JPS 404/10 Future Operations in the Pacific, 29 July 1944.
51. Ibid.
52. JPS 404/11, 4 August 1944.
53. Ibid.
54. Ibid.
55. CincPac File Serial 000563 Op Plan 6–44 Stalemate II, 6 July 1944.
56. Ibid.
57. JCS 713/9 Future Operations in the Pacific, 2 September 1944.
58. Ibid.
59. H.M. Cannon, *Leyte: the Return to the Philippines,* Washington, DC, Center of Military History, 1954, reprinted 1993, provides an excellent description of the decision and timing of the Leyte operation. On the importance of Peleliu see Commander 3rd Fleet Op Order 14–44, 1 August 1944.
60. JCS 713/10 4 September 1944, Memorandum for Joint Chiefs of Staff.
61. JCS 713/14 7 September 1944, Report by the Joint Strategic Survey Committee.
62. Ibid.
63. Ibid.
64. CincPac Serial 00078 Staff Study, 21 June 1944.
65. JCS 713/14 op. cit.
66. JPS 404/13 23 September 1944, Future Operations in the Pacific.
67. Ibid.
68. Ibid.
69. Ibid.
70. JCS 713/18 2 October 1944, Future Operations in the Pacific.
71. JCS 713/19 3 October 1944, Future Operations in the Pacific.
72. Military Archives Record Group 165 OPD Box 1838, Musketeer II, 29 August 1944.
73. Ibid.
74. General Headquarters Southwest Pacific Area Operations Instructions, Number 70, 21 September 1944 and Serial 00851 OpPlan 8–44, 27 September 1944.
75. Record Group 165 Box 1838 op. cit. Musketeer II Intelligence Annex, 28 August 1944.
76. Among the large number of studies on the Leyte campaign and Leyte Gulf battle see Cannon, op. cit., Spector, op. cit., and Samuel E. Morison, *The Two Ocean War*, Boston, Little, Brown and Company, 1963.

Victory

By late 1944 the United States and the Allies dominated the world's battlefronts but the Germans and Japanese were still dangerous opponents. Neither Axis power could by a bold operational stroke reverse its bleak strategic situation, but could delay defeat and drive up the costs of Allied victory. German offensives in 1944 and early 1945 and grim defensive fighting in the Pacific did indeed raise the price of victory but failed to alter either the strategic balance or political outcome of the war.

On 16 December 1944 the Germans struck in the west threatening SHAEF's plans for the final Allied drive to victory. Gathering in great secrecy, twenty-eight divisions, nine of which were armored, with nearly a quarter of a million men and 1,200 tanks and assault guns, struck a fifty-mile stretch of the lightly held American front in the Ardennes. The German objective was not simply to launch a counterblow to delay the Allied offensive but rather to reverse the entire course of the war in the west with a single decisive campaign.

The plan for the Autumn Mist offensive called for two panzer armies, with infantry armies securing their flanks, to break through the American lines and advance to the river Meuse. The advancing forces would then cross the river, march on and take Antwerp and encircle and destroy the entire 21st Army Group as well as a large part of the 12th Army Group. Winter weather, the Germans assumed, would limit the effectiveness of Allied air power, and fuel shortages would be overcome by the capture of Allied depots and storage facilities. The plan was like the Mortain attack, a desperate gamble personally devised by the German head of state.

The outlines of the projected offensive bore certain superficial similarities to the 1940 campaign – a surprise offensive through the

Ardennes, a crossing of the Meuse, and rapid exploitation resulting in a major victory. The balance of forces, however, was so different in 1944 that a comparison of the two offensives is largely irrelevant. In 1944 the Reich was in fact risking the last of its armored operational reserves in the west in an operation that was unlikely to change the war's outcome.

Initially, the Germans attained complete surprise, made substantial advances and rendered several US divisions combat ineffective. They failed, however, to attain operational freedom of maneuver. American soldiers fought doggedly. The shoulders of the breach held. Reserves were rushed forward, and the 3rd Army, attacking in Lorraine, quickly shifted substantial forces in a ninety degree arc to attack the southern face of the salient. The 3rd Army's immediate goal was to relieve the garrison of Bastogne consisting of an airborne division plus several units from other divisions. The Germans had surrounded Bastogne on 20 December, but the garrison refused to capitulate.[1]

Other German divisions advanced about forty miles but, far from threatening Antwerp, never even crossed the Meuse. The Allies halted the drive to the Meuse on 26 December, and on the same day 3rd Army units made contact with the defenders of Bastogne.[2] The Germans launched desperate attacks to cut the corridor. The Americans sought to widen it and to push north in an effort to seal off the entire bulge. Neither side fully succeeded. The Americans maintained and widened the corridor to Bastogne. Inclement weather, however, limited further advances, and the Germans began to retreat thus escaping efforts to trap them. Additional fighting eliminated the Ardennes salient in the second half of January 1945.[3]

The German offensive had failed disastrously as the German army suffered heavy casualties amounting to about 100,000 men killed, wounded or taken captive. The Germans also lost some 600 tanks. A series of attacks in Alsace in the first part of January – Operation Northwind – were also ineffective. The Germans made small initial gains.[4] The commander of the 6th Army Group contemplated withdrawing to better defensive positions further west. The French protested against major retreats in Alsace threatening, if necessary, to fight on alone. Eisenhower, in order to maintain Allied unity, agreed not to make any voluntary withdrawals, and the 6th Army Group soon halted the German attacks.[5]

The Americans suffered 76,000 casualties in the Ardennes and several thousand more in Alsace. The offensives also dislocated SHAEF's timetable for advances into the Reich, but assured that when the attacks did get underway, resistance would be less formidable than might otherwise have been the case had German armored divisions not been squandered in fruitless counterblows. When the Allies moved into Germany, the German army would still be able to offer stiff resistance but would not possess the capability to mount large-scale counter-attacks.

Even as the Allies were completing the reduction of the Ardennes salient, General Eisenhower was planning his own offensives. On 18 January 1945, SHAEF sent a cable to the Combined Chiefs of Staff describing forthcoming campaign plans. Offensive operations were to fall into three broad phases – the destruction of German forces west of the Rhine, the seizure of bridgeheads across the river from which to develop operations into Germany, and the destruction of German forces east of the Rhine.[6] On the same day Eisenhower informed the War Department that his plan included the elimination of the Colmar Pocket by the 6th Army Group and a strong offensive north of the Moselle. The 12th Army Group would continue to drive to the Rhine while the 21st Army Group which now included the US 9th Army would mount the major offensive designed to close on the Rhine north of Düsseldorf.[7]

Closing on the Rhine would provide the Allied armies with a good defensive barrier that could be held with a minimum of forces, thereby freeing additional divisions for operations east of the river.[8] Moreover, defeating the Germans west of the Rhine would further reduce their ability to continue resistance on the east bank. The main Rhine crossings would take place north of the Ruhr by the 21st Army Group. The terrain was suitable for mechanized operations and once across the river Allied forces could envelop the Ruhr from the north and east.[9]

Logistically, the Allies, even using the port of Antwerp, could support only thirty-five divisions for the assault north of the Ruhr. Consequently the 12th Army Group would close on the Rhine north of the Moselle and seek to make additional crossings in order to place extra pressure on German forces.[10] Once across the river, the 12th Army Group would, according to prevailing circumstances, strike north to cut communications from the Ruhr, move northeast on Berlin or advance due east towards Leipzig.[11]

For the offensive the Allies would have seventy-one divisions. They would face eighty German divisions, many badly under strength. SHAEF believed that if the Soviets launched an offensive at about the same time as the Allied attack, the Germans would be unable to reinforce their western front. The Allies could then begin operations in March and have bridgeheads across the Rhine in late April or early May.[12]

The Operations Section of SHAEF issued on 26 January a detailed plan of operations for the advance to the Rhine and the seizure of crossings. By March the Allies would have seventy-three divisions facing eighty-two German divisions of which fifteen were panzer or panzer grenadier. Many German formations were seriously depleted, and because of pressure on the Eastern Front, new troops were unlikely to be available for employment in the west.[13]

The Allied advance would unfold in phases. Closing to the Rhine would occur in two stages. The Allied armies would first advance to the Rhine north of the Moselle and if the opportunity arose seize bridgeheads on the eastern side. The Allies would then attack German forces south of the Moselle and if feasible seize additional bridgeheads.[14] The Allies would then make logistical preparations to support a thirty-five-division advance north of the Ruhr and a fifty-division advance south of the industrial region. SHAEF called upon the field forces to maintain operational flexibility and to be prepared to put maximum effort into the attack that scored the greatest success.[15] The 21st Army Group attack north of the Ruhr still retained the highest priority for logistical support, but the role of the 12th Army Group was expanded and the possibility of shifting priorities remained open.

On 29 January Eisenhower's headquarters issued instructions for operations north of the Moselle. In early February the 1st Canadian Army would launch Operation Veritable involving an advance from southern Holland southeast along the Rhine as far as Xanten. The US 1st Army would assist the advance by clearing the river Roer and the dams. The US 9th Army would then execute Operation Grenade pushing northeast to link up with the Canadians near Wesel, thereby forcing the retreat of German forces facing the British 2nd Army which was located between the Canadian 1st and American 9th armies.[16] The US 1st and part of the US 3rd Army would then advance to the Rhine and attempt to take Cologne and Koblenz[17] in an operation code-named Lumberjack.

143

Additional plans issued on 11 February dealt with additional operations in the Rhineland. After closing to the Rhine north of the Moselle, the Allies would, if possible, cross the river and advance to the east. If it were not possible to cross the Rhine immediately, the US 7th Army would clear the Rhineland south of the Moselle, after which the 21st Army Group would mount Operation Plunder – a major deliberate Rhine crossing north of the Ruhr.[18]

The Allied offensive began on 20 January when the 6th Army Group attacked the Colmar pocket in Alsace. By early February the French 1st and US 7th Army had eliminated the German salient in Alsace while the 12th Army Group began its advance towards the Roer River dams. By 10 February the US 1st Army had control of the dams, but the Germans had destroyed them causing heaving flooding in the region, thus delaying the US 9th Army's advance for two weeks.

The Canadians, meanwhile, launched Operation Veritable on 8 February after heavy preliminary bombardments by artillery and RAF Bomber Command. The Canadians fought over very difficult terrain – the Reichswald and numerous built-up areas which the Germans had transformed into strong points. Nevertheless, by the end of the second week in February, the Canadians were advancing steadily despite desperate German resistance.

On the morning of 23 February the 9th Army launched Operation Grenade, attacking across the Roer. By 2 March spearheads reached the Rhine; by 5 March the Americans had cleared the west bank of the river from Düsseldorf to Moers. The 1st Army had meanwhile launched Operation Lumberjack, reaching the Rhine on 5 March and capturing Cologne two days later. The 3rd Army also advanced rapidly reaching the Rhine on 10 March.

The campaign north of the Moselle had been very successful. In prisoners alone, the 21st, 12th, and 6th Army Groups had captured about 250,000 men and had destroyed more than twenty German divisions. More critically, however, a division belonging to the 1st Army captured an intact Rhine bridge at Remagen. General Bradley promptly ordered the 1st Army to reinforce the bridgehead on the east bank as rapidly as possible.[19]

During the ensuing two weeks the US 1st Army pushed additional troops across the Rhine while the Germans tried to wipe out the Remagen bridgehead. The Germans, however, lacked the forces to mount a major assault. Consequently, they launched a series of limited attacks that not only failed to eliminate the Remagen foothold but also depleted their reserves especially in armor and generally weakened defensive capabilities north and south of Remagen.

As fighting continued around Remagen the 7th Army launched Operation Undertone to clear the Rhineland south of the Moselle. General Eisenhower modified his original plan, directing elements of the 3rd Army to cross the Moselle on 11 March. The 3rd Army was to advance to the southeast in order to assist the 7th Army's drive to the northeast. The 3rd Army quickly smashed the German right flank and moved rapidly towards the Rhine. Both armies reached the river by 21 March. In the process the 3rd and 7th Armies had destroyed one German army and left another holding a precarious foothold on the west bank around Landau. Thus, by 21 March, the Allied armies had for all practical purposes cleared the west bank of the Rhine from Holland to Mannheim and established a firm foothold on the east bank at Remagen. The Germans retained a weak position on the west bank around Landau, but Allied forces held the rest of the western side of the river from just south of the Landau salient all the way to the Swiss border.

The extent of the success of the Rhineland operations convinced General Eisenhower to modify his plans a second time. On 13 March he directed the 21st Army Group to launch Operation Plunder on the 24th. The 12th Army Group was to direct the 1st Army to drive due east from Remagen while the 3rd Army crossed the Rhine and advanced to the northeast. Both armies would then advance on Kassel where they would link up, thereby creating a large force south of the Ruhr equal in strength to forces operating north of the industrial region.[20] The 12th Army Group would then link up with the 21st Army Group to surround the Ruhr.[21] Eisenhower had thus modified his plan from a single major thrust north of the Ruhr to a double envelopment.

On 22 March the 3rd Army made a surprise crossing of the Rhine, and on the night of 24–25 March the 21st Army Group launched Operation Plunder. Massive air and artillery bombardments covered the Rhine crossings by elements of the British 2nd and US 9th Army supported by a large-scale airborne operation. The German defenders were quickly overwhelmed, and Eisenhower had thus obtained operational freedom of maneuver.

On 28 March, SHAEF issued orders for the final campaign against Germany. The 21st and 12th Army Groups would surround and reduce the Ruhr. The 12th Army Group would then strike east in the direction of Leipzig where they would link up with Soviet forces and cut what remained of the Reich in half.[22] He informed Stalin of his intentions, and the Soviet leader agreed that US and Russian forces should meet in the Dresden area as Eisenhower proposed. On 30 March, Eisenhower informed Churchill that his plan, after encircling the Ruhr, called for the 12th Army Group to drive from Kassel to Leipzig while the 21st and 6th Army Group protected the flanks of the 12th Army Group's main advance.[23] By shifting the main weight of the Allied offensive from the 21st to the 12th Army Group, General Eisenhower's plan produced the last Anglo-American confrontation over strategy.

At this juncture the British raised objections to the new plan. Churchill and his Chiefs of Staff wished to continue the primary role of the 21st Army Group and called for an attack directed at Berlin. Churchill and his military advisors evidently had political considerations in mind including British postwar prestige and post-victory relations with the Soviet Union. The British, however, made their arguments on strategic grounds, and Eisenhower, supported by the JCS, rejected them.

On 30 March Eisenhower explained his plans to the War Department. After encircling the Ruhr, his main object was to divide and destroy the main German forces. Berlin as a strategic area was discounted since it was largely destroyed, and the Russians were much closer to the city than were the Allied armies.[24] A drive on Leipzig would divide the enemy roughly in half and give the Allies control of the one industrial area remaining to Germany. An advance on Leipzig would take place over terrain well suited for mechanized warfare and would avoid the necessity of having to cross the Weser and Elbe rivers.[25] The 12th Army Group would, therefore, strike on the Leipzig axis with flank protection provided by the 21st and 6th Army Group. A concentrated drive across the heart of Germany would also leave open the possibilities of exploitation to the north or south or both according to circumstances.[26]

On 2 April SHAEF issued directives to the army groups. The 21st would advance to Bremen and thereafter launch a thrust to the Elbe River while protecting the northern flank of the 12th Army Group.

Upon reaching the Elbe, the 21st Army Group would seize any opportunity of capturing a bridgehead over the river and prepare to conduct operations east of the Elbe.[27] The 12th Army Group would launch its main thrust along the Kassel–Leipzig axis while the 6th Army Group protected the south flank of the 12th Army Group and prepared to advance towards Linz to prevent the possible consolidation of German resistance in the south.[28]

On 4 April the British Chiefs of Staff told their American counterparts that SHAEF's plans did not give sufficient emphasis to the northern drive and ignored the desirability of a rapid capture of Berlin.[29] The American Joint Chiefs of Staff supported Eisenhower. They stated that any psychological advantage derived from taking Berlin before the Russians was far less important than the rapid defeat of Germany. Eisenhower's plan of a powerful drive in the center coupled with provisions for flexible action to either flank was the best means of attaining the basic Allied political and strategic goals. The JCS further noted that Berlin might in fact fall to the Allies. The US 9th Army, back under the control of the 12th Army Group, might, if circumstances permitted, move on Berlin, but the capture of the German capital remained an issue of secondary importance. Such a decision was of course Eisenhower's to make within the overall context of seeking the defeat of Germany.[30] At about the same time, the 12th Army Group issued orders for the advance into Saxony and also included Berlin as a possible target but one subordinate to the main advance on Leipzig.[31]

At no point in the discussions did the British explicitly state their political objectives. American policy, therefore, remained the pursuit of the unconditional surrender of Germany and Japan. The United States sought a rapid conclusion of the European war in order to redeploy forces to the Pacific. General Eisenhower believed that an effort to take Berlin was a political objective. He fully understood that wars were fought for political purposes and stated that if the British and American political leaders changed Allied policy and ordered him to advance on Berlin he would comply without hesitation, but in the absence of a change of Anglo-American policy he would pursue stated goals by the most efficient military means.[32]

Moreover, it was unclear to Eisenhower and others what the Anglo-American coalition would accomplish if they took Berlin. A European Advisory Commission had already drawn the borders of occupation zones for Germany. The British and Soviets had taken the lead in designating the zones based on the principle of a rough equality of territory and population for each area. In September 1944, the Americans accepted the fact that their original design of occupying the northern portion of Germany with the occupation zones converging on Berlin was no longer feasible.[33] Instead the United States accepted a zone in south-western Germany. Berlin was located within the Soviet zone, but the city was to be a separate enclave, and the United States, Great Britain and, later, France were to control about two thirds of the city.[34] Thus, even if American or British forces reached Berlin first, they would have to relinquish their conquest or risk a major confrontation with the USSR before the conclusion of the war against Japan.

Finally, SHAEF did not believe that Allied armies could, in fact, get to Berlin ahead of the Russians. Furthermore, if British and American forces somehow reached Berlin first, taking the city would in all probability be very costly. General Bradley told Eisenhower in late March that any Anglo-American effort to take Berlin would cost an estimated 100,000 casualties. If the Western powers launched an attack on Berlin, the Soviets would almost certainly strike for the city as well, and they were closer. Presuming the Allies reached Berlin first, fighting would have been very bitter. German forces would doubtless have preferred to capitulate to the Western allies rather than the Soviets, but there were elements who would have fought to the end. Berlin had a large garrison, and Hitler was prepared to direct the city's resistance. The Chancellor had no intention of surrendering to anybody. He retained the loyalty of most of the armed forces and would, and ultimately did, insist on extended resistance in Berlin.

Eisenhower wanted to avoid the heavy losses involved in taking a well fortified city that the Allies would have to share with the Russians after the end of hostilities. The Allies would also have to relinquish much of the territory taken in any race to Berlin as a result of prior agreements. Finally, a dash for Berlin might well have convinced the Soviets to seize as much German territory as possible regardless of the zonal agreements, and it was unclear which power would most profit in the race for spoils.

In any event, the Berlin issue was brushed aside by the Americans on strategic grounds, and the British, not having raised policy issues, had to agree. While the debate over Berlin continued, Allied forces

VICTORY

were driving deep into Germany. Early in April, the 9th Army from the north and the 1st Army from the south completed the encirclement of the Ruhr. The pocket with 300,000 prisoners was in Allied hands by 18 April. The 21st Army Group moved rapidly on Bremen, and the 6th Army Group overran the area between Frankfurt and the Czech border, while the 12th Army Group moved to the Elbe.

On 12 April, the 9th Army seized two bridgeheads over the Elbe. A German counter-attack eliminated one foothold but the other held. Lead elements of the 9th Army were fifty miles from Berlin. The Soviets were about thirty-five miles from the city. If the Allies decided to advance on Berlin, 9th Army's leading elements would, nevertheless, need to be resupplied and reinforced before advancing further, but any thought of a quick strike for the city was precluded by the start of a massive Soviet offensive on 16 April. The Americans had been willing to contemplate a drive on Berlin if circumstances permitted. Churchill raised the issue again in mid-April, but Eisenhower flew to London and convinced the Prime Minister on 17 April that his forces could not in fact beat the Russians into the German capital.

General Bradley halted the 9th Army on 17 April and directed the 1st Army to hold the line of the river Mulde. He ordered the 3rd Army to advance to the southeast into western Austria to protect the left flank of the 6th Army Group which was advancing into the Danube valley and western Austria.[35] On 19 April SHAEF issued final directives for the conclusion of the European war. The main effort remained the central drive into Saxony to meet the Russians and cut Germany in half. In the north the 21st Army Group would advance on Hamburg and Lübeck and if feasible liberate Denmark. In the south Allied forces were to move on Salzburg and Linz to preclude the formation of a southern redoubt.[36]

Allied intelligence was not at this point deluded by the myth of a national redoubt in the Alps from which some Nazi elements would continue the war. A report of 7 April from the Combined Intelligence Committee pointed out that the economic resources of any redoubt region could not long sustain a full-scale war effort. Moreover, the mountainous terrain of the Alps, though formidable, nevertheless presented numerous avenues of approach. The best the Germans could do in the south was to continue guerrilla resistance for some time.[37]

General Eisenhower's headquarters noted on 10 April that there were some indications of preparations for a last ditch stand in the south. If the Germans were indeed preparing for a last stand, the redoubt could not in fact offer sustained resistance because of the virtual absence of industrial resources. On the other hand, even a brief campaign in the region would result in additional casualties. To preclude any possibility of prolonged resistance, Allied forces should move into the region.[38] On 16 April SHAEF's Operations Division noted that present evidence concerning a national redoubt was not conclusive but that forces should advance with speed to key points as insurance against the creation of a bastion and the subsequent expensive and time-consuming operations to reduce it.[39]

German resistance by the second half of April was so fragmented that no sustained effective resistance met the Allied drives. There were numerous vicious small encounters, but nothing the Germans could do was able to stop or even seriously delay Allied forces. The Russians surrounded Berlin on 25 April; by April 30 Soviet troops entered the Reichstag, and Hitler committed suicide. By 2 May the Berlin garrison capitulated. In the north the British took Hamburg on 3 May, while in the center the Americans, having linked up with the Russians on 25 April, moved towards the Czech border. In the south, American forces entered Munich on 30 April, and by 4 May US forces in Germany had linked up with Allied armies in Italy. In early May American forces crossed into Czechoslovakia.[40]

The German collapse was complete. A wave of surrenders from individual soldiers to entire army groups began in May, and on 7 May the surviving German government surrendered unconditionally to the Allies. General Eisenhower was thus able to inform his superiors 'The mission of this Allied force was fulfilled at 0241 local time May 7, 1945.'[41]

The campaigns from January to May 1945 worked as well, if not better, than planned. The Germans lost so heavily in the Ardennes, Alsace and around Remagen that their subsequent resistance though dogged could do little more than delay marginally the Allied offensives. Strategic debates between March and May did not have to focus on how to defeat the Germans. Rather, they focused on how to exploit Allied victories. The weakened enemy and growing Allied power enabled SHAEF to formulate and execute plans with the problems and friction of war much reduced.

As the Americans were eliminating the German salient in the

Ardennes, forces of the Southwest Pacific Command began the invasion of Luzon. The Musketeer III Plan of 28 September 1944, like the Musketeer II Plan, dealt not only with the Luzon invasion but also with the liberation of the entire Philippine archipelago.[42]

The primary operation of the Musketeer Plan, code-named Mike One, called for a landing in the Lingayen Gulf by two corps under control of the 6th Army. Once ashore, US forces would advance overland and take Manila.[43] Supporting operations by two divisions and a number of independent regiments from the 8th Army would clear other major islands. General MacArthur also held three divisions in reserve for employment whenever required.[44]

MacArthur's armies expected to face 130,000–140,000 Japanese troops in the Philippines.[45] Despite the losses sustained in the fighting on Leyte, the Japanese deployed substantially more troops on Luzon alone than the Americans expected to encounter throughout all of the islands. The Japanese did not intend to resist the landings on the beaches. Rather, they organized their forces into three major concentrations that would fight a series of delaying actions designed to inflict severe casualties on the Americans and slow the pace of Pacific operations. One group, 152,000 strong, held northern Luzon; a detachment of 30,000 men held the airbase complex around Clark Field, and 80,000 men guarded southern Luzon. More than 100,000 troops were stationed on other Philippine islands.

On 2 January 1945 a bombardment force of six battleships, twelve escort carriers and thirty-nine destroyers left Leyte for the invasion beaches. On their voyage, they were subjected to a series of kamikaze attacks and in two days lost an escort carrier, while a destroyer, two cruisers and an escort carrier suffered severe damage. Upon entering Lingayen Gulf, the suicide planes struck again damaging two battleships, three cruisers and a number of smaller vessels. Suicide planes also sank a destroyer escort. Fortunately for the Americans the Japanese had struck too soon and were almost out of planes when the troop-laden transports and supply ships arrived.

Consequently, when the four divisions of the 6th Army landed on 9 January, there was virtually no air or ground opposition. Within a few days nearly 175,000 men were ashore. The 6th Army directed one corps of two divisions to drive for Manila while the other corps advanced into the mountains to protect the left flank of the advance on Manila. By 23 January American forces had reached Clark Field while other units advanced slowly across the difficult terrain of the central mountains where they met stiff opposition. On 31 January elements of an airborne division landed south of Manila and by 4 February had reached a point four miles south of the city. Meanwhile, the advance from the north captured Clark Field and reached the outskirts of the Philippine capital on the night of 3 February.

The Japanese originally had no intention of contesting control of Manila, but naval troops, not under the command of the area army, decided to fight for the city. The local army commander had little choice but to agree and added several infantry battalions to the 16,000-man naval garrison. As a result, the Americans had to wage a house to house battle for Manila. Fighting continued until 3 March. The Americans lost over 1,000 killed and more than 5,500 wounded. Virtually all the defenders perished along with some 100,000 civilians.[46] The city was largely destroyed, its physical infrastructure shattered and its port facilities demolished.

As fighting raged in Manila, a third corps landed on the west coast of Luzon and retook the Bataan Peninsula and Corregidor by late February. General MacArthur also undertook the liberation of other major Philippines islands.[47] The 8th Army began to conduct fourteen major and twenty-six minor operations in forty-four days. Japanese garrisons usually did not resist the landings but withdrew into the interior of various islands and held out for the duration of the war. On Luzon the 6th Army drove into the island's center where the Japanese forced the Americans to wage a difficult and costly campaign. Though defeated and forced away from any important strategic objectives, Japanese forces held out until the war's end.

While Southwest Pacific forces were recapturing the Philippines, the Central Pacific Command began to move into the Bonins. The JCS had selected Iwo Jima as the objective of Operation Detachment in March 1944. Located about 650 miles from Tokyo, Iwo Jima consisted of about eight square miles of volcanic ash. The island, however, contained three airfields and a radar site and was well located as a base from which fighters could support B-29 raids against Japan.

The Air Corps had shifted the weight of strategic bombardment against the Japanese home islands from China to the Marianas. The loss of airbases in China to a Japanese offensive in the spring of 1944 convinced the Air Force to abandon further efforts to operate from

China. In January 1945, the JCS approved the movement of XX Bomber Command from China to the Marianas to operate with XXI Bomber Command.[48]

If Iwo Jima remained in Japanese hands, B-29s on the way to Japan would have to avoid the island, thereby lengthening the distance flown and fuel consumed with a resulting reduction in bomb load. Moreover, there was no American base between Japan and the Marianas upon which to recover damaged aircraft or planes low on fuel. Therefore, in addition to providing a stepping stone for future moves into the Ryukyus, Iwo Jima was viewed as an important part of the air offensive against Japan. By November 1944, the Central Pacific planners concluded that it was feasible to attack Iwo Jima even while operations continued in the Philippines, and assigned three Marine divisions to execute the assault.[49] D-Day was 20 January 1945, later postponed to 19 February.

The Japanese, however, expected an attack, and although he had no hope of victory, the garrison commander intended to make the American conquest of Iwo Jima as long and as expensive as possible. Civilians on the island were evacuated to Japan in the summer of 1944 and the garrison was reinforced to 21,000 men. Engineers constructed extensive underground fortifications which included positions for more than 350 artillery pieces plus numerous machine-gun emplacements. The commander decided not to contest the initial American landings but to wage a yard by yard defense of the fortified bastions.

American tactical planners understood that they would face formidable opposition and called for ten days of preliminary naval and air bombardment. The Navy, however, was organizing a major carrier raid on Japan while Philippine operations tied up additional air and naval forces. Consequently, the initial bombardment was reduced to three days.

The ensuing bombardment was heavy and often effective, especially near the landing beaches, but when the Marines went ashore on 19 February, most of the island's defenses were still intact. The landings, executed by two Marine divisions – a third remained afloat – met little opposition at the shoreline. As the Marines advanced inland resistance stiffened, and Japanese artillery put the entire beachhead under fire. The volcanic ash made vehicular and foot movement very difficult, and the carnage in the landing zone grew rapidly. But this was only the beginning.

The next morning the Marines resumed their advance, and each forward movement was measured in yards and paid for in blood. The Japanese resisted tenaciously for thirty-six days and took the lives of over 6,800 Marines and wounded some 20,000 more. The defenders died almost to the last man. For the first time in the Pacific, the Japanese inflicted more casualties than they received, but like other garrisons chosen for attack, they were doomed from the start. During the last days of the fighting, captured airfields were already in operation primarily as emergency landing sites for damaged B-29s. By the end of the war over 2,400 aircraft had landed on Iwo Jima's airfields.

Before and during the Iwo Jima battle, the Central Pacific planners prepared Operation Iceberg – the invasion of Okinawa. Located 350 miles from Japan, Okinawa was essential as an air base area and fleet anchorage for the ultimate invasion of the Japanese home islands. In late October 1944, a staff study called for the employment of three Marine and three Army divisions against Okinawa which held an estimated garrison of 48,000 men.[50] In November the JCS increased the invasion force to eight divisions, some of which were to be held in reserve. JCS strategic planners also warned that an invasion force could expect attacks from about 2,000 Japanese aircraft.[51] On 31 December Pacific Fleet plans called for the employment of six divisions in the initial landings plus two more in reserve. Naval forces assigned to Operation Iceberg included sixteen carriers and eighteen battleships.[52] In addition, eighteen escort carriers, 206 destroyer types, 150 LSTs and 800 amphibian tractors were part of the invasion fleet.[53]

The Iceberg Plan called for the seizure of a number of outlying islets around Okinawa followed by the major assault on the island's western coast. The invaders were to quickly overrun the southern portion of Okinawa and then move north.[54]

Unknown to the Americans, the Okinawa garrison numbered over 100,000 men. As at Iwo Jima, the Japanese did not intend to resist the landings and concentrated the bulk of their forces in the southern part of the island intending to offer prolonged resistance. The attack on Iwo Jima had not encountered large-scale suicide plane attacks, but Okinawa was well within range of airfields in Japan. The fields were widely dispersed and well camouflaged and could not be entirely suppressed by US air strikes. With a relatively short flying time to

Okinawa, the Japanese were well positioned to mount large-scale kamikaze attacks on the American fleet.

In late March American forces seized several small islands around Okinawa, and on 1 April 1945 over 1,200 ships carrying over 180,000 troops began the main invasion. There was only light opposition on the beaches. Soldiers and Marines moved rapidly inland and soon overran the northern portion of the island. At the end of the first week, however, US troops came up against the main Japanese positions in the south.

During the following weeks both sides fought furiously and sustained heavy losses. American forces pushed slowly forward while the Japanese launched major counter-attacks on 12–13 April, 4–5 and 25–26 May. They lost thousands of troops and made no significant or permanent gains. Moreover, the Japanese losses weakened their defensive positions, but despite the casualties suffered in the unsuccessful counter-attacks Japanese resistance continued until 22 June.

At sea the Japanese launched massive kamikaze attacks against the American Fleet sinking thirty-eight ships and damaging over 350. Supporting an invasion so close to Japan inevitably limited fleet mobility. Transports, supply ships and their escorts had to remain close to Okinawa and had no choice but to stay and do battle with the suicide planes. Hundreds were shot down but inevitably the US Navy suffered severe losses.

The grim struggle for Okinawa cost the lives of some 12,500 American soldiers, marines and sailors. Over 50,000 Americans were wounded. Almost the entire Japanese garrison along with some 80,000 civilians perished in the fighting. The Americans had won a clear-cut victory but had paid a severe price. The casualties incurred during the Okinawa campaign in turn raised serious questions concerning the projected invasion of Japan.

The Joint Chiefs of Staff had long accepted the fact that in the absence of Japanese capitulation an invasion of the home islands was probably the only way to win the war. On 19 April the JCS planning staff noted that an invasion of Japan was the supreme and culminating point of the Pacific war.[55] On 30 April the Joint Chiefs approved the staff's proposals concerning future strategy.[56] The Combined Chiefs accepted the American strategic view a few days later.[57] In examining Japanese defensive capabilities the Joint

Intelligence Committee reached some unsettling conclusions. Japan's navy represented no significant threat but there were approximately two million soldiers in the home islands backed by 1,400 combat aircraft plus 500 to 600 planes in operational training units.[58]

These unsettling figures led the JCS planning staff on 25 April to explore alternatives to a direct invasion of Japan. A campaign of encirclement, blockade, and bombardment was militarily feasible but would not guarantee that Japan would surrender in a reasonable length of time. Nor would such a campaign necessarily lead to the capitulation of Japanese forces in China, Manchuria, Korea, Southeast Asia and bypassed the Pacific islands.[59] Finally, a blockade and bombardment would involve almost as much manpower as an invasion – twenty-eight divisions for blockading purposes as opposed to thirty-six divisions for an invasion.[60] An invasion could be executed and completed by June 1946 while the less direct approach would take a good deal longer.[61]

The planning staff also noted that although a direct invasion was feasible, it could prove costly. In Pacific land battles the daily casualty rate per thousand averaged 7.45 percent. Naval casualties varied with the length of a campaign.[62] Nevertheless, despite the risk of substantial casualties, the planners concluded that the United States should invade Japan at the earliest practicable date. An invasion was the most rapid and effective means of compelling the Japanese government to capitulate and to include within the terms of surrender forces located outside the home islands.[63]

Meanwhile staff planners in the Pacific were drawing up plans for Operation Olympic – the invasion of southern Kyushu – and for a subsequent invasion of the Tokyo plain – Operation Coronet. The Joint Intelligence Committee estimated on 16 May that Operation Olympic would face a total of 2,300 combat aircraft and up to 2,000 suicide planes, many of which would be committed to the defense of Kyushu. On the ground the Japanese would deploy about 390,000 troops.[64] Despite formidable defenses the Joint Chiefs of Staff directed on 25 May that the Central and Southwestern Commands launch Olympic on 1 November 1945.[65]

On 16 June the JCS planning staff submitted detailed appraisals of both Olympic and Coronet. US forces would launch Operation Olympic on 1 November 1945. The objective was the seizure of southern Kyushu followed by the establishment of air bases for over

2,500 aircraft which would contribute to the bombardment and blockade of the main island – Honshu.[66]

If the loss of southern Kyushu and intensified aerial bombardment failed to compel Japan to capitulate, the Americans would launch Operation Coronet on or about 1 March 1946.[67] By March 1946 the United States intended to deploy thirty-nine Army and six Marine divisions, 8,500 land-based and 3,600 carrier aircraft, twenty-three battleships, thirty-three large and seventy-four escort carriers, 364 destroyers, 326 destroyer escorts and 189 submarines.[68] Casualties in both operations, though not subject to precise estimation, would be substantial, but alternative approaches would take longer and would also lead to heavy losses.[69]

Operation Olympic called for a twelve-division assault and an eight-division follow-up. Naval assault lift included 210 attack transports and 515 LSTs.[70] Coronet required a fourteen-division assault and an eleven-division follow-up.[71] The two operations required 1,026,000 ground troops and 3,300 aircraft. On Kyushu the Americans expected to encounter 350,000 ground troops and up to 2,000 aircraft. Japan had over 1.5 million troops on Honshu.[72]

The magnitude of Olympic and Coronet and the prospect of heavy casualties disturbed the civilian leadership, and on 18 June President Truman met the Joint Chiefs to discuss the Olympic Operation. General Marshall insisted that Olympic was essential either for a campaign of blockade and bombardment or for an invasion of the Tokyo plain.[73]

As far as casualties were concerned the Joint Chiefs noted that it was almost impossible to derive precise estimates. Geographically, however, Kyushu resembled Luzon more than it did the small densely fortified islands of Tarawa, Iwo Jima or Okinawa. There was then reason to believe that losses during the first thirty days of fighting on Kyushu would not exceed the 31,000 men killed or wounded on Luzon.[74] Beyond the first month of operations the Joint Chiefs offered no casualty projections except to note that based on previous campaigns in the Southwest Pacific, Japanese casualties would exceed American losses at a ratio of approximately twenty-two to one.[75]

Admiral Leahy, Chairman of the JCS, offered a gloomier prognostication by suggesting that a battle on Kyushu might well resemble the recent struggle for Okinawa. Troops on Okinawa suffered thirty-five percent casualties. Given the fact that 766,000 troops would be involved in Operation Olympic, losses could amount to 268,000 killed and wounded.[76] Admiral King then offered the opinion that a realistic casualty figure for southern Kyushu would lie somewhere between losses suffered on Luzon and losses sustained at Okinawa.[77]

Admiral Leahy was, nevertheless, sufficiently alarmed by the prospect of heavy losses that he raised the possibility of a modification of the demand for unconditional surrender. The President replied that Congress could, if it wished, alter or modify the government's policy and that he had left the door open for Congress to do so but that he could not act at this time to change public opinion on the issue of unconditional surrender.[78]

General Marshall, the Secretary of War and the Secretary of the Navy all agreed that Operation Olympic was the only feasible strategy. Even if the United States decided to adopt a blockade strategy which according to the Secretary of the Navy might take a year or more to produce a Japanese surrender, air bases in southern Kyushu were an essential prerequisite. The President replied that he hoped to prevent a repeat of Okinawa from one end of Japan to the other but agreed to launch Operation Olympic.[79]

At the 18 June meeting the discussion of possible casualties focused primarily on losses that might be sustained in Operation Olympic especially during the first month of fighting. The President and the service chiefs and secretaries did not directly raise the question of casualties in Operation Coronet except to note that an invasion of the Kanto plain would probably unite the Japanese people behind their government.[80]

On 21 June a report on Japan's air strength provided disquieting information. The Joint Intelligence Committee claimed that the Japanese currently possessed some 4,000 combat aircraft plus 3,500 to 4,000 training planes which could be configured for suicide missions. There existed many Japanese air bases within range of Kyushu, and the Japanese could launch between 400 to 500 combat sorties and 200 to 300 suicide attacks in any given twenty-four hour period. Because of the proximity of an invasion fleet to the Japanese coast, interception would be more difficult than it had been during the Okinawa operations where attacking aircraft had to fly over 350 miles, thereby providing the US Fleet with fairly substantial warning time. Dealing with night attacks, the Committee noted, would be particularly difficult.[81] Another report of 25 July set the number of Japanese aircraft at 5,000 combat and 6,000 trainer types. After 1 November 1945 Japanese air strength would be reduced to 4,000 combat and 3,000 training aircraft.[82] Estimates of ground strength were also disquieting. Some reports placed the Kyushu garrison as high as 600,000 men and total ground strength in the home islands at 2,975,000.[83]

Additional examinations of Coronet indicated that Japan would have two million men on Honshu in the spring of 1946. About 526,000 troops would be stationed in the Tokyo region.[84] After an invasion the Japanese would be able to reinforce the Kanto plain defenders quite rapidly, despite massive American efforts at aerial interdiction. American invaders would also meet resistance by lightly armed home guard regiments. Air strength would have been substantially reduced during the Kyushu fighting, but in March 1946 the Japanese would still have available 1,000 to 2,000 aircraft of all types.[85]

If Japan continued to resist after the loss of southern Kyushu and the Tokyo plain, the War Plans Committee on 26 July called for a series of amphibious operations on Honshu. The operations would require between five and nine divisions and would strike at areas including Kyoto, Kobe, and Shimonoseki.[86] Planners thus contemplated the virtual military conquest of all of the home islands.

A report submitted to the JCS on 13 August, after the use of atomic weapons and the Soviet entry into the war against Japan, estimated that if Japan continued to resist, forces on Honshu to meet an American invasion would include sixty-seven infantry, three armored and fourteen depot divisions with a total of 2.8 million men. About 700,000 troops would be immediately available to meet the forces of Operation Coronet. Rapid reinforcement of the Kanto Plan and violent large-scale counter-attacks would be within reach of Japanese capabilities.[87] Japan would also deploy 3,000–4,000 combat and 4,000 training–suicide aircraft.[88]

Japan's decision to surrender precluded the execution of either Olympic or Coronet. In August 1945, Japan in fact had over 2 million men under arms in the home islands – fifty-six infantry divisions, two tank divisions, seven tank brigades, three garrison brigades and four anti-aircraft divisions. Japan also had some 10,000 aircraft of all types, thirty-eight submarines, and 3,300 suicide boats.[89]

Unlike Germany, Japan capitulated with major forces still intact. By the spring of 1945 the German armed forces had been effectively destroyed; by early May resistance had become sporadic and disorganized. Japan, by contrast, still retained substantial armed forces not only in the home islands but also on the Asian mainland and Southeast Asia. Large units also held out in the Philippines, Rabaul, and other Pacific islands. In the summer of 1945 Japan had no realistic hope of victory or even altering significantly Allied political objectives. Nevertheless, the decision to surrender did result in the capitulation of large well organized forces capable of organized resistance. The surrender, of course, meant that the residual Japanese forces fell into Allied hands without additional combat.

NOTES

1. CCS 761/3, 29 January 1945, SHAEF Report.
2. Ibid.
3. Ibid.
4. Military Archives Record Group 331, Operations "A" Section, Decimal File 1943–45 Box 14 SHAEF G-3 Liaison Sub-Section Report No. 84, 1 January 1945 and 6th Army Group B-22132.
5. Record Group 331, Box 114 op. cit.
6. Military Archives Record Group 331 SHAEF G-3 Decimal File 1943–1945, Box 78, SHAEF, January 18, 1945 Appreciation and Plan of Operations in Winter and Spring, 1945.
7. SCAF176, 18 January 1945 Appreciation and Over-All Plan.
8. Record Group 331, Box 75 op. cit. and Military Archives Record Group 331 Box 75 PS-SHAEF (45) 4, 26 January 1945, Development of Operations 1945.
9. SHAEF (45) 4 op. cit.
10. Ibid.
11. Ibid.
12. Ibid.
13. Military Archives Record Group 331 SHAEF G-3 Division, Box 75, 26 January 1945 Development of Operations 1945.
14. Ibid.
15. Ibid.
16. Military Archives Record Group 331 SHAEF G-3 Decimal File 1943–1945, Box 76, 29 January 1945 Closing Rhine in North.
17. Ibid. and Record Group 331 HQ 12th Army Group TS Decimal File, Box No. 68, Outline Operation Plan, 23 February 1945.
18. Record Group 331 SHAEF G-3 Box 78 op. cit., 11 February 1945 Development of Operations 1945.
19. HQ 12th Army Group Letter of Instructions, Number 17, 13 March 1945.
20. HQ 12th Army Group Letter of Instructions Number 18, 25 March 1945.
21. Ibid.
22. HQ 12th Army Group Letter of Instructions Number 19, 28 March 1945.

23. Military Archives Record Group 331 SHAEF G-3 Division Future Plans Section Decimal File 1943–1945, Box 76.
24. SCAF 260, 31 March 1945.
25. Ibid.
26. Ibid.
27. SCAF 261, 2 April 1945.
28. Ibid.
29. CCS 805/4, 4 April 1945 Plan of Campaign in Western Europe.
30. CCS 805/5 6 April 1945 Plan of Campaign in Western Europe.
31. Military Archives Record Group 331 SHAEF G-3, Box 37, 12th Army Group Letter of Instructions Number Twenty, 4 April 1945.
32. Stephen E. Ambrose, *The Supreme Commander. The War Years of General Dwight D. Eisenhower*, New York, Doubleday & Co., 1970, p. 641.
33. JCS 577/10 Allocation of Zones of Occupation in Germany, 24 April 1944.
34. JCS 577/24 Protocol on the Zones of Occupation in Germany and Administration of 'Greater Berlin', 12 December 1944.
35. Headquarters 12th Army Group Letter of Instructions Number Twenty-One, 17 April 1945.
36. Military Archives Record Group 331 SHAPE G-3 Division, Box 76, Operations after reaching the River Elbe, 19 April 1945.
37. CCS660/4, 7 April 1945, German Capabilities for Continued Resistance in the South.
38. Military Archives Record Group 331 G-3, Division Decimal File 1943–1945, Box 80 SHAEF, Intelligence Committee, 10 April 1945.
39. Ibid., G-3 Division GCT370-69 Plans, 16 April 1945.
40. Headquarters 12th Army Group Letter of Instructions Number Twenty-two, 4 May 1945.
41. Ambrose, op. cit., p. 668.
42. Military Archives Record Group 165 OPD Box 1838, Musketeer III, 28 September 1944.
43. Ibid.
44. Ibid.
45. Ibid.
46. Spector, op. cit. has a detailed account of operations on Luzon.
47. Record Group 165, Musketeer III, op. cit.
48. JCS 1190/4, 15 January 1945, Movement of XX Bomber Command from China.
49. 7 October 1944 Detachment Staff Study Serial 00019 and 25 November 1944 Serial 0001027 Op Plan 11–44.
50. Military Archives Record Group 165 OPD, Box 1819, 25 October, United States Pacific Fleet and Pacific Ocean Areas Iceberg, October 25, 1944.
51. Ibid., November 1944 Studies JWPC 116/4.
52. CincPac Serial 000193 Op Plan 14-44, 31 December 1944.
53. Ibid.
54. JWPC 393/2 Examination of Iceberg, 2 January 1945.
55. JCS 1316, 19 April 1945 Operational Priorities for the Continuation of the War against Japan.
56. JCS 1316, 30 April 1945.
57. JCS 1316 – CCS 824/2, 5 May 1945.
58. JIC 269, 23 April 1945, Japanese Defensive Capabilities.
59. JCS 924/15, 25 April 1945, Pacific Strategy.
60. Ibid.
61. Ibid.
62. Ibid.

63. Ibid.
64. JIC 191/7 16 May 1945, Japanese Reactions to an operation against Southern Kyushu.
65. JCS 1331/3 25 May 1945, Directive for Operation Olympic.
66. JCS 1388 16 June 1945, Details of the Campaign against Japan.
67. Ibid.
68. Ibid.
69. Ibid.
70. Ibid.
71. Ibid.
72. Ibid.
73. JCS 381 Japan – Extracted from Minutes of Meeting Held at the White House, 18 June 1945 at 1530.
74. Ibid.
75. Ibid.
76. Ibid.
77. Ibid.
78. Ibid.
79. Ibid.
80. Ibid.
81. JIC 191/8 21 June 1945, Japanese Reaction to an Operation against Southern Kyushu.
82. JIC 307 25 July 1945, Capabilities of Japanese Air Forces.
83. JIC 218/9 10 July 1945, Japanese Reactions to an Assault on the Kanto Plain (Tokyo) of Honshu.
84. Ibid.
85. Ibid.
86. JWPC 333/1 26 July 1945, Operations in Japan following 'Coronet'.
87. JIC 218/11 13 August 1945 Japanese Reaction to an Assault on the Kanto (Tokyo) Plain.
88. Ibid.
89. HQ USAFFE and Eighth U.S. Army (Rear) *Homeland and Operations Record*, Monograph No. 17, p. 139.

Conclusion

With fifty years of hindsight, it becomes somewhat easier to determine the factors that produced the often stark differences between the intentions of American strategists and the reality of battle. Of course, most major war plans are simply a starting point, and war itself inevitably forces changes – real war is different from war on paper. During the Second World War, plans and execution frequently differed so substantially that the explanation of the difference must be more complex.

The United States fought a global war against formidable enemies. Moreover, America waged war as a coalition partner working closely with Great Britain and the Dominions and more distantly with the Soviet Union. The global context of the war, the decisions of the major Axis powers, the complexities of Alliance decision making and the impact of logistics were among the more important factors in determining the relationship between strategic plans and actual operations.

The United States entered the war with a predetermined grand strategy. American planners had decided that in case of hostilities against both Germany and Japan, the nation would focus its efforts and resources on the defeat of Germany while standing on the strategic defensive in the Pacific. After the defeat of Germany, America would transfer resources to the Pacific to crush Japan – an early version of the win-hold-win strategy revived and quickly abandoned by the Pentagon in the early 1990s. US strategists also assumed that America would act in close concert with Great Britain and, prior to Pearl Harbor, Anglo-American staff talks produced a basic agreement on the 'Germany first' strategy.

The initial Japanese offensive was, however, so devastatingly effective that the United States had to alter the pre-war grand strategy. To contain the Japanese in the Central and South Pacific and to secure the lines of communication to Australia and New Zealand, the US had to deploy substantial forces to the Pacific. Not until late in 1943 did American strength in Europe and the Mediterranean equal and begin to surpass force levels in the Pacific.

Even after halting the Japanese at the Coral Sea and Midway, American strategists realized that it would be dangerous to revert to a defensive strategy. Japan would use the time to exploit conquered resources and expand and train its armed forces, especially carrier-trained aviators who were in desperately short supply after Midway. The JCS, therefore, approved the initiation of offensive operations in the early spring of 1942. Thus, by mid-1942 the United States was not only involved in a global war but also was committed to the waging of offensive operations in both Europe and the Pacific.

The war in the Pacific was primarily an American enterprise notwithstanding significant British efforts in Burma and India. In Europe and the Mediterranean, however, Washington and London had to work in tandem. Both nations agreed to the 'Germany first' strategy and to the absolute requirement to conduct operations in such a way as to provide assistance to the Soviet Union. The USSR, after June 1941, fought against the bulk of the German army. American and British political and military leaders were vividly aware that if Russia were defeated or signed a separate peace treaty with Germany, the United States and Great Britain would face a bleak strategic situation. Victory would become at best improbable or vastly more expensive in lives and treasure than even the most pessimistic planners predicted. Beyond the basic Anglo-American strategic agreements, however, there was a wide divergence of views of how best to implement Allied strategy.

Driven by the need to keep the Soviet Union in the war by alleviating pressure on the Eastern Front, by logistical considerations and by the military doctrine of concentration of force, the American military wanted to build up forces in the United Kingdom, invade France and engage the German army as soon as possible.

The British were reluctant to undertake a direct invasion of northern France. Having been defeated by the Germans in Norway, the Low Countries and France, Greece, Crete and Dieppe British strategists were apprehensive about attempting a major amphibious invasion against a well entrenched enemy. The specter of defeat haunted England's political and military leaders. Memories of the stalemate and slaughter on the Western Front in the First World War raised concerns that even a successful landing would not be the key to victory. Britain's manpower resources were limited. In late 1943 Churchill told Roosevelt and Stalin that the United Kingdom could expand the army no further. Battles of attrition in northern Europe would not only reduce Britain's army but also undermine London's post-war position. Finally, the British had large forces fighting in the Western Desert where Axis forces periodically threatened the imperial lifeline between the British Isles and the Far East. London, therefore, wanted to secure the south shore of the Mediterranean and then strike directly at Italy.

As early as 1941 the British made it clear to the Americans that a cross-Channel attack would have to be the end rather than the beginning of a process. Only after German forces had been worn down by losses in Russia and the Mediterranean, the war economy shattered by aerial bombardment and morale undermined, would the Allies strike across the Channel and finish the war. London's strategic approach clashed directly with Washington's emphasis on a direct assault on France, producing the first of several serious disputes concerning the strategy for defeating Germany.

Compromise was necessary if the coalition was to survive, but Anglo-American military conferences in 1942 reached a complete deadlock. The American Joint Chiefs recommended to President Roosevelt that if the British persisted in refusing to invade France in 1943 the United States should adopt a 'Pacific first' strategy. The President, however, overruled his military advisors. Despite the Joint Chiefs' warning that operations in the Mediterranean and North Africa would delay a cross-Channel assault until 1944, Roosevelt, in order to maintain coalition unity and get American forces into battle against the Germans in 1942, ordered the US military to join with British forces in an invasion of North Africa.

The arguments surrounding Torch versus Roundup – the peripheral versus the direct approach – were to characterize Anglo-American strategic decision making until the summer of 1944. Moreover, the strategic debates indicated that the Anglo-American alliance had no clear-cut overall strategy for the defeat of Germany. After every major campaign, the Western Allies had to confer, often acrimoniously, about the next operation, a process that went on until the last days of the war in Europe. The Allied war effort was negotiated every step of the way. Consequently, American plans were often subject to modification or change in the overriding interests of maintaining coalition unity. Moreover, German reactions to Allied moves contributed additional elements in the strategic equation that forced the Americans to modify their war plans.

The invasion of North Africa was supposed to produce a rapid defeat of the Axis forces. The Germans, however, occupied Tunisia before the Allies could move into the area from Algeria. Consequently, American and British forces had to fight until May 1943 before completing the destruction of Axis forces in North Africa. The duration of the campaign in turn shattered any lingering American hopes of a cross-Channel attack in 1943. Consequently, there was little inter-Allied disagreement concerning an invasion of Sicily which appeared to be a logical subsequent move. Forces were already in North Africa and could not readily be moved back to the United Kingdom in time to invade France in 1943, and the conquest of Sicily would help secure the sea lines of communication in the Mediterranean and weaken Italian willingness to remain in the war.

After the Sicilian campaign, the logic of events led the Americans to agree to an invasion of the Italian mainland in return for which the British agreed to a cross-Channel assault in the spring of 1944 and to an intensification of American offensives in the Pacific. The British also agreed to an invasion of southern France at the same time as the cross-Channel attack based on the presumption that operations in Italy would be quick and decisive. Allied planners expected that after landing in Italy, German forces would retreat rapidly north. The Allies would establish their forces well north of Rome in 1943, and consequently there would be forces available to strike into southern France. The optimistic assumptions of Anglo-American strategists were again undone by the German response to Operation Avalanche.

Far from retreating to the Pisa–Rimini line or even the Adige river, the Germans decided to fight well south of Rome. The Allies found themselves engaged in a bitter campaign of attrition and by November 1943 were bogged down along the Gustav Line. The United States was thus involved in a two-ocean war, waging offensives in the Pacific, which had not been foreseen in pre-war plans, and in the Mediterranean which the Joint Chiefs regarded as a diversion from the main objective of invading northwest Europe.

The British had agreed to invade France in the spring of 1944, but in late 1943 began to call not only for a continued offensive in Italy but also for operations in the eastern Mediterranean even at the price of delaying Overlord by several months. Such delays might, because of weather conditions, have in fact, precluded Overlord in 1944. American and British military leaders could not reach a compromise and, unlike the decision to invade North Africa, neither could the heads of state. Roosevelt and Churchill, in fact, left the decision on the future of Anglo-American strategy to a third party – Joseph Stalin.

Stalin sided with the American strategic position, and once again the British agreed to launch a cross-Channel attack and an invasion of southern France in May 1944. While British and American officers worked to plan and organized Operation Neptune, the German reaction to Allied operations in Italy imposed further changes on American and British strategy.

To break the stalemate in Italy, the Allies launched an amphibious operation to turn the right flank of the Gothic Line. The forces initially set ashore at Anzio were not, however, strong enough to threaten the German positions to the south, and offensives to break the Gothic line and link up with the forces at Anzio failed. The Allies were thus faced with another stalemate that lasted from January to May 1944, and German counter-attacks even threatened the integrity of the Anzio beachhead. To sustain the troops at Anzio, resources that were supposed to be transferred to the British Isles for the forthcoming invasion had to be retained in Italy. General Eisenhower ultimately had to agree to delay the invasion of southern France until after the Normandy landings.

Planning for Operation Neptune on the whole went smoothly although differing views on the role of airpower caused severe strains and inter-service disputes within the British and American staffs, and even the successful D-Day invasion did not put an end to inter-Allied differences. German actions continued to have a significant influence on American and Allied strategy. Having failed to defeat the invasion at the water's edge, the Germans, instead of retreating, sought to contain the Allied forces in Normandy. The Allies consequently fell well behind their planned schedule of advance, but the Germans lost so heavily in their defensive efforts and in the ill-conceived Mortain counter-attack that when the Allies did break out there were no forces left to offer a coherent defense short of the Dutch–German border. By early September Allied armies were not only well ahead of schedule but also commanders were convinced that the German armies in the west were finished.

During the battles in Normandy and Brittany the British suggested cancellation of the invasion of southern France. Instead, the British wanted to push on into northern Italy and then advance into Yugoslavia and Hungary. The Americans insisted on Anvil, and after heated arguments that ultimately involved directly the President and Prime Minister, the American view prevailed.

After the Allied breakout, General Eisenhower and General Montgomery had a substantial difference of opinion over the course of operations. Eisenhower always intended to launch his main drive north of the Ardennes towards the Ruhr. Montgomery's Army Group would have the primary responsibility for the final thrust into Germany, and, therefore, received the lion's share of available resources. Montgomery, however, requested that American armies operating south of the Ardennes assume a completely defensive posture to free additional resources for operations further north. Eisenhower refused to immobilize a large portion of his forces although he did increase the allocation of supplies to Montgomery.

Growing logistical problems and a rapid German recovery soon dashed Allied hopes for a rapid conclusion of the war. The Allied advance in the summer had outrun the capabilities of the logistics system to sustain the drives. In their retreat, the Germans left garrisons in the Channel and Brittany ports. The garrisons either held out until the end of the war or demolished the port facilities in the face of Allied assaults. The absence of a major port near the front in turn imposed severe constraints on the field armies which desperate expedients failed to alleviate, and the capture of Antwerp with its facilities intact was negated by the failure to clear the port's approaches.

As logistical problems slowed the Allied advance, the Germans were rapidly reconstituting their shattered forces. When Eisenhower agreed to the Market-Garden operation instead of immediate moves to clear the approaches to Antwerp, both he and Montgomery were pursuing a final effort to cross the Rhine and win the war without having to pause to rectify the supply situation. However, the Germans had reconstituted forces sufficient to halt the assault. On other parts of the front the Germans were also able to slow Allied advances to minor gains, and Allied commanders reluctantly concluded that the war would in fact go on into 1945.

In December the Germans launched a major counter-attack in the Ardennes and in January 1945 launched a second attack in Alsace. Like the counter-thrust in France the previous summer, the German strikes worked to the benefit of the Allies. Despite substantial casualties in American forces, the Allies halted the Germans, who suffered losses so severe, especially in armored vehicles, that their ability to resist renewed Allied offensives was substantially reduced.

The final Allied campaigns in 1945 produced additional Anglo-American friction. After clearing the Rhineland, crossing the Rhine and encircling the Ruhr, General Eisenhower decided to drive on Leipzig and cut Germany in half. Prime Minister Churchill then demanded that the Allies drive on Berlin. Since Churchill posed his demand on strategic grounds, Eisenhower rejected it although he added that if the United States and Britain wanted him to advance on Berlin for political reasons, he would certainly comply. Thus, even in the final days of the European war, the United States and the United Kingdom continued to debate Allied strategy.

American strategy in the European conflict was subject to delay, modification and setbacks. London and Washington never established an overall theater strategy, and every campaign was the subject of serious debate. From 1941 to late 1943 the British dictated the course of Allied strategy. After Stalin's intervention in favor of the American approach in November, the balance shifted. In 1944 and 1945 London gave way to Washington's views. Fortunately, both the Americans and the British understood that coalition unity was essential in order to defeat Germany and that almost any price in terms of altering strategic preferences was worthwhile in order to keep the Alliance together.

American strategy in the Pacific also suffered from internal friction, not between heads of state but rather between strategists in Washington and operational theater commanders. Differing service perspectives both in Washington and in the field added additional complexities to the problem of devising a series of campaigns to defeat Japan.

By 1942 the United States was committed to offensive operations but the first American offensives took place in areas – New Guinea and the Solomons – that had not been considered strategically important in pre-war plans. Nonetheless, having moved forces to the Southern Pacific for defensive purposes, offensive operations in the area seemed a reasonable subsequent move. By late 1943 the expansion of US naval power permitted additional operations in the Central Pacific, a region well suited to the deployment of major fleet assets. Thus, just as the United States fought on two fronts in Europe, American forces were committed to a dual advance in the Pacific.

The dual offensive presented American forces with useful opportunities. It was a classic response of a power with superior resources fighting an enemy with the advantage of interior lines. Attacks in more than one area made it difficult for Japan to use its geographic advantage by moving forces from a quiet region to reinforce a threatened position. The problem with the dual advance in the Pacific revolved around the allocation of resources between the operational theaters, caused in large measure by the absence of an overall strategic plan for the defeat of Japan.

The Joint Chiefs of Staff organization in Washington initially wanted to emphasize the Central Pacific thrust in the direction of the Philippines. Reconquest of the Philippines would cut the Japanese Empire in half and set the stage for the blockade, bombardment and perhaps the invasion of the home islands. The growth of US naval power then convinced the planners to call for bypassing the Philippines and driving instead on Formosa which was a better platform upon which to base long-range air power assets.

General MacArthur, for personal and strategic reasons, called for a drive to reconquer the Philippines. Initially, he proposed an advance along the New Guinea coast followed by an invasion of Mindanao. After the occupation of Mindanao, US forces would move north towards Luzon. Later, MacArthur proposed a direct invasion of Luzon. Naval commanders in the Pacific tended to accept MacArthur's strategy of recapturing the Philippines but wished to achieve the objective by waging naval and amphibious operations in the Central Pacific. Air Corps planners tended to support the Central Pacific strategy since they wanted to capture the Marianas in order to establish bases for the deployment of long-range bombers.

Up to the summer of 1944 the issue of overall strategy did not have to be resolved. Operations in the Central and Southwest Pacific moved steadily forward and Formosa and Luzon were sufficiently distant to allow strategists the luxury of delaying a final choice.

Unlike German resistance in Europe, Japan had been unable since early 1943 to influence seriously the American campaigns. The Japanese had imposed substantial delays on operations in the Solomons and New Guinea but to do so they had fought a war of attrition, especially in the air, that they could not win. Losses in air battles in the Solomons coupled with additional casualties inflicted by the Pacific Fleet could not be readily replaced. Periodically, the Japanese Fleet had to retreat while new pilots trained at home, but the new recruits simply lacked the time and experience to deal effectively with US air power. Thus, as the Americans advanced they faced progressively less well trained Japanese pilots flying aircraft that could not match newer American types. The Japanese could still inflict heavy casualties in ground operations, but without tactical air and sea power garrisons could either be bypassed or assaulted and taken, although at a heavy price.

By mid-1944, however, the Americans had to decide where to strike next. All agreed that Leyte should be the next target since the island could be used as an air power platform for subsequent advances either to Luzon or Formosa. In some respects the decision to invade Leyte was a serious mistake since the island's terrain was unsuitable for airfield construction. It is still hard to understand why the Americans, who had ruled the Philippines for more than four decades, did not know this. On the other hand, the Japanese decided to wage a major battle on Leyte thereby weakening their forces on Luzon. Japan also committed what was left of its fleet in a futile effort to reverse the tide of the war in one Mahanian stroke.

The Americans also decided to invade Luzon rather than Formosa when planners discovered that the conquest even of the southern portion of Formosa would require resources from Europe that were unavailable because of extended German resistance. Fighting on Luzon, despite the loss of many of the best Japanese divisions in the campaign on Leyte, was long, difficult and costly. Fighting in Manila nearly destroyed the city, and although defeated on Luzon and other islands in the Philippines, some Japanese forces held out until the end of hostilities. Some planners had earlier suggested that American forces seize Mindanao as an airbase area, bypass both Luzon and Formosa and strike directly at the Bonins and Ryukus. The difficulty of attacking Formosa and the lure of recapturing Luzon effectively precluded other options.

As fighting continued in the Philippines, American forces struck into the Bonins thus continuing the dual advance down to the last months of the war. The final blows against Japan including the loss of Okinawa, the conventional and atomic bombings of Japanese cities, and Soviet intervention, convinced the Japanese government to surrender. Unlike the German capitulation, Japan turned over to the Allies substantial organized residual forces in the home islands, China, the East Indies and island garrisons in the Pacific.

Japan began a war in 1941 that it had no realistic expectation of winning. Given the fundamental imbalance in human and material resources, Japan's main prospects for emerging from the conflict with some initial conquests intact lay in profiting from a major American strategic blunder or using a collapse of national will to obtain a reasonably favorable negotiated peace. Neither event happened. American strategy was perhaps not perfect, but US planners and commanders made no crucial errors. After the attack on Pearl Harbor, a collapse of American morale was at best unlikely.

Taken by surprise, the Americans entered the war without a Pacific strategy. Pre-war plans had dramatically underestimated Japanese capabilities and the defensive posture called for was, in fact, based on highly optimistic assumptions that were quickly torn to shreds during the first months of hostilities. After halting the Japanese drives, the decision to launch a counter-offensive was sound, but the Americans in effect had to devise strategy campaign by campaign and each advance was the subject of extensive discussion among military leaders and planners.

The dual advance which evolved as much by accident as by design was a reasonable approach with marginal attached risks. Problems arose in determining the relative emphasis attached to each line of advance. Thus, Pacific strategy became the subject of debate and compromise. Internal discussion had more influence on US strategic decisions than Japanese counter moves.

War plans are always subject to change when they meet the reality of battle. During the Second World War the United States and its Allies achieved the common political objective of the unconditional surrender of the major Axis powers. America entered the war with a strategy previously worked out with Great Britain, but enemy actions and coalition politics imposed substantial changes. 'Germany first' became a two-ocean offensive war, and in both Europe and the Pacific the United States found itself waging a dual offensive. The issue of priorities among the offensive options became a contentious issue in Europe and the Pacific. Fortunately, all participants in the arguments surrounding strategic decisions made the compromises necessary to produee victory.

Initially, enemy actions often dictated American and Allied strategy. As the Grand Alliance became stronger, enemy actions had progressively less impact. Moreover, numerous enemy decisions worked to the ultimate benefit of the Allies, and towards the end of the war Allied leaders found themselves in the situation of reacting to major victories instead of defeats. Sometimes the question is asked, why didn't the Allies with all their advantages pursue a more effective strategy and end the war sooner? The answer is – perhaps they did.

Maps

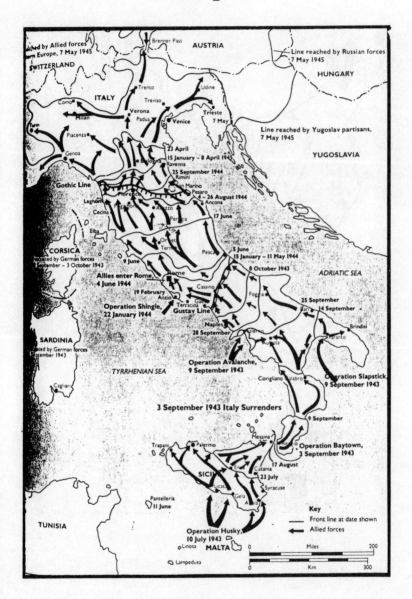

Map 1: The Italian Campaign

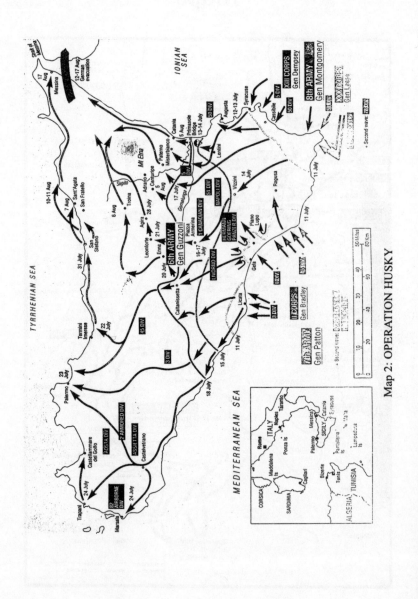

Map 2: OPERATION HUSKY

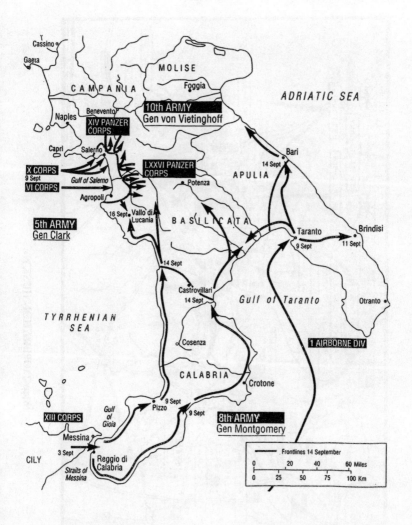

Map 3: OPERATION AVALANCHE

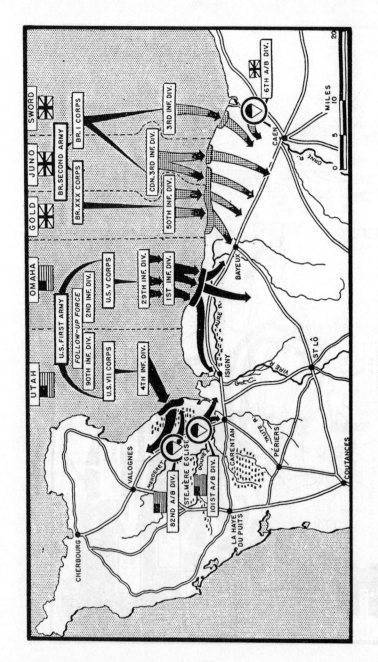

Map 4: OPERATION NEPTUNE

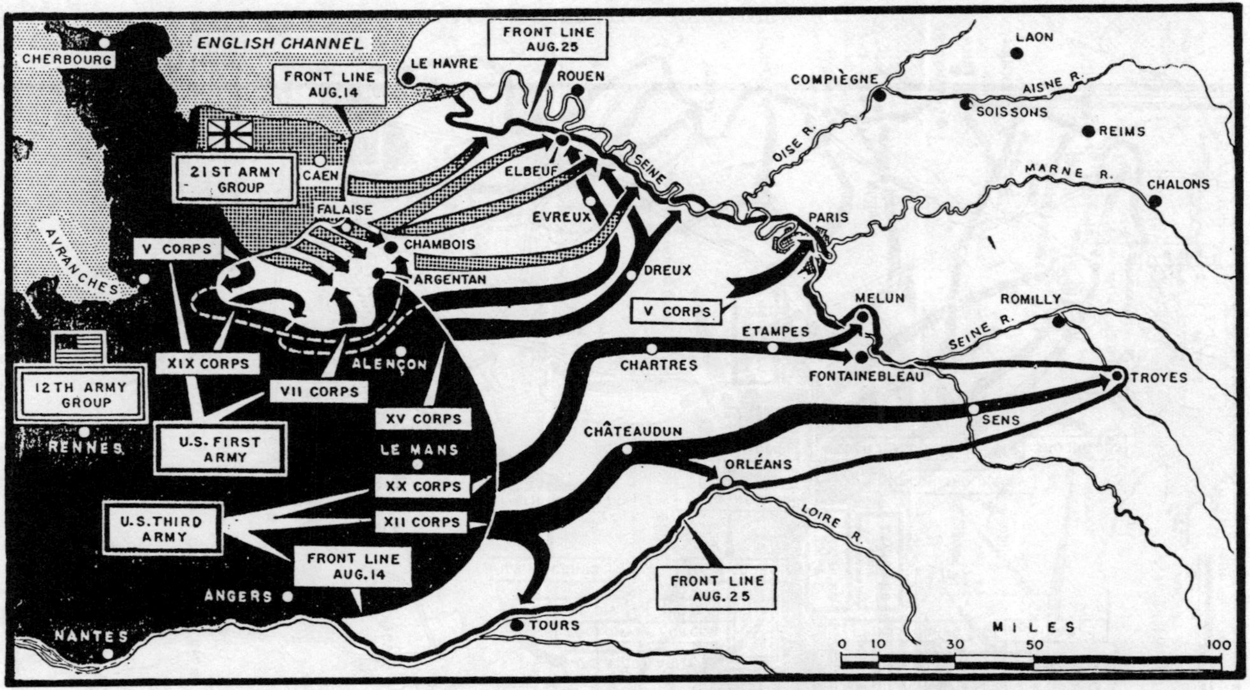

Map 4: OPERATION NEPTUNE

CHALONS

REIMS

AISNE R.

LAON

SOISSONS

MARNE R.

TROYES

COMPIÈGNE

ROMILLY

SEINE R.

SENS

OISE R.

MILES

PARIS

MELUN

FONTAINEBLEAU

ÉTAMPES

ORLÉANS

FRONT LINE AUG. 25

SEINE

ROUEN

DREUX

V CORPS

CHARTRES

CHÂTEAUDUN

LOIRE R.

FRONT LINE AUG. 25

LE HAVRE

ELBEUF

ÉVREUX

TOURS

FRONT LINE AUG. 25

CAEN

FALAISE

CHAMBOIS

ARGENTAN

ALENÇON

XV CORPS

LE MANS

XX CORPS

XII CORPS

ENGLISH CHANNEL

FRONT LINE AUG. 14

21ST ARMY GROUP

VII CORPS

FRONT LINE AUG. 14

CHERBOURG

V CORPS

XIX CORPS

U.S. FIRST ARMY

U.S. THIRD ARMY

ANGERS

AVRANCHES

12TH ARMY GROUP

RENNES

NANTES

0 10 30 50 100

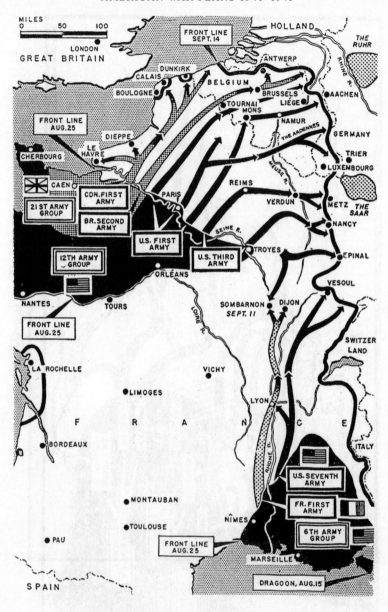

Map 5: France, Summer 1944

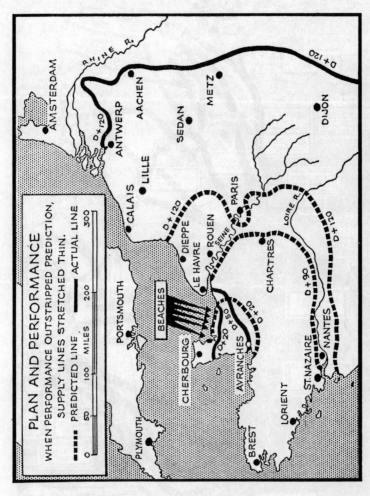

Map 6: The Tyranny of Logistics – Plan and Performance 1944

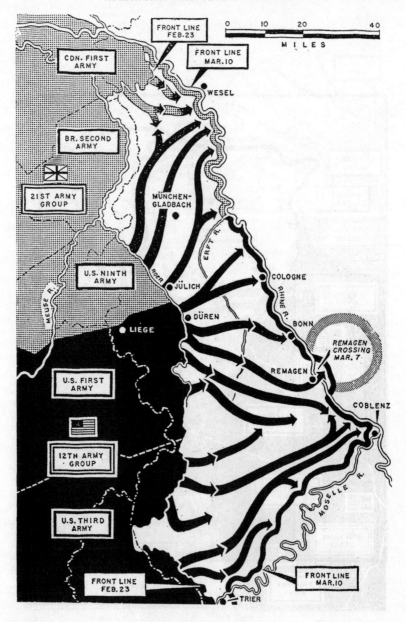

Map 7: Germany, 1945

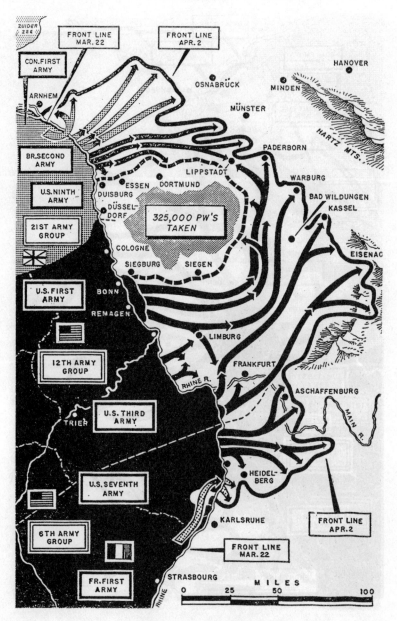

Map 8: Germany, 1945

183

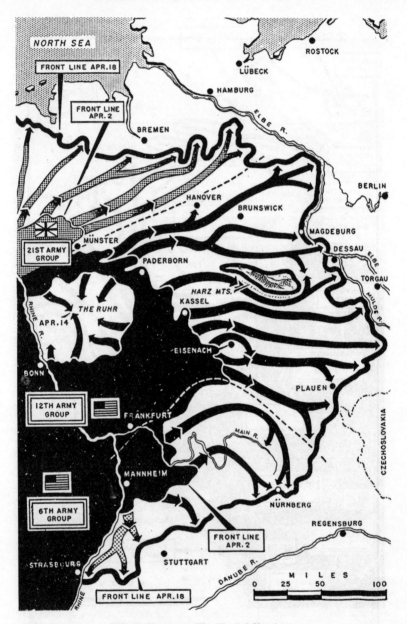

Map 9: Germany, The Final Offensive

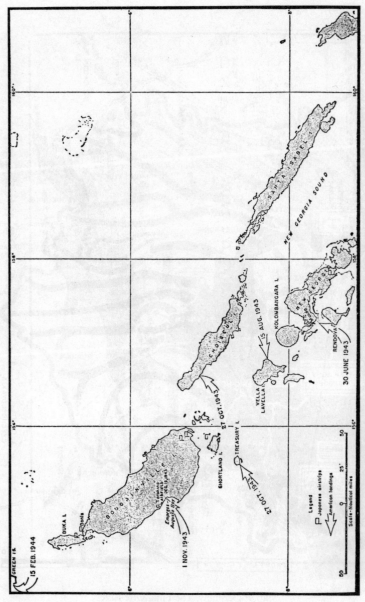

Map 10: Landings, Central and Northern Solomons, June 1943–February 1944

185

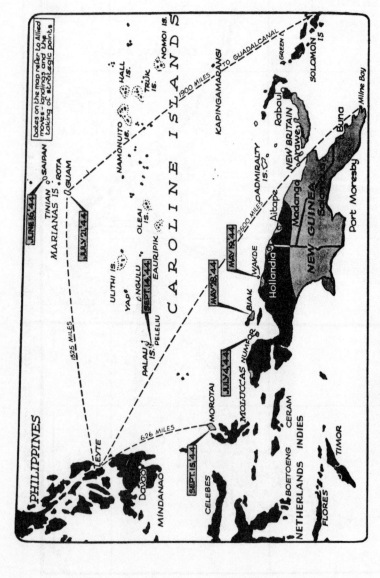

Map 11: Allied Moves and Landings in the Pacific May 1944–September 1944

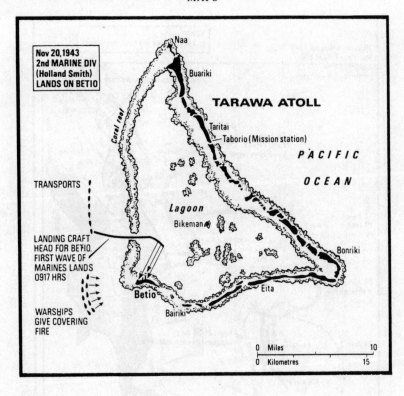

Map 12: OPERATION GALVANIC

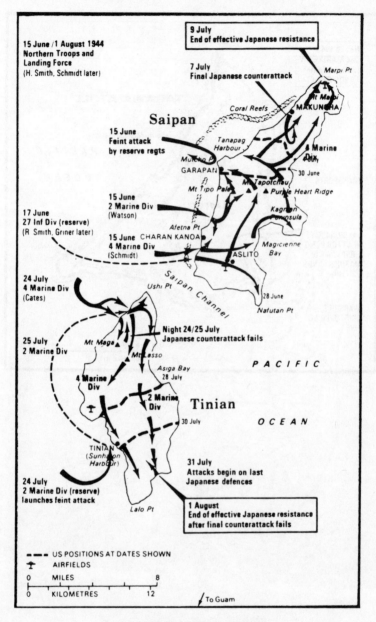

15 June /1 August 1944
Northern Troops and
Landing Force
(H. Smith, Schmidt later)

9 July
End of effective Japanese resistance

7 July
Final Japanese counterattack

Marpi Pt

Coral Reefs

Mt Marpi
MAKUNSHA

Saipan

15 June
Feint attack
by reserve regts

Tanapag
Harbour

4 Marine
Div

Mucho Pt
GARAPAN

30 June

Mt Tipo Pale

Mt Tapotchau

Purple Heart Ridge

15 June
2 Marine Div
(Watson)

Kagman
Peninsula

17 June
27 Inf Div (reserve)
(R. Smith, Griner later)

Afetna Pt

15 June
4 Marine Div
(Schmidt)

CHARAN KANOA

Magicienne
Bay

ASLITO

Saipan Channel

Ushi Pt

24 July
4 Marine Div
(Cates)

28 June

Nafutan Pt

Night 24/25 July
Japanese counterattack fails

PACIFIC

25 July
2 Marine Div

Mt Maga

Mt Lasso

Asiga Bay
28 July

4 Marine
Div

2 Marine
Div

Tinian

OCEAN

30 July

TINIAN
(Sunharon
Harbour)

31 July
Attacks begin on last
Japanese defences

24 July
2 Marine Div (reserve)
launches feint attack

Lalo Pt

1 August
End of effective Japanese resistance
after final counterattack fails

- - - US POSITIONS AT DATES SHOWN

✈ AIRFIELDS

0   MILES   8
0   KILOMETRES   12

To Guam

Map 13: OPERATION FORAGER

188

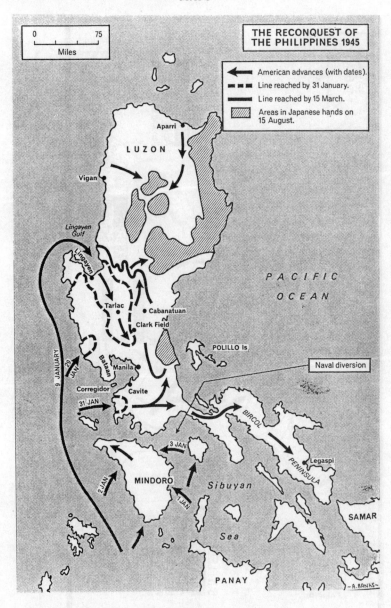

Map 14: OPERATION MUSKETEER

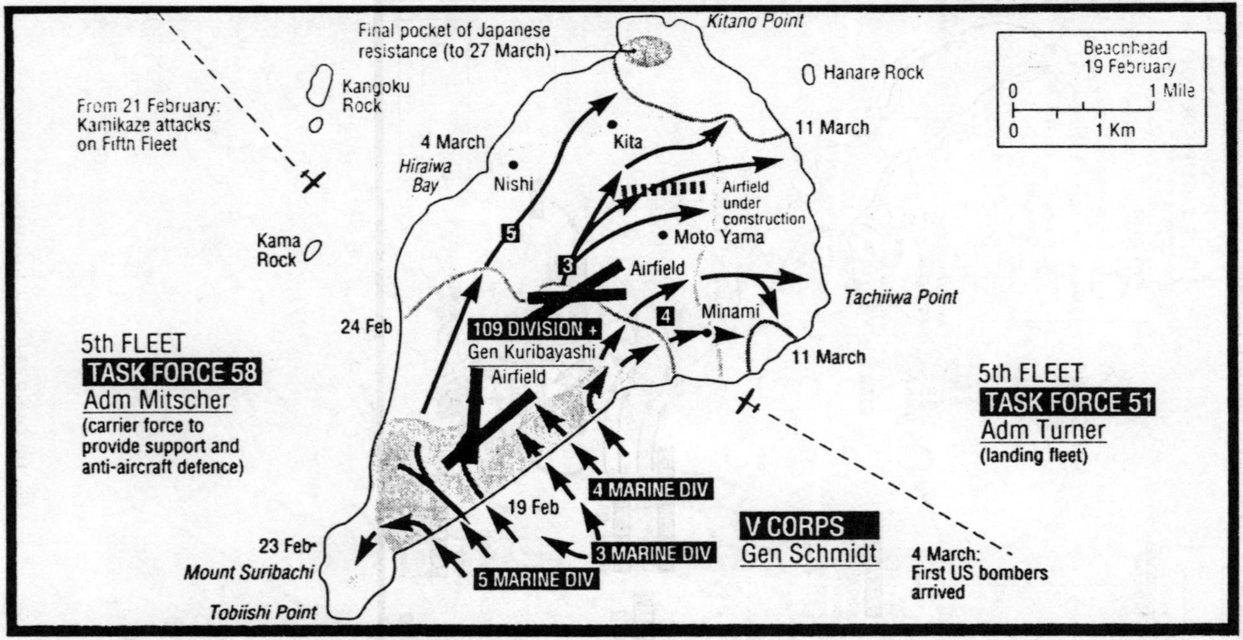

Map 15: OPERATION DETACHMENT

Beachhead
19 February

0   1 Mile
0   1 Km

Kitano Point

Hanare Rock

Tachiiwa Point

11 March

11 March

Airfield
under
construction

Moto Yama

Minami

Airfield

Kita

3

109 DIVISION +
Gen Kuribayashi

Airfield

Nishi

5

Hiraiwa
Bay

4 March

24 Feb

Kangoku
Rock

Final pocket of Japanese
resistance (to 27 March)

Kama
Rock

From 21 February:
Kamikaze attacks
on Fifth Fleet

5th FLEET
TASK FORCE 58
Adm Mitscher
(carrier force to
provide support and
anti-aircraft defence)

23 Feb

Mount Suribachi

Tobishi Point

19 Feb

5 MARINE DIV

3 MARINE DIV

4 MARINE DIV

V CORPS
Gen Schmidt

4 March:
First US bombers
arrived

5th FLEET
TASK FORCE 51
Adm Turner
(landing fleet)

190

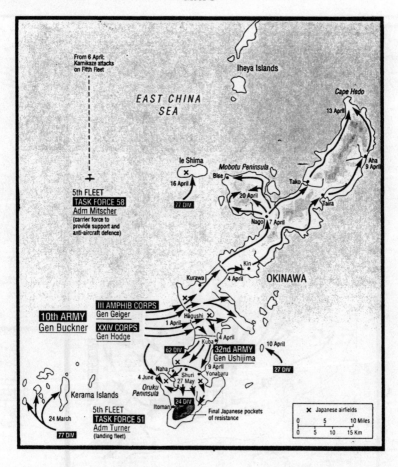

Map 16: OPERATION ICEBERG

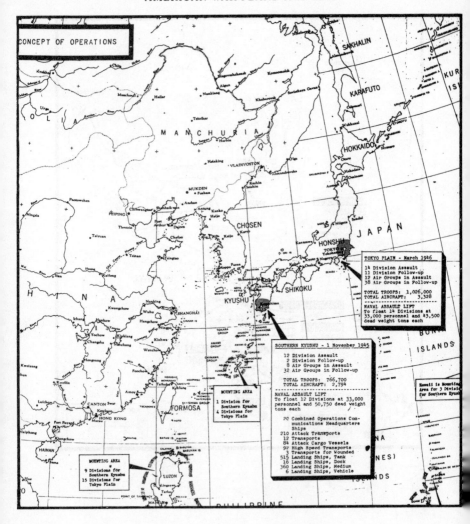

Map 17: OPERATIONS OLYMPIC AND CORONET

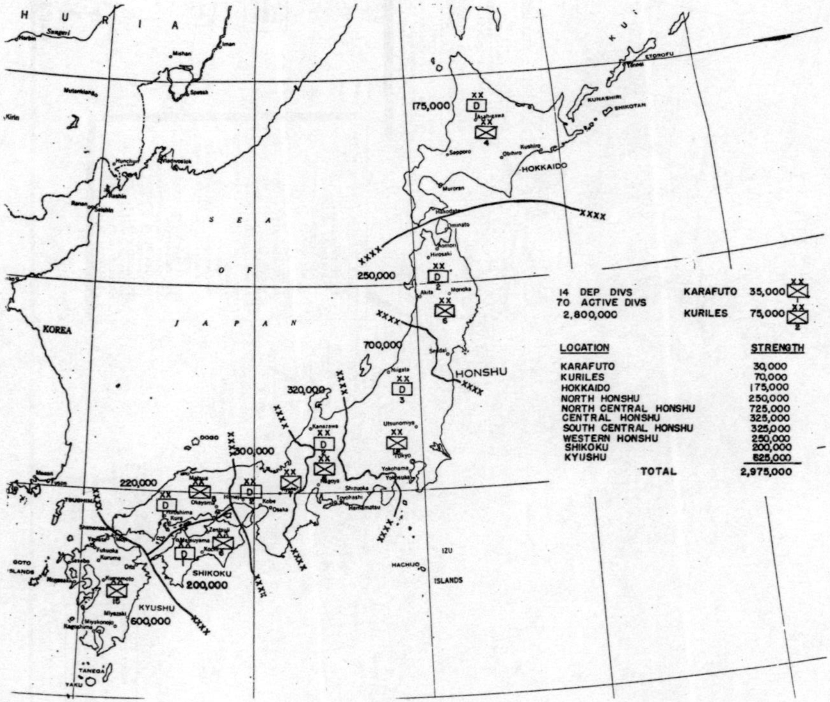
14 DEP DIVS
70 ACTIVE DIVS
2,800,000
KARAFUTO 35,000
KURILES 75,000
LOCATION STRENGTH
KARAFUTO 30,000
KURILES 70,000
HOKKAIDO 175,000
NORTH HONSHU 250,000
NORTH CENTRAL HONSHU 725,000
CENTRAL HONSHU 325,000
SOUTH CENTRAL HONSHU 325,000
WESTERN HONSHU 250,000
SHIKOKU 200,000
KYUSHU 625,000
TOTAL 2,975,000
SEA OF JAPAN
KOREA
HOKKAIDO
HONSHU
SHIKOKU
KYUSHU
175,000
250,000
700,000
320,000
300,000
220,000
200,000
600,000
IZU ISLANDS
HACHIJO
GOTO ISLANDS
TANEGA
YAKU
ETOROFU
KUNASHIRI
SHIKOTAN

Map 18: OPERATIONS OLYMPIC AND CORONET

Selected Bibliography

United States Government Archives

Archives of the Department of the Army, Modern Military Branch, Military Archives Division, National Archives and Record Service.

Record Group 165. Records of the War Department General and Special Staffs: American-British Conversations File, Civil Affairs Division File, Operations Division Decimal and Executive Files, War Department Chief of Staff Army File, and War Plans Division Decimal File.

Record Group 331 Records of Allied Operational and Occupational Headquarters, World War II Supreme Headquarters, Allied Expeditionary Forces, G-3 and Secretary General Staff Files

Operational Archives of the Naval History Division of the Department of the Navy, Washington, D.C., Operational Division Plans COMINCH, COMSOPAC, CINCPAC.

Published Government Records

Records of the Joint Chiefs of Staff Part I (Microfilm) Frederick, MD, University Publications of America, 1980.

Minutes of Meetings of the Combined Chiefs of Staff. Washington, D.C., Office of the Combined Chiefs of Staff, Washington, D.C., 1942–1945, 19 vols.

Ross, Steven, ed., *American War Plans 1919–1941*. New York, Garland Publishing Co., 1992, 5 vols.

Official Histories

Birtle, Andrew J., *Sicily*, Washington, D.C., CMH Pub 72–16, U.S. Government Printing Office, n.d.

Blumenson, Martin, *Salerno to Cassino, U.S. Army in World War II: The Mediterranean Theater of Operations*. Washington, D.C., U.S. Government Printing Office, 1969.

Cannon, M.H., *Leyte: The Return to the Philippines U.S. Army in World War II. The War in the Pacific*. Washington, D.C., U.S. Government Printing Office, 1993.

Cline, Ray S., *Washington Command Post: The Operations Division. U.S. Army in World War II: The War Department*. Washington, D.C., U.S. Government Printing Office, 1951.

Conn, Stetson and Byron Fairchild, *The Framework of Hemispheric Defense. U.S. Army in World War II: The Western Hemisphere*. Washington, D.C., U.S. Government Printing Office, 1960.

Craven, Wesley F. and James L. Cate, eds. *The Army Air Forces in World War II*. Chicago, University of Chicago Press, 1948–1949, 7 vols.

Crowl, Philip A. *Campaign in the Marianas. U.S. Army in World War II. The War in the Pacific*. Washington, D.C., U.S. Government Printing Office, 1993.

Crowl, Philip A. and Edmund G. Love, *Seizure of the Gilberts and Marshalls. U.S. Army in World War II. The War in the Pacific*. Washington, D.C., U.S. Government Printing Office, 1993.

Fisher, Ernest F., *Cassino to the Alps. United States Army in World War II. The Mediterranean Theater of Operations*. The Mediterranean Theater of Operations, Washington, D.C., U.S. Government Printing Office, 1977.

Garland, Albert N., and Howard M. Smyth, *Sicily and the Surrender of Italy, U.S. Army in World War II: The Mediterranean Theater of Operations*. Washington, D.C., U.S Government Printing Office, 1965.

Greenfield, Kent R., *American Strategy in World War II: A Reconsideration*. Baltimore, MD: The Johns Hopkins University Press, 1963.

——, ed., *Command Decisions*. Washington, D.C., U.S. Government Printing Office, 1960.

Hammond, William M., *Normandy The U.S. Army Campaigns of World War II*. Washington, D.C., U.S. Government Printing Office, n.d.

Harrison, Gordon A. *Cross-Channel Attack. U.S. Army in World War II. The European Theater of Operations*. Washington, D.C., U.S. Government Printing Office, 1951.

Howard, Michael, *Grand Strategy*, Vol. 4, *August 1942 – September 1943*. United Kingdom Military Series. J.R.M. Butler, gen. ed., *History of the Second World War*. London: HMSO, 1972.

Howe, George F., *Northwest Africa: Seizing the Initiative in the West. United States Army in World War II, The Mediterranean Theater of Operations*. Washington, D.C., U.S. Government Printing Office, 1985.

Leighton, Richard M., and Robert W. Coakley, *Global Logistics and Strategy 1940–1943 U.S. Army in World War II: The War Department*. Washington, D.C., U.S. Government Printing Office, 1955.

——, *Global Logistics and Strategy, 1943-1945. U.S. Army in World War II: The War Department*. Washington, D.C., U.S. Government Printing Office, 1968.

Matloff, Maurice, *Strategic Planning for Coalition Warfare, 1943–1944. U.S. Army in World War II: The War Department*. Washington, D.C., U.S. Government Printing Office, 1959.

—— and Edwin M. Snell, *Strategic Planning for Coalition Warfare 1941–42. U.S. Army in World War II: The War Department*. Washington, D.C., U.S. Government Printing Office, 1953.

Miller, John, *CARTWHEEL: The Reduction of Rabaul. U.S. Army in World War*

II: The War in the Pacific. Washington, D.C., U.S. Government Printing Office, 1959.

Morison, Samuel E. *History of U.S. Naval Operations in World War II.* Boston, Little Brown and Co., 1947–1962, 15 vols.

Morton, Louis, *Strategy and Command: The First Two Years. U.S. Army in World War II: The War in the Pacific.* Washington, D.C., U.S. Government Printing Office, 1962.

Pogue, Forrest C. *The Supreme Command. U.S. Army in World War II: The European Theater of Operations.* Washington, D.C., U.S. Government Printing Office, 1954.

Ruppenthal, Roland G., *Logistical Support of the Armies Volume I: May 1941 – September 1944. U.S. Army in World War II: The European Theater of Operations.* Washington, D.C., U.S. Government Printing Office, 1953.

Smith, Robert Ross, *Triumph in the Philippines. U.S. Army in World War II: The War in the Pacific.* Washington, D.C., U.S. Government Printing Office, 1963.

Watson, Mark S. *Chief of Staff: Prewar Plans and Preparations. U.S. Army in World War II: The War Department.* Washington, D.C., U.S. Government Printing Office, 1950.

Wright, Burton, *The Eastern Mandates. The U.S. Army Campaigns of World War II.* Washington, D.C., U.S. Government Printing Office, n.d.

General and Specialized Studies

Ambrose, Stephen, *D-Day June 6, 1944: the Climactic Battle of World War II.* New York, Simon and Schuster, 1994.

——. *The Supreme Commander. The War Years of General Dwight D. Eisenhower.* Garden City, N.Y., Doubleday and Co., Inc., 1970.

Baer, George, *One Hundred Years of Sea Power. The U.S. Navy 1890–1990.* Stanford, Stanford University Press, 1994.

Barbey, Daniel, *MacArthur's Amphibious Navy. Seventh Amphibious Force Operations 1943–1945.* Annapolis, U.S. Naval Institute, 1969.

Blair, C., *Silent Victory. The U.S. Submarine War against Japan.* New York, J.B. Lippincott Co., 1975.

Blumenson, Martin, *Anzio: The Gamble That Failed.* Philadelphia, Lippincott, 1963.

Buell, Thomas, *Master of Sea Power: A Biography of Fleet Admiral Ernest J. King.* Boston, Little, Brown and Co., 1980.

——. *The Quiet Warrior. A Biography of Admiral Raymond A. Spruance.* Boston, Little, Brown and Co., 1974.

Calvocoressi, P. and G. Wint, *Total War: the Story of World War II.* New York, Pantheon Books, 1972.

Dallek, Robert, *Franklin Roosevelt and American Foreign Policy 1932–1945.* New York, Oxford University Press, 1979.

D'Este, Carlo, *Decision in Normandy.* New York, E.P. Dutton, 1983.

——. *Fatal Decision: Anzio and the Battle for Rome.* New York, HarperCollins, 1991.

Divine, Robert A., *Roosevelt and World War II*. Baltimore, MD.

Frank, Richard, *Guadalcanal*. New York, Penguin Books, 1990.

Funk, A.L., *The Politics of Torch: The Allied Landings and the Algiers Putsch, 1942*. Lawrence, The University Press of Kansas, 1974.

Gailey, H.A., *Bougainville 1943–1945*. The University Press of Kentucky, 1991.

Goulter, C.J.M. *A Forgotten Offensive: Royal Air Force Coastal Command's Anti-Shipping Campaign 1940–1945*. London, Frank Cass, 1995.

Graham, Michael B., *Mantle of Heroism. Tarawa and the Struggle for the Gilberts November 1943*. Novato, CA, Presidio Press, 1993.

Griffith, Samuel B., *The Battle for Guadalcanal*. New York, Ballantine Books, 1963.

Hamilton, Nigel, *The Battles of Field Marshal Bernard Montgomery*. New York, Random House Inc., 1994.

Hastings, Max, *Overlord. D-Day and the Battle for Normandy*. New York, Simon and Schuster, 1984.

Hayes, Grace P., *The History of the Joint Chiefs of Staff in World War II: The War against Japan*. Annapolis, Naval Institute Press, 1982.

Higgins, Trumbull, *Soft Underbelly: The Anglo-American Controversy over the Italian Campaign, 1939–1945*. New York, The Macmillan Co., 1968.

———. *Winston Churchill and the Second Front, 1940–1943*. New York, Oxford University Press, 1957.

Horne, Alistair, *Monty: The Lonely Leader 1944–1945*. New York, Harper-Collins, 1994.

Howard, Michael, *Studies in War and Peace*. New York, Viking Press, 1972.

HQ, U.S. Army Japan, *Monograph 17*.

———. *Monograph 37* Tokyo, Office of the Chief of Military History, n.d.

Hughes, T. and J. Costello, *The Battle of the Atlantic*. New York, Dial Press, 1977.

Isley, J. and Philip A. Crowl, *The U.S. Marines and Amphibious War*. Princeton, Princeton University Press, 1951.

James, Clayton D. *The Years of MacArthur 1941–1945*. Boston, Houghton Mifflin, 1975.

Keegan, John, *Six Armies in Normandy*. New York, Viking Press, 1982.

———, ed., *The Times Atlas of the Second World War*. New York, Harper & Row, 1989.

May, Ernest, ed., *The Ultimate Decision: The President as Commander in Chief*. New York, George Braziller, 1960.

Mayo, L., *Bloody Buna*. Garden City, N.Y., Doubleday & Co., 1974.

McNeil, William H., *America, Britain and Russia: Their Cooperation and Conflict 1941-1946*. London, Oxford University Press, 1953.

Middlebrook, Martin, *Arnhem 1944*. Boulder, Westview Press, 1994.

Moulton, J.L., *Battle for Antwerp*. London, Ian Allan Ltd., 1978.

Murray, Williamson, *Luftwaffe*. London, George Allen and Unwin, 1985.

Newcomb, Richard F., *Iwo Jima*. New York, Signet Books, 1965.

Overy, R.J. *The Air War 1939–1945*. New York, Stein and Day, 1980.

Pogue, Forrest, *George C. Marshall*. New York, Viking Press, 1963–1973, 3 vols.

Potter, E.B., *Nimitz*. Annapolis, U.S. Naval Institute Press, 1976.

Rentz, John N., *Marines in the Central Solomons*. Washington, D.C., U.S. Government Printing Office, 1952.

Reynolds, Clark G., *The Fast Carriers: The Forging of an Air Navy*. New York, McGraw Hill, 1968.

Runyan, T.J., and J. Copes, eds., *To Die Gallantly: The Battle of the Atlantic*. Boulder, Westview Press, 1994.

Ryan, C., *A Bridge Too Far*. New York, Simon and Schuster, 1974.

Sakai, S., with Martin Cardin, *Samurai*. New York, Dutton and Co., 1957.

Smith, Gaddis, *American Diplomacy During the Second World War, 1941–1945*. New York, John Wiley and Sons Inc., 1966.

Snell, John, *Illusion and Necessity: The Diplomacy of Global War, 1939–1945*. Boston, Houghton Mifflin Co., 1963.

Spector, Ronald H., *Eagle against the Sun*. New York, The Free Press, 1985.

Starr, Chester G., *From Salerno to the Alps. A History of the Fifth Army 1943–1945*. Washington, D.C., Infantry Journal Press, 1948.

Stoler, Mark A., *The Politics of the Second Front*. Westport, CT, Greenwood Press, 1977.

United States Army War Department *First Army Report of Operations*. Washington, D.C., 1946, 3 vols.

——. *U.S. Fifth Army* n.p.n.d., 9 vols.

——. *12th Army Group* n.p., 1945, 11 vols.

——. *Seventh United States Army*. Heidelberg, Aloys Graf, n.d., 3 vols.

Weigley, Russell F., *Eisenhower's Lieutenants. The Campaign of France and Germany 1944–1945*. Bloomington, Indiana University Press, 1981.

——. *The American Way of War. A History of United States Military Strategy and Policy*. New York, Macmillan Publishing Co., 1973.

Weinberg, Gerhard, *A World at Arms. A Global History of World War II*. Cambridge, Cambridge University Press, 1994.

Willmott, H.P., *The Great Crusade. A New and Complete History of the Second World War*. New York, The Free Press, 1989.

——. *June 1944*. Poole, Blandford Press, 1984.

Articles

Bix, Herbert, 'Japan's Delayed Surrender: A Reconsideration', *Diplomatic History*, Vol. 19, no. 2, Spring, 1995.

Cohen, Eliot, 'A War That Was Not Left to the Generals', in *Joint Force Quarterly*, Summer 1995, number 8.

Conn, Stetson, 'Changing Concepts of National Defense in the United States 1937–1947', *Military Affairs*, 28 (Spring, 1964).

D'Este, Carlo, 'Falaise: The Trap Not Sprung', *Military History Quarterly*, Vol. 6, no. 3, Spring, 1994.

Franklin, William N., 'Zonal Boundaries and Access to Berlin', *World Politics*, 16 (October, 1963).

Leighton, Richard M., 'Overlord Revisited: An Interpretation of American

Strategy in the European War', *American Historical Review*, 68 (July, 1963).

Moshe, Tuvia Ben, 'Winston Churchill and the Second Front: A Reappraisal', *The Journal of Modern History*, Vol. 62, no. 3 (September, 1990).

Murray, Williamson, 'The Meaning of World War II', in *Joint Force Quarterly*, Summer 1995, number 8.

Pundeff, Marin, 'Allied Strategy and the Balkans', *World Affairs Quarterly* 29 (1958).

Strange, Joseph L., 'The British Rejection of Operation Sledgehammer, An Alternative Motive', *Military Affairs*, Vol. 46, no. 1 (February, 1982).

Weigley, Russell, 'Fighting with Allies: The Debate Fifty Years On', in *Joint Force Quarterly*, Summer 1995, number 8.

Index

MacArthur, Gen. D. xv, 26, 50–2, 55,
70–1, 75–6, 78, 130–1, 151, 170
Marshall, Gen. G.C. 28, 30–1, 33, 43,
84, 158
McClellan, Gen. G.B. xvii
Moltke, Count H. von xviii–xix
Montgomery, Gen. Sir B.L. 58, 98,
100, 105, 126, 167
Morgan, Lt.–Gen. F.E. 94
Napoleon xiv, xv, xvi
Nimitz, Adm. C.W. 50, 75, 77, 130–1
Ramsay, Adm. Sir B. 100
Sherman, Gen. W.T. xiv
Spruance, Adm. R. 73, 78
Stark, Adm. H.R. 6–8
Tedder, Air Marshal Sir A. 58
Voroshilov, Marshal K.E. 84
Conferences and Talks
ABC 1 Conference 1, 9–13, 28
ABD Conversations 13
Arcadia Conference 21, 22–3
Argentina Conference 16
Casablanca Conference 43, 94
Eureka Conference 82, 83–5, 121
Pacific Military Conference 51
Quadrant Conference 62, 72, 98
Quebec Conference 131
Sextant Conference 74–5, 81–2, 85
Teheran Conference see Eureka
Conference
Trident Conference 46, 48, 68, 95
COSSAC see United States-British
Co–operation and Conflict: Chief of
Staff to the Supreme Allied Commander

Deception xii, 94, 105–6, 108

First World War xiv, xv
France
armed forces
1st Army 129, 144
Vichy forces in north Africa 36–7
plans to invade north–western France
46, 47, 81–2, 85, 94–100, 101–5
plans to invade southern France 84–5,
119–23

Germany
Allied plans to defeat first 9, 17, 21, 47

armed forces
5th Panzer Army 119
7th Army 119
British plans for defeat of 28–9
combat losses 90, 119, 141
US plans for defeat of 28
see also United States–British
Co-operation and Conflict
Great Britain
American forces in 29, 46, 105
Chiefs of Staff 30, 46, 147
strategic aims 18
see also British Armed Forces and United
States–British Co-operation and Conflict

Intelligence xvi, 49, 61, 118
Interservice Co–operation xiv–xv, 45–6
Italy
plans to eliminate from the war 46–7
plans to invade mainland 61–3
plans to invade Sicily 43–4

Japan
Allied underestimation of 12, 18
capitulation 159–60
combat losses 27, 57, 74, 134, 155
offensive in 1942 23
plans to invade 155–9
strategic plans to defeat 68, 74
strength and deployment in southern
Pacific 53–4
JCS see United States: Joint Chiefs of
Staff

Leadership xvi–xix
Logistics xiv, 103, 124–7, 129, 168

Mediterranean
plans for 80–1, 83
Mussolini, B. 62

New Zealand Armed Forces 53, 55, 78–9

Operations and Plans: Named
A–WPD1 15
Anvil 85–6, 89–90, 99, 119–23, 168
Autumn Mist 140
Avalanche 63, 166
Bolero 28–30, 44, 46, 94